CAREER STAGES

Books by Auren Uris and John J. Tarrant

The Victory Principle
How to Keep from Getting Fired
Getting to the Top Fast
How to Win Your Boss's Love, Approval and Job

Books by Auren Uris

The Executive Deskbook
Action Guide for Job Seekers and Employers
Mastery of Management
Over 50—the Definitive Guide to Retirement
Executive Dissent
Techniques of Leadership
Realworld Management Deskbook (work in progress)

Books by John J. Tarrant

Leavetaking
Drucker: The Man Who Invented the Corporate Society
How to Negotiate a Raise
The Corporate Eunuch
How to Make It Big on Your Own

CAREER STAGES
SURMOUNTING THE CRISES OF WORKING LIFE

Auren Uris & John J. Tarrant

Seaview/Putnam
New York

Mr. Shiung Y. Lo
P.O. Box 10567
Chicago, Ill. 60610

Dedication

The authors dedicate this book to the generous men and women—beginners, high flyers, the serene veterans and the expert observers—who shared their experiences, opinions and feelings with us so that others might benefit, and that a new vision might light up the world of work.

Copyright © 1983 by Auren Uris and John J. Tarrant
All rights reserved. This book, or parts thereof, may not be reproduced in any form without permission in writing from the publisher. Published on the same day in Canada by General Publishing Co. Limited, Toronto.

Library of Congress Cataloging in Publication Data

Uris, Auren.
   Career stages.

   1. Job satisfaction.   2. Vocational guidance.
I. Tarrant, John J.   II. Title.   III. Title: Crises of working life.
HF5549.5.J63U74 1983   650.1'3   82-19209
ISBN 0-399-31005-3

Printed in the United States of America

Contents

Introduction

Stage I: Getting Ready

1	On the Threshold	25
2	Heading for the First Job	29
3	People in Crisis: Four Cases	38

Stage II (20–30): The Learning Decade

4	Entering the Dark Cave	57
5	The First Day	63
6	The Achievement Crisis	69
7	The Crisis of Individuality	73
8	The First Crisis of Failure	80
9	Crises of the Spirit	87
10	Getting a Job Offer: An Early Crisis of Decision	93
11	Relocating	99
12	Making Sergeant	104

Stage III (30–40): The Power Decade

13	Thrusting Toward the Summit	111

14	The Crisis of Reassessment	116
15	When Faults in Planning Appear: A Crisis of Redirection	123
16	The Crisis of Responsibility	129
17	Depression: A Complication of the Power Crisis	132
18	The Crisis of Management	135
19	Cutting Corners	139
20	Workaholism	145
21	Love Among the Laborers	149
22	Biology vs. Economics	152
23	The Motherhood Decision	157

Stage IV (40–50): The Win/Lose Decade

24	Time's Winged Chariot Keeps Rollin' Along	167
25	Some Inner Consequences of Leadership	172
26	The Great Disillusionment—a/k/a/ Burnout	175
27	The Crisis of Frustration	178
28	Falling Through the Status Gap	184
29	When the Axe Falls	192
30	The Crisis of the Heights	200
31	The Crisis of Authority	205
32	Quitting	211

Stage V (50–60): The Consummation Decade

33	Frosting on the Cake	217
34	Obsolescence and Push-out: A Climactic Crisis of Competition	221
35	Midlife Anger: A Crisis of Success/Failure	228
36	The Crisis of Identity	236
37	Looking Back and Accepting What You See	248
38	Retirement on the Job: A Crisis of Adjustment	252

Stage VI (60–70): The Wrap-up Years

39	Over the Top	263
40	The Group, Broadbrush	269
41	The Age Gap	275
42	Retirement: The Final Identity Crisis	282
43	The Final Crisis of Self-Assessment	285
44	A Few Words About Retirement Planning	290
45	Another Kind of Retirement	295

Preface

AUREN Uris and Jack Tarrant met and became good friends as fellow employees in the editorial department of a business publishing house we will call Apex. Apex sold business guidance in the form of newsletters and programs aimed to help supervisors, field sales people, managers and top executives to become more effective in their jobs.

Tarrant was a successful writer with experience in marketing and sales. Uris, on the other hand, won his place on the Apex writing staff mostly because of his business background.

For both men, life at Apex was educational and enjoyable. The organization was young, the professionals were a feisty, sophisticated and fun-loving lot. They were specialists who could write—economist/writers, tax expert/writers, labor lawyer/writers, management expert/writers, sales expert/writers. And, of course, this professional core was surrounded by all the other people needed to operate a business organization, from president down to department managers, secretaries, and personnel to run the mailroom and copying units.

One fact became a continuing subject of discussion between Uris and Tarrant. Despite the comparatively high level of sophistication of its personnel, and even though the organization was in the business of purveying management guidance to the world at large, Apex itself was susceptible to all the human problems that beset companies in general.

People were hired and failed to work out. Bright new people came on staff, scored early successes, and then became so obnoxious in their overreactions that they had to be let go. Cliques formed and spawned organizational tensions that created partisanship and unfairness in dispensing the largesse of promotions and salary increases.

Most of these incidents Uris and Tarrant saw up close, in terms of the exhilaration or the agony, the pleasure or the pain of friends and colleagues. But they also saw them as cases in management, as revelations of working relationships on the job to be probed and analyzed for professional reasons.

For years afterward, as friends, colleagues, and collaborators, Auren Uris and Jack Tarrant talked about their Apex days—all those gifted people, many suffering, miserable, others riding the crest.

They tried to make some sense out of it; the chaos of conflicting emotions, the fears, hates, envies, and despairs, the excitement, the striving, the many triumphs.

Could they apply any yardsticks that would make these crises-on-the-job less terrifying, more understandable and surmountable? Could they chart them? Could they classify or quantify them?

Something began to emerge. While few of the key developments that confronted people at work were foreseeable, they were not *surprising*. They had happened before to others, many others. As a matter of fact, they were, without exception, *repetitive*. For a case of Colleague X who had quarreled with his boss and had to decide how to deal with the aftermath, Uris or Tarrant could come up with similar cases involving other people in other organizations. No matter what the difficulty, a parallel came to mind, in some instances from the writer's own firsthand experience.

Furthermore, each of the difficulties in which the respective people were involved was somehow appropriate *for that stage of the person's career.*

Maybe it was possible that certain kinds of work-related crises happened over and over again, to many people, at roughly the same times in their lives. And perhaps these crises were not unrelated to what Erik Erikson and others were beginning to say about life cycles and the fact that existence can be charted along an observable course. Certainly, life on the job was just as real—in some ways even more so—as life away from the work scene.

What can be charted can be predicted.

Uris and Tarrant began then to talk about a book that would delineate the major critical points of the working life. The book would say some useful things about job-related crises, the forms in which they come, and the effects they have on people—not just in terms of their careers but in terms of their total emotional selves.

Equally as important, perhaps one could predict the points at which certain kinds of crises would occur. If you could do this, you could show something of the effect that an earlier crisis has on subsequent attitude and later response to problems. You could, too, investigate the degree to which there was harm when crises came contrary to the pattern, afflicting young persons with the kinds of major dilemmas usually faced at a later stage and vice versa.

The career paths of the two authors diverged, reunited, diverged again. They collaborated on several books—each had left Apex in his own critical fashion—and they wrote books on their own.

But they continued to talk about *this* book. And then, in 1978, they began to do something more than talk. They began the systematic course of interviewing and research, analysis and discussion and writing, writing, writing, which led them here.

Introduction: The Idea that Grew and Grew

WHAT you do has a lot to do with what you are. Yet, people think of the hours they spend on the job as separate from the remainder of life. It's assumed that different rules apply on the job. And there is a related assumption that causes even more bewilderment and pain, the assumption that crises of working life should not strongly affect us. "It's not for real" is the way one interviewee put it.

When a mother abandons a child, it is expected that the child may suffer severe emotional anguish. When long-time lovers break up, pain usually follows. When close friends fall out, it is understood that each may suffer psychic wounds.

But when people betray each other on the job, this is often written off as "office politics." It is widely assumed that while you can get fired if somebody stabs you in the back, your soul will remain intact. This is how the personal crises of work are compartmentalized and assigned a lower order of hurt to job trauma. In ways direct and indirect, individuals suffer from the repressed reality.

It's not just among lay people that the impact of work crises has been overlooked or underestimated. Indeed, during the early part of the twentieth century, psychiatrists tended to feel that nothing happening to the individual after childhood had much impact.

In 1944 the psychoanalyst Heinz Hartmann coined the term *social compliance,* referring to the way in which the social structure influences behavior. Hartmann later observed that the "attention of analysts has been perforce directed to the object relationships of childhood, for these are infinitely more important to the development of personality than those of later life. . . ." While acknowledging the dominant role played by childhood and the family, Hartmann noted in *Essays in Ego Psychology* that "our patient's current social environment constantly enters the analytic picture."

While psychologists and psychoanalysts today pay more heed to the social context of behavior than was formerly the case, they still tend to focus on interpersonal relationships off the job. "For a long time," one analyst told us, "work to me was off limits when the patient brought it up. This, I thought, is the province of the industrial psychologist. Now it seems to me we have done great harm in setting up that artificial classification, 'industrial psychology.' In any event, I now know that, with many of the people I see, what happens in their jobs has a most profound significance. I was going to say 'significance in their lives'—but that, you see, is compartmentalizing. Their work *is* their lives."

One of the most significant things about work is that it involves dependence on other people. Once it was commonplace to view the successful achievement of adulthood as a freeing of the self from dependency, similar to the butterfly's emergence from the cocoon. It is viewed differently now. The infant, of course, is altogether dependent. Continuation of excessive dependency needs beyond childhood can lead to severe neurotic disorders. However, that mature and healthy adults have deep dependency needs is recognized—though these needs may be disguised as desire for reassurance, approval, love. When Barbra Streisand sings "People

Introduction

who need people," she is stating a psychological finding of recent vintage.

There are, of course, the exceptions, the people so bound up in their work that they "take the job home with them." The accepted wisdom is that this is always bad—you should be able to leave the job in the office. The fact is that the job comes home with you whether you want it to or not. The workplace is a community in which employees at all levels spend much of their lives. What happens there can have a more profound effect than what happens in the living room or the bedroom. Work shapes the psyche.

Because work is society. It is the universal social environment most familiar, often most alive. And if there is a San Andreas fault in the office parquet underfoot, when it goes, it will split the ground not just on the job but through the entire length and breadth of your existence.

In *Passages,* Gail Sheehy emphasized the importance of chronology in human experience. She described the crises that link up with life's milestones, presenting opportunities as well as problems. *Career Stages* does the same for working life.

This book is based on certain premises:

- It is practically impossible to be unhappy in your job and happy out of it. Work is *you.*
- Career crises are inevitable. Success does not lie in the avoidance of crisis but in the management and understanding of crisis.
- The salient crises of a career can be predicted.
- Careers are cyclical. They may be divided into stages of about ten years. Each stage has its own character, its own opportunities, its own dangers.
- A happy and successful working life calls for successful transition from one stage to another.

Stages is a word heard constantly during space missions: "Successful staging has been achieved," etc. Successful staging for a space capsule involves accurate guidance, achievement of the necessary velocity, and total disengagement from the empty rocket that fueled the previous stage. Similarly, the individual who moves successfully through career stages must have accurate direction and push—and must also be able to cut away the useless paraphernalia of the past.

The word *stages* in the title as well as the text refers to the division of work life into six successive parts. The pages ahead sketch out job experience from prejob preparation—Stage I—in ten-year cycles, to stage VI—age 60–70.

Each stage is marked by crises, by psychological transitions, by decisions to be made: The executive headhunter calls and hints at a job opportunity that is extremely tempting, even though you like your present affiliation. You've made a mess of a critical assignment—should you start looking for another job?

Many crises naturally fall into one or another stage. "Which job offer shall I accept in entering the world of work?" is a Stage I question. Stage VI is the natural point at which crises involving retirement must finally be resolved.

Some crises are not limited to any one stage; they are repetitive. The crisis of identity—Who am I, really? And what am I doing here?—recurs again and again. These crises have been assigned to the stage at which, in the authors' opinion, they have the greatest impact.

Career Stages examines six definable stages. Following the period of the late teens, Stage I–Getting Ready (in which important attitudes are formed and career decisions begin to be made), comes Stage II, The Learning Decade (20–30). Here the reader experiences crises of adjustment—Learning to be an employee; crises of decision—What shall I do with my life?; crises of the spirit—Am I becoming a hypocrite?; etc.

Stage III, The Power Decade (30–40), brings its own set of crises: fear of failures (or in some cases the *need* to fail); severe home/job strain; the onset of cynicism.

The Win/Lose Decade (40–50), Stage IV, involves another set of crises: midlife doubt; the point of no return; alienation and loneliness of success; bitterness of failure.

During the Consummation Decade (50–60), Stage V, the individual confronts a set of crises centering on the need to acknowledge and accept the fact that all the major life-

Introduction 15

moves have been made. Ruefulness and regret may color the work-related problems met at this stage. And for others comes the feeling, "I have wrought well."

Beyond the Consummation Decade, the individual moves into Stage VI, The Wrap-up Years, a period of questions regarding retirement and how to live a rich and full life with less or no work involvement.

The book identifies and analyzes a wide range of crises typical of each stage. It is based on hundreds of conversations—interviewers sat across countless executive desks, buttonholed undergraduates and M.B.A.s in college corridors, talked with experts across the country by phone—and refined the results of years of research. One major aim is to tell how people are surmounting job problems and carving out successful careers that provide deep emotional satisfaction.

There is both insight and opportunity in the stage concept. Once a career is seen as a series of stages in which success may vary—rise, fall, and rise again—one is weaned away from seeing one's working fortunes as a monolithic structure, more or less uniform throughout. An individual who has had a mediocre Stage I or II may go on to a brilliant Stage III. Understanding that each stage may mean a new deck and a new game, you can use the experience of earlier stages to capitalize on new opportunities.

Career Stages offers you a time road map. With it in hand, you can review where you've been and how you have met the challenges—that is, the crises—of the *past;* you can assess where you are in your *present* stage; and do strategic thinking and planning about your career *future*.

In the context of this book, crisis is seen as a decisive or crucial point, usually one in which the individual undergoes considerable stress and a degree of psychic trauma. You don't face a crisis every time something goes wrong. You do face a crisis when what goes wrong has a deflecting effect on your life.

When you examine the crises that stud the typical working life, they begin to fall into categories. Some kinds of categories are common in certain decades; others are rare.

Crises of Adjustment

Going from here to there causes problems. It involves change, and change is resisted. The new is often difficult to accommodate. Resistance to change is a phenomenon frequently observed—and usually deplored—on the business scene. Management efforts to change a work procedure, physically move departments about, inaugurate new policies almost always meet with reactions ranging from open antagonism to thinly veiled suspicion. And yet it's really strange that the human being, whose development has been marked by the greatest changes and adaptations of any of God's creatures, still should be subject to the wariness of the new and unfamiliar shown by the lower orders.

Even when change is not threatening, it can be difficult, often critically so. When you move into a new situation, you have to adjust behavior and attitudes. It's not easy. For some people, it's almost impossible.

The phenomena that accompany adjustments to a new situation do not always constitute a crisis. Usually they amount to no more than some shimmying as you accelerate. But at other times the struggle to adjust is agonizing.

Crises of adjustment are abundant during the early years. The world of work itself is a new experience, sometimes a shocking one. The young person entering it is coming not so much out of a world of school or a world of family, but out of a world of self. The individual cannot grow without, in Piaget's term, escaping from egocentricity and creating a universe.

The universe of work is malleable. When one creates his or her particular part of it, rather than just being in it, a successful career begins.

Crises of the Spirit

Crises of the spirit strike deep into the self-image or the view of what the world should be like. A trusted one betrays; a cherished maxim turns out to be false; a mistake causes one's self-esteem to totter. Usually life begins with a reasonable store of self-confidence. If that supply is depleted by too many crises of the spirit, it may run short before the end of the journey.

Crises of Competition

Careers take place in arenas. Combat is a commonplace. Many crises grow out of the prevalence of competition. Competition is not the crisis. If one feels that it is, then most careers are out of the question. But the side effects of competition, and its aftereffects, can be extremely critical. Crises of competition may run like a thread throughout a career.

Crises of Failure/Success

The two most obvious aftermaths of competition are failure or success. They involve a special set of psychological phenomena that constitute a separate category of crisis.

Failure is something to pity or abhor in others, and fear for oneself. And yet it is so natural. If there is to be success, there must be failure. Throughout the working career, failure is omnipresent. Even those who seem *never* to fail go around in terror. They hear the eternal beating of wings and cringe at the thought of the talons.

Success brings just as many problems as failure. It wears disguises, and may not become critical right away. But it is a crisis just the same.

One subset of the success/failure category is the *crisis of limitation,* in which the individual is simply unable to meet the demands of the situation. Another is the *crisis of risk*. However, risk is not only inevitable, it is to be sought out and curried in a successful career. But when you risk, you may lose. When you put it all on the line, you can lose it all. Yet out of hopelessness can come new resolve, new directions, new triumphs.

Crises of Decision

A career is charted along a path of decisions. You cannot escape crisis by shunning decision. The decision is still made—by other people, or by time and fate. Should I take that job? Should I adopt that course of action? Should I go this way or that way?

Just about any critical career point calls for the individual to decide one way or the other. That act can be fraught with significant implications: personal ethics vs. professional expediency; family vs. job; today vs. tomorrow; contentment vs. power. As you climb higher, your decisions become more crucial, if only because you have farther to fall.

Crisis-Fearers and Crisis Junkies

Some people are crisiphobic. They avoid crisis at all costs. When confronted with major problems or decisions, their instinct is to flee. But satisfactory working life is impossible when the individual's paramount motivation is the avoidance of crisis. It used to be thought that one could evade climactic events by becoming a monk or a nun. Nowadays the world, with its crises, has invaded even these sanctuaries.

Other people are crisiphiliacs—crisis junkies. Strife is their métier. When there is no trouble, they create some. They are emergency-prone.

Being a crisis junkie can be as exhilarating as being a dope junkie. But there is a price: not addiction, but stress.

The *stress response* is a recently identified but age-old phenomenon. When the human being—like the lower mammals—is confronted with danger, a signal goes out from the hypothalamus in the brain. "Condition Red!" radiates along the network of nerves. Body elements go to action stations. The pituitary gland injects hormones into the blood to alert the adrenal and thyroid glands. These glands, in turn, shoot added energy to every part of the body.

Blood vessels constrict. The tiny capillaries just under the skin close off altogether. Your digestion stops in its tracks; all activities not relevant to defense are stopped. Muscles tense. Sight and hearing become more acute.

Some people *like* to feel this way. They may not realize it, but they have come to take pleasure in the altered state into which the body is plunged by the imminence of danger. And so some people climb mountains, shoot rapids, drive fast cars. Others make waves on the job.

Crisis is inevitable. To the prepared and the capable, it is red meat. To the ambitious, it is the way to win your spurs. But beware of addiction.

Greek Gods in the Executive Suite

The mind has a survival mechanism that helps it weather crises, the turns and twists of the future. It *anticipates*. In primitive cultures, tribal wise men traditionally looked for omens and portents. The joking observance of Groundhog Day is a bit of antiquity that persists: If the groundhog emerges from his burrow on February 2, Candlemas Day, and sees his shadow, then supposedly six more weeks of winter are due.

On the job, the reading of portents is a popular occupation. The Big Boss has just bought a new car and it's not a Caddy but a Buick. What is he trying to say?

It certainly makes sense to develop expectations based on a reading of the "signs." Knowing of a crisis soon to flower, you are in a better position to deal with it.

But the reading of the signs—spotting causes and looking for logical effects—is hampered by a misleading assumption. Being aware of it strengthens our crisis-coping capability.

It is generally assumed that, in business, logic prevails and superior ability is rewarded. The curricula of most of the graduate schools, featuring computer models and "decision trees" and all the rest of it, are still based on this optimistic assumption. The top management of an enterprise is seen as the God of Judeo-Christian tradition: all-knowing, all-seeing, and, above all, *just*. The organization, in this view, may be strict, but it is compassionate and fair.

Actually, most top managements resemble the Greek gods. In *Mythology,* the classic scholar Edith Hamilton observes that, until the Greeks, gods were nonhuman, towering colossi or strange beasts. "The Greeks," she says, "made their gods in their own image." The Greeks felt at home with their gods: "They knew just what the gods did . . . what they ate and drank and where they banqueted and how they amused themselves. Of course they were to be feared; they were very powerful and very dangerous when angry."

The fact is, Hamilton wrote, the gods "often acted in a way that no decent man or woman would." They were incalculable: "One could never tell where Zeus's thunderbolt would strike."

There isn't much justice or logic in the Greek pantheon. The gods were petty, mean, and nasty. They would interfere with, disrupt, or utterly destroy human beings for poor reasons, ignoble reasons, or no reason at all. You could be promoted by a god to kingship or queenship—or even godship. Or you could be turned into a goat. Zeus was asked by one of the godesses, Aurora, to do something nice for her husband Tithonus, so he made Tithonus immortal. Zeus forgot, however, to arrange for Tithonus to remain young; so the poor fellow just got older and more senile but never died. His wife finally turned him into a grasshopper. This reminds us that on Mount Olympus, as in many an office, even the publicly expressed favor of the big boss is no guarantee of success or happiness. He or she can do you a favor that does you no good.

But whether the echelon gods smile or scowl, crises go on forever. They are inescapable in part because the goals of work are often at odds with the generally accepted ethics of human behavior. Fights are supposed to be fought fair and clean. But an executive intent on pushing his ideas is not going to be reasonable in battling the opposition. One predictable result: crisis. He will acquire a few gray hairs wondering, How far can I go in destroying the opposition—who are also friends and longtime colleagues?

Familiarizing yourself with the catalog of crises, particularly in their order of appearance, prepares you for their occurrence and improves your ability to deal with them.

In the pages immediately ahead, you will find yourself at Stage I of the career road map that describes the terrain, the highroads and low roads, the pitfalls, and the opportunities that await first-job seekers at the career starting gate.

Stage I:
Getting Ready

1.
On the Threshold

THE threshold years—when adolescence is assumed to have ended but adult life has not yet begun—constitute a period in which a multitude of early, first-time, only-time crises take place. This is the case even though the career has not yet begun. In fact, it is *because* the career has not begun that the crises erupt.

Young people in their late teens and early twenties are confronted during the threshold period with profound decisions that may set the course for their whole lives. The conditions under which these people must make these decisions are daunting; in many cases terrifying.

Erik Erikson, whose work has given depth and shape to our view of the psychology of youth, remarks that the young person coming to the end of adolescence "now looks for an opportunity to decide with free assent on one of the available or unavoidable avenues of duty and service, and at the same time is mortally afraid of being forced into activities in which he would feel exposed to ridicule or self-doubt."

Erikson's comment is packed with meaning, and it resounds with ramifications of the dilemmas faced at the threshold of working life. For example, the term "available or unavoidable avenues of duty and service": Today, the whole world is assumed to open up before the young person, with an unlimited range of options. A couple of generations ago, the individual might have found the choices quite limited. Certain options were simply ruled out—because your family didn't have enough money, or because you hadn't gone to the right schools, or because people in your station of life did not aspire to certain careers, or because God had ordained otherwise for you.

Nowadays, people are relatively free of such limitations. The opening up of a wide range of options has been greeted with jubilation, as one of the triumphs of modern society. And, no question about it, it is a very good thing; but it has side effects. The concept of unlimited options can be difficult for people of any age; when you are young, it can be extremely severe. Those who stand on the threshold of working life can see career options all the way to the horizon. But they are all sealed boxes. You don't know what's inside, and you don't know whether the contents will be right for you until you open them.

The trouble is that you are burdened with the feeling that once you open *one* of the boxes, *all the others are forever sealed to you*. Worse, you have the feeling that if you open the wrong box, you will be trapped within that box for the rest of your life.

So you have to think very clearly and very hard. This is a vital decision. But you find yourself in a state that is the seething opposite of the emotional tranquillity needed to deliberate and choose in important issues.

One of the authors was once aboard ship in a typhoon in the Pacific. Vital decisions had to be made about the course, speed, and ballast—sink-or-swim decisions. But how could anybody think with the wind shrieking in the rigging, the waves driving the hull over onto its beam-ends, the green water surging through the broken doors of the wheelhouse? Survival was pure luck.

Young people in the late teens and early twenties are

likely to be going through similar emotional storms. They are striving, sometimes in agonizing turmoil, to get a sense of their identity, the new identity that will come with their first job.

In *Identity: Youth and Crisis,* Erikson writes: "In general it is the inability to settle on an *occupational* identity which most disturbs young people." (Emphasis ours.) Elsewhere *(Toys and Reasons: Stages in the Ritualization of Experience),* he writes: "The *work role,* which we begin to envisage for ourselves at the end of childhood, is, under favorable conditions, the most reassuring role of all, just because it confirms us in skills and permits us to recognize ourselves in visible works. But the unrest of puberty and the necessity to leave childhood behind, and the unrest of the times, combine to produce a variety of conflicting self-images, just at the age when we must envision ourselves not only as worker, but also as mate, parent and citizen...."

So here is the person in the threshold stage:

- under pressure to make momentous decisions;
- lacking satisfactory information about the options available;
- undergoing the physical and emotional stresses that come with the emergence from the cocoon of adolescence;
- feeling naked and vulnerable;
- terribly afraid of making the wrong decision; one that will bring doom and a life of unhappiness.

It is no wonder that in this situation young people will often try to delay the decision for as long as possible. They stay in school, or take off, or drop out (before ever dropping in), or just do nothing.

The crises faced by those on the threshold of working life grow out of these factors. Overloaded by the responsibility for making profound choices, fearful of being trapped, striving to shape an identity, the individual comes up against challenges like these:

- Crises of compromise—in which the dreams of youth must be altered and cut down to fit the mold of practicality.
- Crises of judgment—in which the desire to be judged

favorably is twisted by uncertainty as to who is doing the judging and by what standards.
- Crises of commitment—or lack of commitment—caused by aversion to the ultimate plunge into a life-channel.
- Crises of need for approval from a wider and more indifferent world than one has ever encountered before.
- Crises of identity, centering on the search for self.

Those who stand on the threshold know they will have to cross it. It is the mysterious darkness which lies beyond that underlies the greatest difficulties of this first stage.

2.
Heading for the First Job

Two cousins, college seniors, meet at a family get-together. One is graduating from Stanford with an M.B.A.; the other has a B.A. from Alfred, a small college in upper New York State.

STANFORD: Done anything about a job?

ALFRED: Some. The job market is miserable. How about you?

STANFORD: Big headache. I've narrowed the choice between IBM and Exxon, and I can't decide. What kind of job are you looking for?

ALFRED: Anything that pays.

Both men are in a crisis situation, but with an obvious difference. The Stanford cousin with marketable training can pick and choose. His concern is to decide between two of the best employers in the country. The liberal-arts cousin will go with anyone who will pay him a salary. He may have to settle for an entry-level job with any organization that will have him.

Even a man from Mars could detect the contrast in

preparation, attitude, and prospects of these two people. Preparation, attitude, and prospects—these three factors form a tight braid on which hangs an individual's fate in that terra incognita known as "first-job country." In that land, uncertainties of a dozen kinds lurk like predators in the underbrush. The intensity of worry makes the first job hunt one of the most severe crises the careerist will ever face. Listen to one recent graduate, embittered and unemployed:

"I put in four years at college and might just as well have spent them in Disneyland. Here I am out of school eight months and the best I can do to earn money is part-time typing." She adds, "Some people get it right. A B.A. who roomed with me in my junior year—she majored in art history—got herself a job as a management trainee. But she knew someone in the company."

Lack of preparation punishes about a third of those who have been educated but not vocationally trained. As one authority puts it, "Students who come out of school without marketable skills have been taught how to solve all the world's problems except one—how to find a job."

Not all people are banged about by doubt and uncertainty. Some find in the graduation-to-job situation all the ingredients of a grand ball. Buoyed up by the cresting wave of graduation, they go surging along toward the job world, confident that they are headed for good jobs, good pay, good future.

But they are a lucky minority. Even among these are some with insecurity lurking beneath a thin crust of optimism. Most are less hopeful. They expect struggle and adopt a take-the-best-you-can-get goal—which may not be much.

Talk to people undertaking a voyage and you find, underneath the excitement, a pervasive anxiety. The level of uneasiness is highest among those who don't know what to expect at the other end.

College graduates looking up at the work-world heights have a varied range of expectation. For most, the trip from academia to the first job seems more like a trip to the moon than between any two points on the planet Earth.

Alvin Toffler coined the phrase *culture shock* and used it as the title of his book describing the convulsive reaction people register as our society heads into the momentous changes of the future. It can well be applied to the first foray into the world of work.

A complication for the college undergraduate is that he or she faces two crises: one immediately past; one impending. Just as the level of bliss at becoming a senior is attained, the job hunt darkens the horizon. The ultimate school stage, instead of being a restful plateau, proves to be a catapult wound up and ready to toss graduates willy-nilly into a world that not only didn't they make, but one that seems to promise quick anointment into victimhood.

Here's the way that experience seemed to undergraduate Alan G. Ampolsk, '81, in the *Columbia Spectator*.

> For years I have heard about being a Senior in College. Whenever I felt frustrated by the present my family would remind me about it. "Someday," they said, "you'll be a Senior in College." I knew what it meant, too. Immense freedom. The end of confinement. A future overflowing with possibilities ...
>
> "Welcome to your Senior year in College," said the letter from the Dean. He was enthusiastic. "I see you're a religion major. That's excellent, just excellent. You know we have so few Liberal Arts majors these days ... any medical school would be happy to have you...."
>
> "So," asked my family, "What's it like being a Senior in college?"
>
> My advisor smiled. "What do you plan to be doing this time next year?"
>
> "Ah ... living ... somehow ..."
>
> "Nothing more specific? You ought to give some thought to where you want to wind up ..."
>
> I thought again. "Something fulfilling ... that I won't regret ... fulfilling and just ... and stimulating ... and relatively prosperous."
>
> "Well, law schools are glutted. Graduate schools aren't, but that's only because there's no work...."

The responses registered by those experiencing the transition from school to work constitute a unique syndrome, a career equivalent of *mal de mer* that may reach extremes of frustration and sense of failure. Some people—those who are more aware—feel the roots of childhood and youth being ripped up. They sense the difference between the life being left behind and the one they are about to enter. And the realization dawns that they are not tourists passing through. Whatever the land of their destination turns out to be, they must live there.

Professor Anthony Athos of Harvard says, "The average young graduate leaving the campus today rents a cap and gown, shakes hands with the college president, accepts his diploma amidst a burst of ceremony. . . ." Following which he tries to find a niche in an alien environment and then "the real world hits him hard and right between the eyes."

If you talk to people who are breasting the job market, the deep levels of their emotions usually come through. Here are three comments from among those we queried about their anticipations:

Jason Eppley, 23 years old, at Baruch College, City University of New York, has positive feelings about his employability. "I feel free at last, almost the way Martin Luther King meant. My first job is going to give me the liberty I want, financial independence, getting out from under my parents' control, entering a new world. I'll be a man, man."

Sarah Deland, twenty-two and a communications major at a West Coast college, was considerably less sanguine. "It's like going into a dentist's office. I know it will be unpleasant. People aren't going to be throwing welcome mats at my feet. I've heard my brother moaning and groaning about having a tough boss, being part of a demoralized work group—and that's all after you get the damn job.

"And even at this late date, my mother is nagging me to learn steno and typing so that I can get a job in a big company with eligible men around. I feel as though I'm being pulled in seven directions, and I don't want to go in any of them."

This young woman's outlook was dismal enough. But of all our interviewees, a graduate of a small college in Pennsylvania gave us the most chilling answer. He said, "I got out of college two months ago. I remember my graduation day clearly. After the ceremony, I walked down the stairs of the main building, and I knew I was leaving my best days behind me."

For those graduating into a less protective world, it is not only school that is being left behind. The world of teachers and texts is but part of the cocoon that is cast off. The first two comments we quoted reflect that broader world.

Jason Eppley, exulting in his impending freedom, mentions the restrictions from which he is escaping—parental control, financial dependence—as he passes from youth to adulthood in a kind of ecumenical bar mitzvah offering liberty that, unfortunately, may be matched by built-in servitude.

And Sarah Deland speaks of the family influence that converts her indecisiveness into anxiety. She is blocked from anticipating some of the possible benefits of change because her mother's marriage hints prevent her from committing herself to the challenges of the job world.

To the outsider looking in, the tensions of first-job seeking seem exaggerated. One assistant personnel director who interviews job applicants says, "These young people seem to think they are in a life-and-death situation. This is unreal. Although the people I see are generally not from affluent homes, they do have resources that can keep them healthy and well fed indefinitely. Yet many get to the hysterical point before they land something."

This could be the cool view of the uninvolved practitioner who has adjusted to others' discomfort by an emotional callus. However, the observation may be explained not by hysteria but by a below-surface struggle as powerful as it is unconscious.

The theater has a word for it: A director will talk of the action of a play and refer to the *subtext,* the hidden feelings and motivation that give the drama its richness. It is the subtext that explains why Goethe's *Faust* continues to grip the imagination of audiences. We empathize with Faust not because he is fighting the machinations of Mephistopheles but because we see in his struggles our own, our tragic resistance to old age and death.

Or consider *King Kong*. Why are we so fascinated by the story of an apelike monster fighting his human captors? We sense a symbolic confrontation of which we are a part, a primitive force struggling against an implacable civilization that eventually promises to crush him and us.

In the same way, the struggle of the young graduate is not simply to find a job. It is to do a number of other things that contribute muted but powerful concerns. For example:

To prove oneself; to show others—family, peers, friends—one's capability and worthiness.

To start a career that *may* reach admirable heights and satisfy aspirations, or confine one to pits of mediocrity and low levels of accomplishment.

And above all, to establish identity, to update the answer to that continually urgent question, "Who am I?" in a favorable way.

It is the hidden elements of motivation that intensify the crucial aspects of job hunting. Feelings become clear when you ask job hunters, "What is your real concern? What are you really worried about in looking for a job?" Some answers:

"No one may want me"—from someone who is concerned with acceptability and fears rejection.

"I'm not sure I can hold a job"—from a person with low self-esteem.

"I want to get married." This from a young man who sees a job as the economic foundation for starting a family. If the job is poor, marriage becomes less practical, and not finding a job at all holds a threat of interference with a deeply rooted social and biological desire.

Members of the preworker group reveal behavior that reflects underlying feelings about themselves, and their ways of handling these feelings. Their approaches to job seeking provide some interesting insights.

Five Types of Job Hunters

Take the group of college students in all its variety of background, intelligence, level of school achievement, capabilities and aspirations. Homogenize that mix, then stand within the portals of a placement office, and you see a kind of fractionating of the group according to the way they go about looking for jobs.

Here's how one expert observer, Florence Brand of Columbia's placement service, describes the five categories into which most of her interviewees fall.

- *Got-it-together people.* "There is a substantial percentage," Brand says, "who are objective, intelligent, and capable of planning an effective job hunt. A typical person in this group will come in and say, 'I'm graduating next spring. I'll have a B.A. with a major in English and creative writing. What should I start to do now that will help me find a job?'"

- *Passive-dependent people.* Of these, Brand says, "They are mildly neurotic and hope to be given specific directions in every phase of the job hunt. Usually their view of what is involved is unrealistic. Even if they have skills or qualifications that can be sold on the job market, they are either unaware of the fact or don't know how to capitalize on their assets."

This category can be especially helped by the placement services offering a range of assistance—for example, in résumé writing, or suggesting how to strengthen training or experience by study that will enhance key skill or knowledge areas.

- *Railroad-track people.* "These are the easiest ones to work with," Florence Brand says. "They have built a straight road from school to employment." Typical of this group are the prelaw or premed people looking for secure jobs, often in civil service. An average job market usually can absorb these individuals readily. On their part, they are looking for an organization that will take them on, help develop their careers, and in which they will stay until retirement.

- *Side-road wanderers.* Brand says, "These are individuals who are more interested in living than in working. They are not career-minded and consider work merely as an opportunity to earn enough money to take care of their needs. Generally they don't object to travel and will change their line of work readily if a good opportunity arises."
- *The walking wounded.* Most placement offices and employment agencies are familiar with people who are only marginally employable. They may have emotional problems and need emotional support as much as they need practical help. Some in this group seek another person to depend on; others come into a service or agency office just to be heard. They are eager to talk about themselves, their experiences, their interests—including highly personal reminiscences.

Since the average person in this group is not in a position to follow through on a job quest, agencies seldom offer practical aid for a job-finding program. But their needs seem to be satisfied when they are listened to and encouraged in whatever kind of action they decide on.

Most of the people fall into the first two categories. While some of the points covered apply to the third category—railroad-track people—most do not. The railroad-trackers do not constitute a large group. They are a select few who have known exactly what they wanted to be since age five, and have never departed from this path. Most people, uncertain about the right career, do far more meandering.

For many people, the crux of the decision boils down to this: Should they go with the hard facts, or the dream?

"I studied art and I'm good at it. But I've got to earn my living. Do I try to make it as an artist, or do I teach?"

"I love archaeology, I'm right in tune with Leakey and Aarons and people who devote their lives to trying to decipher the past. But my father has a good business—and he wants me to go in with him."

It's a basic dichotomy that lurks for many, and making a choice is not only an internal struggle. There are plenty of well-wishers in the wings who are positive they know "what is best for you."

Remember the scene in the film *The Graduate,* in which Dustin Hoffman in the title role is cornered at his graduation party by a doting uncle who whispers fiercely, "Plastics!"

That was a key word in an earlier time. But there are others pushed on you today. Recently, 900 high-school students listened to a mass recommendation: "Energy!" A day's program was sponsored by the National Energy Foundation, whose members include U.S. Steel, Brooklyn Union Gas, and Ebasco Services, which builds power plants.

Career goals summed up in single words abound. Which one you hear depends on who your relatives, friends, and parents are. Don't be surprised if it's computers, oil, biological engineering, or the hotel business. Employment hot spots keep changing. Your children will be put on to a good thing in lunar real estate.

The fact is, the future is enigmatic. No matter what your choice, it seems right—at first—and ten years later may come the dismal realization that the other one probably would have been better. Or, you soon know you've made the wrong choice, and you either feel there is no turning back or you try to and there are obstacles—the previous opportunity has disappeared. Resign yourself: Every choice has its risks. And there are few situations for Stage I people in which initiative and enlightened opportunism won't suggest a next step, or a new direction.

3.
People in Crisis: Four Cases

PEOPLE in the prejob category are generally aware of the change they are going through. If you have recently observed young adults in the about-to-look-for-a-job group, you will probably see behavior like this:

An unusual interest in the image that stares back from the mirror.

Curiosity about life on the job, such as "What's your boss like?" or "What if I don't make out?"

Preoccupations like these reflect awareness of the molting process by which they will shed a prejob persona and assume an as yet unperceived one.

As people reach the first-job threshold, they are confronted by a new and troubling sense of self. It is one of exposure, of vulnerability to unfamiliar forces. The comforts of known places, people, and patterns fade, and the individual stands at the edge of an abyss over which there arches a bridge—but is it strong enough to bear one's weight? And does the individual have the fortitude to try to cross it?

First-job hunters are often short on perspective. Elements of all kinds swirl about, some seeming large, some small, most triggering exaggerated reactions because complexities are not understood and frame of reference is lacking. But their confusion becomes understandable when it is realized that they are exposed not to a single crisis but to many. And each crisis has a different potential for trouble for each about-to-be worker. There are four categories of crisis faced by this age group—often in combination.

"Must I Commit Myself?"

Many hold back, asking themselves whether they are ready to take the step, commit themselves to the world of work. You'd think the committing referred to a mental institution rather than to the Big Time, that part of life that offers unmatched challenge, potential for accomplishment and self-fulfillment at least equal to any other. It's a game that in terms of stakes makes other endeavors seem like little league. Then why the hesitation?

What is being reflected is a kind of claustrophobia, a fear of being locked in and helpless.

Lisa and Dan talked about how they were going to pack it all in and go away together. Out west. Dan could be a forest ranger or something. Lisa would be a great painter. No way were they going to let their lives be tailor-made for them.

But when high-school graduation came, there was a change. Lisa seemed as gung-ho as ever. But one night she took Dan's face in her hands and looked him in the eye and said, "You're gonna go to college, aren't you?" And Dan mumbled, yeah, he thought he might give it a try, just for a year, not that he and Lisa weren't eventually going to take off on their own, but just, you know . . .

Lisa—talented—refused to go to college, but stayed around their Connecticut suburban home, commuting to New York to take classes at the Art Students League. Dan went to Brown. He did very well there—so well that he seemed to feel he had to explain it to Lisa: "Not that I really care about all that shit, it's a lot of useless stuff, but it doesn't hurt to have the degree."

"Degree? You mean the whole four years?"

"Sure. What's the sense of starting and not getting it? I mean . . . "

Although they still talked about taking off someday, and although neither of them said anything about any lessening of commitment, Dan and Lisa were both seeing other people.

When Dan decided to go on to get an M.B.A., Lisa had had it. Dan tried to explain that, while it was all a crock, maybe it would help when they set up their little business together in Montana. Lisa said, "Dan, you're not going to Montana. You're not going anyplace." She took off.

Dan missed her, but graduate school absorbed so much time and energy that the wound didn't seem to hurt so much. He distinguished himself. As graduation approached, he was the target of various recruiting efforts. Dan could pick and choose among career possibilities.

And one morning it came to him that he did not want any of them. He broke two appointments. He just sat in his room. He wondered where Lisa had gone, whom she was with, what was happening with her. Somebody had said she was in New Mexico, Santa Fe or someplace. Maybe if he went there. . . .

Dan Ehrlich was suffering—over a prolonged period— through a severe crisis of commitment, or rather a crisis of inability to commit. There were several paths open at this stage. Dan continually froze at the thought of taking any of them. He drifted wherever the current would take him, decided as little as he could.

He found himself experiencing a series of fast-changing ideas about his future. The first, strangely enough, was that he would study art. But after some thought, he suspected this was simply a means of competing with and possibly triumphing over Lisa. His next thought: He would take up deep-sea diving and join the glamorous group of people seeking treasure in the ocean depths. (This came after Peter Gimbel's feat of recovering a safe from the sunken *Andrea Doria*.) A few weeks later, another thought came, and lingered with its promise of sylvan solitude and an absence of pressure. Becoming a forest ranger, as he had once discussed with Lisa, seemed a good way to go. . . .

Unprepared to tie themselves to a specific career path, people like Dan will wrestle with desperate strength—of mind and ingenuity—to prevent the sunny open fields from turning into a constraining tunnel.

Dan Ehrlich's struggle to stay out of the job mainstream is duplicated by many who, for one reason or another—lack of aggressiveness to face the change to the working life; fear of failure; laziness—can't bring themselves to make the commitment.

"Fantasy employment" is one placement counselor's phrase for the occupations that some hesitaters dream about. Dan's idea about becoming a forest ranger fits into that category. Material returns from such professions may be meager, but for those to whom commitment to a "regular job" seems humdrum, the aura of the offbeat activity—in which performance judgments are difficult to make—often feels right. (You don't judge a forest ranger by the usual yardstick of affluence—expensive car, kids in private school, luxury home and so on.)

Of course, it is wise to distinguish between those for whom an exotic job title like forest ranger or poet is an indulgence and those for whom it is a serious calling.

Several paths are open to men and women who seek an alternative to going from study desk to work desk.

• *More school.* It used to be said that one benefit of college was that it offered four years to make up your mind about what you wanted to do in the world of work. To whatever extent this may have been true, the implied promise that a college degree automatically qualifies the holder for desirable employment is less true in today's climate of specialization and the need for technical training. The advanced degree now holds out the same promise of more time to think through a career decision and thus avoid premature commitment.

• *First the world, then the yoke.* Some students decide

they want to see more of life before taking the job plunge. This may mean travel—backpacking on the slopes of Mt. Everest, hitchhiking through Europe, squaring the Arctic Circle—or it may mean taking part in an exotic project, usually on a volunteer basis, such as working on an archaeological dig. One graduate of the University of Pennsylvania, fascinated by Africa, turned up in Nairobi and presented herself to a Quaker-run community-service organization. She was assigned first to help build a school on the outskirts of town, then to teach in an all-girl school 250 miles out in the Kenyan flatlands.

The journey, the experience, goes on until the thirst for adventure is slaked, or, as one cynical placement counselor puts it, "until a sense of guilt grows heavy enough to balance the goof-off." Then the deferrers are ready to fit themselves into the working world—as a preliminary, putting the best face on their adventures so that they look good on a résumé.

For some who resist seeking employment, the desire is to have a fling, to sow oats tame as well as wild. For others, it is a conscious effort to stretch horizons, reinforce their vocational thinking. John Shingleton, director of Michigan State University's placement services, makes a distinction between drifting and "stopping out." In his book *College to Career,* he says:

> The concept of "stopping out" is not novel. Goethe referred to *Wanderjahr*—meaning "the year of wandering about" that precedes settling down. In 1973 some 100,000 students took a year off between high school and college to gain real-life work experience. . . .
>
> Stopping out is not a new euphemism for copping out. It often has been successful. The key difference, apparently, is that stopping out implies a plan, a goal, an objective. You do not take a year off merely "to think." You have something specific to think about. And you also have gained another year of maturity. . . .

Feelings about plunging into the job mainstream or seeking alternatives reflect not only individual preferences but also contemporary values. The old work ethic has been beaten lustily about the ears by the poets and politicians of the counterculture. It is not uncommon for young adults to want to avoid an establishment they look on as venal, materialistic, and exploitative. As a matter of principle, it must be respected. Despite many efforts, business has not been successful in selling itself to the world at large and especially to the group to which it looks for a freshener of its human resources.

First-job seekers who worry about the thought of commitment would feel better if work were not seen as a nose-holding way of earning a living but as a part of life with its rewards and punishments, just like any other.

Without embracing the imperative of the traditional work ethic, many people come to the first-job portal with good feelings about their prospects. Some anticipations have already been mentioned: independence, financial and emotional; the excitement and challenge of the world of work; the prospect of satisfaction and fulfillment in being successful at whatever your job proves to be. People may overcome the commitment problem. But another hurdle looms for some.

"Will I Make the Right Start?"

Here's one college senior's explanation of her concern about her first job: "Recently I was talking to my uncle, who had just retired at the age of sixty-five. He worked for a paint company and never got very far; he ran the storeroom. He told me, 'I never expected to stay in the company. I started there on a temporary job and after thirty-five years it became permanent.' "

To many people, the first job becomes a pair of gears that grasps you, and doesn't loosen up to permit a second chance.

Another one of our interviewees put it a little differently: "Taking on my first job is the biggest gamble I've ever made." The assumption is that starting a job casts the fateful die forever. Yet the average person's career seldom shows less than three or four employers—and sometimes many more. As a group, the 20- to 30-year-olds show a particularly high average of job changes.

True enough, a first job may prove a key factor in setting career direction. But many people have taken a first job, disliked it, and gone on to a better second choice. And some may even fail in the first job and go on to better things with a second employer.

Peter Tremayne was the son of an affluent New Orleans builder. The Tremayne name made life easy for Peter, and being an outstanding quarterback at Tulane gave life a free-candy-counter feeling. Moreover, Peter Tremayne's endowments went beyond a husky frame and good reflexes. He had a 140 IQ, a good sense about people, and enjoyed working with them whether on the football field or in other school activities.

One of his schoolmates was a New Yorker whom Peter visited during vacations. The size, complexity, and excitement of the city seized Peter's imagination. By the time graduation came around, he had decided that he would go up to New York and find a job.

He had already made several other decisions. One was that he wasn't going to play professional football. His ambitions ran beyond investing the next ten or fifteen years of his life in an activity that basically he felt would keep him in a kind of permanent immaturity—and with imminent risk of life and limb.

Also, he had shrugged off the offers of people who wanted to take their college hero into business with them. But the idea of parlaying his football exploits into a career, regardless of the Tulane alumni's good intentions, meant to him that he wouldn't really have done it on his own. Besides, the big game of New York seemed a more appropriate next stage.

Finding a job, unexpectedly, was not easy. Despite some assistance from his friend, who helped him find an apartment and gave him some leads, a firm offer of a job failed to materialize. The country was going through one of its periodic recessions and jobs were hard to come by, par-

Stage 1: Getting Ready

ticularly for a young man who had majored in football. On lonely nights, he had reason to regret what in retrospect seemed a quixotic attitude in refusing jobs from his hometown admirers. After four or five months of employment agencies, personnel directors, and nothing but promises of something "later on," he seemed to be stymied. But his father had a card to play, and he phoned one evening to play it.

"Peter, take down this name and telephone number," and he gave his son the name of a college friend of his who might help. "He's the president of an interesting company, Miller and Huggins Management Systems. Talk to him. He's expecting your call."

The meeting between Peter Tremayne and Al Miller went very smoothly. And Al Miller's company, a management consulting firm, opened new vistas to Peter. The concept of organizations in the business of telling other businesses how to run their business, how to solve basic problems, how to approach the marketplace, how to restructure themselves for greater efficiency, reeked of enough godliness to satisfy the same ego needs fed by his football quarterbacking.

Miller took him on, starting as an assistant field representative. The job required visiting customers, making sure that there were no hitches or dissatisfactions with the firm's services.

Peter Tremayne's first six months in the field were supervised by a senior partner by the name of Andy Anderson, large, jovial, and sharp. Time spent with Andy was the equivalent of a cram course in business management. He got close-up views of a number of companies—the inner workings, the politics—and observed firsthand the fear and quaking of supposedly secure top executives and the rapaciousness of younger men out to do in their bosses and take over.

Tremayne was smart enough to know that this kind of firsthand experience, when backed up by selected reading, put him in a strong position to move ahead. He loved his job and his prospects.

Al Miller kept in touch with young Tremayne's progress and saw that it was good. At the end of six months, they had a meeting.

"Peter, Andy tells me you've been doing a fine job, and I'm inclined to agree. Furthermore, he tells me that you are good at working with clients. I've decided to make you a regional manager, put you in charge of part of the Chicago field operation."

That night Peter phoned his folks to tell them the big news. His father couldn't have been happier and his mother cried profusely. Peter hung up with the same feeling he had had when his team won the conference championship.

But three months after Peter Tremayne took on the management job, he was in trouble. The negative reaction of the field representatives hadn't been anticipated. They had liked Tremayne as an occasional visitor from headquarters. As a boss, he was too inexperienced, and they resented the leapfrogging that had put him in charge. Tremayne made several bad mistakes in judgment, intervening between field consultants and their clients, and increasing rather than decreasing the heat. The disagreements, the quarrels, finally caught up with him. He made an enemy of the vice-president in charge of marketing. As a result, he had a talk with an unhappy Al Miller, who told him things weren't working out. Perhaps Peter had better start looking for another job.

The world collapsed for Peter Tremayne. He wasn't used to failure, certainly not one as personal and total as this. Peter was left stunned and shaken. The sleep he had lost in the job-hunting days came in a poor second to the galloping case of insomnia he developed as his plight rankled, angered, then scared him. He had had his big chance and fumbled it.

It was Andy Anderson who got him back on track.

"Peter, I know you've got the stuff. And Al Miller does too, but he can't do a thing for you without having a revolution on his hands. That's organizational politics. In this case, the big man is only as big as others let him be. Things didn't work out because you got boosted too far too soon.

Stage 1: Getting Ready

But you've had good experience. Here is a list of six companies that could use your abilities to work with customers. In each case I've given you the name of a top person to see."

The fourth name on Andy's list was a winner. Tremayne met Greg Danziger, president of Danziger Industrial Engineering Management. Two weeks later, Peter was on the DIEM payroll as assistant marketing manager. And in this new position, things began to click, even better than at Miller and Huggins. A year later, his boss had a heart attack and retired. He was made acting manager and six months later got the job permanently. He had earned it.

For people who fear getting fly-papered by a first job, the Tremayne case makes it clear that the first job can be a stepping-stone to bigger and better things.

There were good reasons for Peter Tremayne's second success. For one thing, he brought experience to his new job. And even more important, the second job had requirements that, both in obvious ways and in subtle ones, were much better suited to Peter's strengths. The people he supervised now were less temperamental and more cooperative than the field experts who reported to him at Miller and Huggins. They not only liked him, they respected him—which made his life a good deal easier.

There are advantages to downplaying the idea that a first job represents a critical choice. One obvious advantage is that it allows you to be more relaxed. The second is that it makes you more capable of being objective in appraising job possibilities. Then you can use the same cool judgment in evaluating the experiences a first job brings and shorten the time it takes to get you into the "job-wise" category. You learn how to do your job better, and about the world of work in general.

Peter Tremayne's case makes an instructive point: A first job, even when it doesn't work out, can boost you upward.

Nervousness over entering the working world through a proper door, as well as anxiety about the commitment it seems to require, are both Stage I experiences. The next crisis strikes those who tend to look ahead, to anticipate situations beyond the immediate future.

"How Will I be Judged?"

The critic Wilson Meisner is given the credit for the insightful statement, "A person could live out his whole life in the twentieth century without discovering whether or not he was a coward." Apparently in our civilized society the occasions are generally lacking that might test an individual's courage.

People standing at any threshold of importance—whether it leads to a social event or to a new way of life—wonder whether they have what it takes to successfully pass the tests that the environment will impose. If it is a formal dinner, will they have the conversational skills to favorably impress diners at either side and be able to follow the dining rituals? If it is a new way of life, as the working world will be, will they have the job skills and the social qualities that will mean easy adjustment to the exigencies of the workplace?

From the first day on the job, people know they will be tested in a number of ways, new and ominous. And many of the trials are not detectable by the naked eye.

There's a story told about Henry Ford, unusual because its narrators sometimes tell it with approval and sometimes with derision. Ford was seeking an engineer to put in charge of one of his planning departments. Eventually the choice narrowed down to two individuals. Henry usually liked to make key personnel choices himself, and so invited the likelier of the two prospects to have lunch with him.

During the meal, the candidate ordered soup, which was placed before him. He picked up the saltshaker and shook it heartily over his soup bowl.

Ford's manner changed from interest to indifference. The meal was finished quickly and the job candidate bid-

Stage 1: Getting Ready

den farewell. Shortly thereafter, he learned that the job had been given to someone else.

Ford told his personnel director: "I would never hire that man; he salted his soup without even tasting it." To Ford, this showed that the engineer made decisions off the cuff without first making sure of his ground.

Perhaps you will agree with the relevance of Ford's test and perhaps you won't. But the anecdote suggests the personal and unpredictable tests of performance that may exist in the business world. The sense of being judged is uncomfortable enough, but when you're not sure of what you're being tested for, nor of the test, anxiety understandably increases.

If you hadn't known before that Moose Glazebrook was touchy about criticism, you would have realized it when Moose punched the sports editor of the high-school paper in the mouth. The sports editor had written that Moose dropped three passes in Saturday's game. While this comment was accurate, Moose took exception to it. Since at 6'3" and 225 pounds he was twice the scribe's size, his rebuttal had force if not logic.

The sports editor should have known: You just do not knock the Moose. You do not even say things that he might interpret as knocking him.

Unfortunately, Moose's athletic scholarship took him to a state university at which the coaching staff did not care whose feelings they hurt. Furthermore, Moose was now playing with teammates who showed no mercy in commenting on his slowness and occasional clumsiness. And they were big. Moose couldn't punch everybody in the mouth.

When it became clear that he had no future as a college football player, Moose was relieved. The president of the local soft-drink bottling company, a heavy sports fan, gave him a job in marketing. Moose was to learn the ropes, and there was a good chance that he could enjoy a tremendous business future.

But it was a nightmare. It was, Moose thought, worse

than high school. All these people looking at you and judging you: the sales manager, the training director, the senior route manager who was his immediate supervisor.

One day the sales manager had a little chat with Moose. He said that he liked Moose's energy, his ability to cut right through the nonsense and get to the heart of situations, his ability to handle tough customers.

Then the sales manager said, "About the way you plan your day . . . "

"What's wrong with the way I plan my day?"

"I didn't say anything was wrong with it. Yet. But now that you ask, you don't leave yourself enough flexibility to stay with the bigger customers a little longer if questions come up. It's just a matter of experience. But you see—"

Moose told him off in no uncertain terms and walked out. He wondered where he could get a job where they weren't always watching him, waiting for him to make a mistake.

Tests in the school situation are simple in that the process is clear-cut. Students know a great deal about testing under school conditions. They are used to taking tests by the dozen. For example, you take a test on last week's chapter in a biology text or on a particular set of theorems in mathematics. But you can't study as precisely for the tests the work scene may set. The subject areas are less readily identifiable, the standards not always clear, and results sometimes arguable.

Yet, by this somewhat vague process you will be judged, your achievement verified, your status in the group determined, to say nothing of salary and promotability. And along with your boss's approval or disapproval, your reputation will be enhanced or tarnished. If an assignment is sufficiently major, your career may be affected for better or for worse by the way it is performed.

Talk to individuals about to start their first jobs and you get the immediate feeling that judgment by a superior is both anticipated and feared. It's accepted that value judgments made by parents and teachers are "different."

Stage 1: Getting Ready

Job tests are not so much of what you know but of what you are. Your ingenuity, your intelligence, your ability to solve problems, your ability to take the initiative and make decisions come under review. These are personal qualities. You are operating much closer to the ego level than you ever have. It is the consequences that count. Materially, the employee may get a raise if he or she does well, a reprimand if results are under par. And psychically, doing well on an assignment, solving a problem, means success, the respect of peers, recognition by the boss—in this new "real" world.

In short, the judgments may have weighty results, and the interest and wariness of about-to-become workers is not misplaced. They have reasons for concern in the trials of the new life.

"For the Second Time, Who Am I?"

School provides the context for becoming aware of and resolving the individual's first identity crisis. Shaped by both exterior events and their interior lives, most students have developed a recognizable self-image by the time they're ready to leave college.

For those on the job threshold, just as the struggle for one's school identity is completed, a new and greater one looms. And what if the results are less satisfactory than those of the school years? Here's one person's story.

Little happened at Charlotte Raglin's alma mater without her being involved. She had written scripts for two senior plays—the first at the end of her junior year, the second just before graduation—and had parlayed a lively sense of humor into two smash presentations. Not incidentally, she played the lead in both. Her homeliness—at the age of 23 she had the drooping features of a 50-year-old, and her round-shouldered figure traversed the stage with a sideways shuffle—helped her in the comedic roles. She ran for president of the senior class and won a landslide victory. Any undergraduate, and sometimes members of the faculty, who wanted to get anything going in the school—whether it was to raise funds to redecorate the student lounge or stage a protest against nuclear proliferation—started with Charlotte.

In short, Raglin's name became *the* campus conjure phrase, her last year a surging triumph of public acclaim and admiration. Had there been a yearbook feature with the traditional *mosts* and *most likelies,* Raglin would easily have come off with the "most likely to succeed" designation.

Friends who asked were told her plans: "Something in the theater," she said. "I've got a couple of scripts that are pretty good. One's just right for Woody Allen."

The self that Charlotte Raglin had grown at school didn't succeed in the outside world. Her two scripts—which would have done well on any college stage in the world—were considered sophomoric and unsuitable for professional production.

She went down the well-traveled path from Broadway producers to Off Broadway, then to Off-Off Broadway groups and their adherents and supporters.

Finally, with the help of 3,000 sweat-earned dollars contributed by her doting and hopeful family (her college success had confirmed their idea of her worth and eventual triumph), one of her scripts, *Zingers and Zongers of the Southland,* a topical review, made the boards in a little East Fourth Street theater, where it struggled and gasped for two weeks, then expired.

Charlotte was not deterred. She eventually made a belated move, looked up some of the more affluent people in her class—or their relatives. Initial reactions were hearty: "The great Charlotte Raglin? I've been watching the theater pages for your stuff, Charlotte. . . ."

After many months, her requests shifted from theater-related matters to employment of any kind. Initial pleasantries died at direct requests—for a job in the friend's father's company, or for an introduction to an executive who might give her a job, and so on. But the qualifications that might have made her the newest Broadway success didn't look so good on a résumé.

Stage 1: Getting Ready

Eventually, her mother's cousin, who was a partner in a Wall Street brokerage house, helped her get a job as a tab-punch operator. Down to her last few dollars, Raglin took the position, thinking up some witty comments to use in telling people what she was doing: "The president of the firm wants me to learn the business from the outside in. . . ." Or, "Thought I'd do a couple of months of research for a satire that will rip Wall Street wide open. . . ."

Charlotte Raglin met and married a man who owned a dress shop in New Jersey. "Sweet guy," she said, not only because she thought he was but also to cover the fact that he was not in the theater. To everyone's surprise, including Charlotte's own, after she had gained some experience in the family shop, she did well selling. Once again she was popular; the customers enjoyed her wit. The humor that didn't go on Broadway played well in a boutique in Ridgewood, New Jersey.

Of course, she still talks of making it on Broadway. "I'm finishing up a script that Marty [her husband] thinks is terrific. . . ." And from time to time she sees producers' agents or performers' agents. "Something's got to give someday" is her public conviction and her private defeat.

Those about to enter the job world are preoccupied by two questions.

The first is how the transition will be made from a present familiar self into an as yet unformed image. What does one do? What can one initiate?

Second: What if the new image is less worthy than the previous one? Fortunately, the odds are against the Charlotte Raglin fate, or the one implied by an interviewee mentioned earlier: "When I left college, I knew my best days were behind me."

For every Charlotte Raglin, there are many who make it in the more common avenues of employment, and find there a world of challenge, and form a new identity based on acceptance and achievement.

The qualified and the capable needn't worry whom

they will find when they find themselves in the working world. And the happy discovery will reflect not only the external factors of money and status but also the ego needs involved in fitting into the adult world of work in some self-fulfilling way.

The more insightful individuals understand that the likelihood is for drastic change in self-image. Whatever the persona may have been, it will recede into the past.

There is especially good news for some. Those who fared poorly during the indentity-crisis-laden school years now may see improvement—the cliché confrontation of the college nonentity, successful in a new job and radiating an aura of accomplishment, meeting the college star selling newspapers on the street. Charlotte Raglin, typical of the latter group, made a fatal and avoidable error. She assumed that the personal qualities that made for college triumph would apply in another milieu. She was wrong.

What many people don't realize is that the world of work is geared for their success. But it takes some cooperation, and a willingness to adapt.

Those undergoing initiation into the world of work eventually benefit from a crucial fact: The difficulties of the initiation itself are not an inherent part of the world, but are a rite of passage, a transition phenomenon; when it's over—that means being on someone's payroll—the individual is ready to start one of life's great adventures. And the future, as has never been the case before, is fluid, shapable by the new citizen.

Stage II (20–30): The Learning Decade

4

Entering the Dark Cave

FEAR of the unknown is our primordial heritage. What must our early ancestors have felt like when they ventured into cavernous darkness, not knowing what kinds of dangers awaited them?

The brightly lit and lavishly furnished office can be a dark cave. The crises of the 20–30 stage may arise from the fear of the unknown and the shock of the new. They are crises of adaptation, of self-doubt, of disillusionment, and of fear. Working is fundamentally different from anything else.

School is a rough—sometimes very rough—socializing experience. But there is very little in the adolescent days in school or camp or in clubs or on teams to prepare us for the structured world of work.

That's why the first crisis of adjustment often coincides with the first weeks on the job. Individuals learn, sometimes with incredulity, that they are expected to *take orders;* that they are at the mercy of persons strictly because of their seniority and rank; that they are supposed to accept a whole list of customs and rules developed for their governance by people they have never seen and who in some cases are long since dead.

One major issue is authority. In your life you get to know three authority figures. Parents are the first institutionalization of authority in our consciousness. During school years, teachers tell you what to do and what not to do, praise and criticize, punish and reward. College provides a hiatus rather than a transition. There are, of course, authority figures; but the dominant mode is to scorn and reject them (except for a few favored instructors).

In the working years, the boss takes on the mantle of power. At this point, some people have a problem: They have trouble making the transition from the two previous kinds of authority to the third. The similarities are perplexing. True, the boss has authority and creates a superior-subordinate relationship that can yield benefits as well as confusion. But the sooner one realizes that a boss is not a parent or a stand-in for a favorite or even disliked teacher, the sooner reality can season the relationship. As benign as a boss may be, he or she represents an establishment that is unsentimental. For dependent individuals, this hazard is particularly threatening.

When freedom is suddenly trammeled, when the tether tightens and the self-image is sharply assailed, the results can be distressing and hurtful.

This is what happens when you start to work. You are no longer free. You are at the beck and call of a boss and a tradition; a way of doing things. And your self-esteem is sharply attacked. The assault on self-esteem comes in several ways.

You are no longer in control. The qualities that were important in earning respect and admiration no longer seem important. And the work you are doing is simply not that challenging. You are the low person on the totem pole—something it seemed you would never be again.

All of this becomes more critical because of the urgency placed on each word and action when you start work. It is difficult to "weight" the innumerable questions and

Stage II (20-30): The Learning Decade

problems that come up every day. A casual word at a meeting may be trivial or earthshaking. At any given time, you might do something that will do immense damage to your future—*and you won't even know it.*

In difficult times, facing dangers and mysteries, the newcomer forms bonds with the people met on the job. These bonds can be a source of great comfort and assistance. But friendship and trust in the workplace are not always repaid. Sometimes they are *betrayed.* Herein lies another rich vein of crises.

During the past two decades, there has been some very significant research into the subject of *attachment behavior.* Orthodox psychiatric thinking once held that bonds developed between creatures *only* if both individuals had needs that were fulfilled by the association; needs like food, sex, dependence. This theory never really seemed to cover the variety of astonishing attachments formed by humans; attachments in which at least one party gets little or nothing out of it. One novel of the many books that have explored such relationships is *Of Human Bondage,* the whole point of which is the senselessness of Philip Carey's obsession with the sluttish and worthless Mildred.

There is a considerable body of evidence showing that strong bonds can develop between individuals without any rewards being given or needs met. A young monkey will cling to a soft dummy that provides no food and reject a hard figure that does provide food. This is attachment behavior. Psychologists have been saying that the individual engages first in attachment behavior; then sexual bonding; then caretaking behavior. To many observers it is now clear that attachment behavior is not only the first but also the strongest of these bonding mechanisms. Even more to the point, attachment behavior does not stop with adulthood. It is a normal element of human nature throughout life.

During the twenties, attachments are formed with people at work: attachments with bosses and with colleagues. The attachments between comrades-in-arms can be very strong, so a number of the crises in this period might be called "crises of attachment." Someone you trust betrays you. Later in your career, armored by cynicism, you might shrug it off. At this point, it is traumatic.

Then, too, there is the attachment crisis that may be precipitated by the conflict between the lure of another job and the bonds one has formed on the present job.

And of course there is the attachment of sex. That people who work side by side will go to bed with each other is not surprising. It would be surprising if it were not prevalent. This is why articles enjoining us to avoid office love affairs have a Canute-like ring. What happens when close attachments with working colleagues—bosses or peers—are shattered? The results often add up to severe personal crisis.

Yet another class of crises met in this decade grows out of the fact that you are involved in the roughest *learning process* of your life.

There are various learning theories. Those grouped under the heading "S-R Theories" are based on the concept that learning consists of association of stimulus and response. Pavlov's dog, salivating at the sound of the bell, is the ultimate simplification (and absurdification) of this theory.

B. F. Skinner broadens the range of stimuli from the particular to the universal. To Skinner, every aspect of the environment is a possible influence on learning. One of the most flamboyant enterprises of the great behaviorist was the "air crib," a glassed-in, controlled environment within which he installed his infant daughter for two and a half years.

More recent theories depart from tradition in various ways. Whatever the particulars of the theory, there are several salient facts about learning that are central to our consideration of the decade of the twenties:

- Learning means changing behavior as a result of experience.
- When behavior is reinforced, it becomes part of our makeup.

Stage II (20-30): The Learning Decade

- When behavior is penalized, we tend not to learn it.
- We continue to learn as adults; and the years between 20 and 30 involve heavy and sometimes difficult activity.

Learning experience means not just "practical" experience but formal teacher-pupil situations as well. During our school days, the trial-and-error nature of learning is not apparent, because the curriculum has been predigested. Whether this is good or bad is a matter for the educationists to debate (and they do). When you start work, however, most learning is acquired in the crucible of trial and error. This rough-and-ready learning process lies at the heart of many of the crises faced in this stage.

The issue is complicated by the fact that the new arrivals in the world of work are likely to feel that they have changed the rules in the middle of the game. A college senior has become familiar with a certain set of criteria by which the individual is judged: academic criteria and the criteria applied by peers. Influenced by these criteria, the young person has a view of self and of the world.

But entry into the world of work brings the necessity to learn, and to be judged by, a whole new set of standards. Many of these standards are in contradiction to those that applied in the prework world. Some of the criteria appear trivial; others ignoble. And many of the standards, along with the process by which they are applied, are extremely mysterious. In fact, they are Kafkaesque.

Franz Kafka's name has become a commonplace for the paradoxes and absurdities of modern life. In his unfinished novel *The Trial,* he presents a bank assessor, Joseph K., who is accused of an unknown crime by a faceless authority, and is brought to ruin by forces that remain totally mysterious and impersonal. Something similar happens during this decade. The newcomer to work becomes acquainted with what *seems* to be an orderly set of rules: listen, weigh the alternatives, decide judiciously, etc. The *real* rules are several levels deeper. The struggle to reach this level underlies many crises.

Actually, the vagaries of the working world are more likely to resemble the pantheon of the Greek gods, whose wonderful whimsies we discussed in the Introduction. Rewards and punishments flash down from the Olympian executive suite without any apparent connection with merit.

And from *this* you are supposed to learn? Well, you try to learn. And you hope you'll get used to it.

"You'll get used to it." They are among the most familiar words in job language. During the first few weeks, you can usually count on the comforting presence of someone "older"—in experience if not years—who offers reassurance as you confront the bewildering world of work.

What you are told you'll "get used to" are particular things: the foibles and crotchets of a particular person ("Andy seems pretty abrupt when you first meet him, but his bark is worse than his bite"), the oddness of specific rules and regulations ("Right now you may wonder why we do it that way, but pretty soon you'll see the reason for it"); the unique peculiarities of the company ("IBM has its way of going about these things and we have ours"). But in a broader sense, what you are getting used to is the world of work itself.

"What is work? And what is not work?" asks the *Bhagavad-Gita,* adding that "these are questions that perplex the wisest of men." Puzzlement about the nature of work feeds the flames of crisis.

What you are undergoing is intended to introduce the "individual animal" into society; in other words, to tame you. Some people just will not make it. They ask, "Why the hell *should* I get used to it?" And they never do. Unfortunately, some of these same people remain in the world of work that they reject, always at odds with it, always in conflict with its concepts.

A new world; new and fragile attachments; new hopes and fears; new and difficult things to get used to. No wonder crisis is rampant. But at the same time you *learn*. And if you learn well in the Stage II Decade, you become much better prepared for the crises of later working life.

5.
The First Day

THE first thing Dorothy learns on landing in Oz is that her house has crushed a person. But the small citizens who cluster around are not accusatory, they are exultant.

One strange thing leads to another for Dorothy. Why should the Witch of the West be such a *kvetch?* Why do the trees throw apples at her? Why are some creatures hostile for no apparent reason?

Culture shock.

Dorothy's tumultuous arrival in the Land of Oz is perhaps more bizarre than the first day on your first job. But for many, it's a fair parallel.

For most of us, the first day on the job does not constitute a crisis per se. However, it gives you a series of "coming attractions"—foretastes of crises that will be met, and resolved, throughout the Learning Decade. The paramount quality of this first day is its *strangeness.* The rules, the ethics, the structure, and the priorities of the working world seem significantly different from what came before. It is the process of acclimating ourselves to these new standards—of *internalizing* what at first seems alien and apart—that defines the Learning Decade.

Janet Carpenter, after receiving her M.B.A., had accepted a job with Arcturus Dynamics, Inc. On the morning of her arrival, she spoke with Andrew Hassler, her department head.

"We're all on a first-name basis here, Jan. Please call me Andy. You'll be going through the usual personnel-department routine with the forms and the lectures and all the rest of it. Don't worry about the personnel people. They take themselves very seriously, but you're in a line department. Right now, though, I thought we could just chat. We want your input."

Jan began to talk about how excited she was, and how she intended to do her first assignment. Hassler listened for a minute, then said, "Jan, please do it the way you're instructed to. Missy, my secretary, who is a tower of strength and the real brains in this department, will show you the format I prefer. Well, I think we're really off to a great start, Jan. Good luck, and I'm sure we're both going to be very glad you chose ADI."

This is, for Janet Carpenter, orientation to a new job. But it is considerably more. It is the first step in *initiation into a culture*. She is beginning to learn more about the *universal* customs existing in business and also the particularized customs and folkways of the microculture she is entering: Arcturus Dynamics, Inc.

Within this brief exchange are threads of some of the major elements of the business culture: rites of passage, ordeals, incantations, the nature of the priesthood.

But of course Jan will get used to it. She will even learn how to read her way through mixed signals, the surface appearance of gentility and sweet reasonableness, and the flinty underlying reality of power (sometimes masking insecurity), greed, egotism, bias, and favoritism.

She'll get used to it. But for right now, Janet's talk with Andy is a bewildering mix of contradictions and cloudy messages. Does he want my input or doesn't he? Does he want to tell me what to do or doesn't he? Does he want an informal relationship, or am I supposed to keep my distance?

Stage II (20-30): The Learning Decade

Involved here is what S. I. Hayakawa calls the "meta-message," the real message behind the words. Children catch on quickly. But it is not so easy in the world of work, because the rules and structures are different from what you've gotten used to in dealing with parents, friends, teachers, etc. "When I use a word," said Humpty-Dumpty to Alice, "it means just what I choose it to mean—neither more nor less."

You are suddenly receiving messages that are shaped by a hierarchy . . . pecking order . . . greed for power . . . *fear*. (Never underestimate the extent to which you, as a new person, will be perceived as a threat by people who seem to be safe and secure beyond imagination.)

Even the surface language of business is hard to understand. The messages underlying this surface language may be hard to read. They are in *code*. Many of the crises of these years revolve around misinterpretation or refusal to accept the code.

For others, the "welcome" to the world of work is a stone wall. Caroline says that she was in her first job for two weeks before anyone gave her any guidance at all. Her boss was pleasant but simply said, "Don't worry. You'll pick it up." Co-workers didn't exactly snub her, they just seemed to act as if she did not exist.

And then there is the situation in which newcomers to the work scene encounter hostility that seems to have no basis whatever. "I had never met any of these guys before," says Vincent, "and here they were trying to louse me up. And it wasn't even as if I was in competition with them. They just did not want to accept me."

They did not want to accept him. They rejected him—as the body will often reject a transplanted organ.

Much of the difficulty you meet when you first go to work will involve this tendency of the organism to reject anything that is added to it. As a matter of fact, you will run into the same thing throughout your career, every time you take a new job; but later you will have adjusted to it.

When you first enter the workplace, though, it will

seem new and strange. You are one small cell, trying to find a place in the complex organism. But at the same time, the organism has to shift—even if ever so slightly—to accommodate you. The critical shock you feel may be mirrored by the shock your arrival causes somewhere else.

It's all part of *structure-building.*

The first multicelled animals were sponges. The sponge is a loose aggregation of specialized cells: Some cells form the skeleton; some form the flagella, which beat the water in search of food; some cells transport food to other parts of the sponge's body; and so forth.

You can force a sponge through an extremely fine mesh, separating it into millions of tiny parts. If you leave this heap of disconnected parts alone, the cells will reassemble themselves into a sponge, each cell finding its proper place in the structure.

Structure-building, whatever its initial cause, is a characteristic of organisms that was essential in the evolution of more and more complex animals.

At a certain point on the evolutionary scale, structure ceases to be purely biological and begins to include nonphysical factors. The pecking order; the social organization of the wolf pack—these are just two examples of this other sort of structure-building.

Human beings are psychic structure-builders. During the Learning Decade, you fabricate your own environments, including a place to live, nonfamily relationships, life-style. One of the most important elements of the psychic structure that is built during this time is establishment in a workplace.

As you begin to find your place, the shock of strangeness abates. But there will be moments of panic; nightmarish, like those terrible dreams in which you wander lost through a strange place, turning down one lane and then another, always finding blank walls and indifference from people who look human but don't act the part.

It is because the instinct for structure-building is so strong within us that the failure to find one's place in the structure leads to crisis. "I don't know what I'm doing!" is a lament that can really mean "Everyone around me seems to be part of the structure, to have a role in the functioning of the complex organism. But I am an outsider. *Will I ever be safely on the inside?"*

Some years ago, the psychologist Leon Festinger formulated a theory to explain why and how people get used to things, even unpleasant things, and come to accept them.

For example, someone you like walks out on you. You're desolate. The person was warm, caring, interesting. Six months later you remember that person as cold, selfish, and dull. What happened? Festinger called the process "cognitive dissonance."

In effect, said Festinger, the mind gradually pushes a bitter shock below the surface of consciousness and then later brings the same experience to the surface in a more pleasant and palatable form.

One way researchers tested this theory was to ask teen-agers to list their ten favorite records in order of preference. Then they told the teen-agers that they would be giving them three of the records on the list. However, the gifts were not numbers one, two, and three. Instead, a teen-ager might be given number three, number five, and number nine from his list.

A little while later, these same young people were again asked to list their ten favorite records. Almost invariably the gift items would move far up on the list, often winding up as numbers one, two, and three.

It is cognitive dissonance that causes people to pay particular attention to the advertising for expensive items after they have bought them. People study ads for cards, stereo and video systems, and big-ticket appliances after the purchase is made. Somewhere inside they still have doubts. They are resolving their cognitive dissonance.

Here's one way this phenomenon operates in the world of work.

Harriet was assigned to Alberta Walker's group when she joined the company. Harriet thought the sun rose and set on Alberta. Alberta's observations were law. Her criticisms were Holy Writ.

And then one day, just like that, Alberta was fired. Harriet was moved to Mary Gallieni's group. Casually, Mary began to dismantle the edifice that Alberta had been building, by saying, "You've got a future here, kid. Don't louse it up by sticking with some of those idiot notions Alberta was so fond of."

Harriet kept her mouth shut. With painstaking care, she unlearned what Alberta had taught her and learned it Mary's way—but it was agony.

That is, it was agony for the first couple of weeks. Then Harriet did not think about Alberta much anymore, if at all. Four months later she was able to say to a friend—and really mean it—"I was lucky to get away from Alberta in time. She really was a loser."

The process of resolution of cognitive dissonance can be cruel, but it is necessary. The trouble is that some dissonances may not stay resolved. Ten years later, even twenty, there are people who have not resolved their basic dissonances about the world of work. They are hostages, doing what they're told, but resenting every minute of it. One way to view their failure: Their own psychological makeup has let them down by not adjusting to the reality of work.

6.

The Achievement Crisis

IN the normal course of events, the confusions and uncertainties of a new workplace dissipate. As familiarity with the milieu of work increases, what's expected and how to perform become clear.

Then a new thought begins to sound in the mind: How do I get ahead? How do I boost my paycheck, get a better job? The thrust of this question originates from two sources. First, our culture in general has a get-ahead tradition. But a secondary source—and in some companies more than others—is that there's a kind of stimulation in the air. A large percentage of people become preoccupied with the idea of advancement. Many companies foster this attitude by making their employees aware of the desirability of and the potential for advancement. By sparking a spirit of competitiveness, top management hopes to get a livelier, more result-oriented group of employees and a consequent improvement in performance.

When the realization hits, the Stage II individual is immediately beset by the question "How? How does one get ahead?" By what strategies and tactics does one begin to forge ahead of one's peers?

There's one ready answer. It's the "good" reason, the one you'll hear from your boss: "Work hard, do your work well, and you'll eventually get recognition." But as Winston Churchill said, "There are always two reasons for something happening—a good reason and a real reason."

Despite the implied cynicism of the Churchillian statement, the good reason—hard, result-getting labor—often does apply. People have progressed in their job situations by outstanding performance. However, there are other factors that make for job success—factors that your boss is less likely to stress. They are luck and opportunity.

Consider the matter of luck. James Cagney, one of the outstanding movie stars of the thirties and forties, described a key episode in his professional life:

"I heard they were hiring actors for a show and I turned up at the audition hall along with dozens of other would-be's. After a while a man came out—I later learned it was George Kelly, the playwright. He looked over the big crowd, suddenly spotted me and said, 'O.K., you. You've got the job.' " Cagney agrees that this break was the bit of good luck that launched him on the way to stardom.

There is no question that luck plays an important part in many careers. The only problem is that it's generally unpredictable and uncontrollable. True, many people say you can "make your own luck," but when you analyze what they mean, it turns out that they are really talking about learning how to manipulate the second factor just mentioned, opportunity.

People who develop a sensitivity to situations and directions that promise a big payoff for them are doing a good deal to resolve the achievement crisis. But opportunity is a funny thing. It seldom is $2+2=4$. As a matter of fact, if the opportunities are too obvious, there can be a wild scramble in which you are just one of several competitors. If someone on the echelon above you is moving out, you probably won't be the only one entertaining the idea of a possible promotion.

Stage II (20-30): The Learning Decade

Opportunity spotting can be a highly creative act. It requires imagination to analyze the situation and see how it can be turned to advantage.

For example, during the Vietnam action, Tom Brett, coming out of Boston College, decided to become a conscientious objector. He went to the draft board of his small town outside Boston and requested CO status. As Tom tells the story in later years, somewhat ruefully, "After considerable hassle, the board eventually agreed to give me CO status. They didn't do it out of respect for my principles, but because my family was well known and respected in town."

As alternative service, the board told Brett he would have to serve as an orderly in a local institution devoted to the care of retarded people. Obviously no picnic.

Brett began his three years of service. Although he liked the idea of helping handicapped individuals, the work itself ran the gamut from stomach-turning to barely tolerable. But as the months went by, Tom Brett realized that he was in an unusual situation that offered vocational opportunity. In line with this idea, he began to learn as much as he could about institutional operations, both from his own firsthand experience and from self-programmed studies. He familiarized himself with as many of the departmental and specialized activities as he could.

His strategy eventually paid off. The week after he finished his three years of service—the Vietnam adventure had finally come to an end—there was a staff opening for a deputy director. Of the fifty candidates, Tom Brett was easily the best qualified and got the job.

For the careerist, the how-to-get-ahead question is a repetitive crisis. Keep in mind as you move ahead through the different stages that as your personal situation changes, the shape and appearance of opportunity tend to change. For example, in Stage II, a good move may be to get yourself transferred into a job where you will be working with a manager who is a good teacher. You will learn more and faster.

By Stage III, developing opportunity may be a matter

of figuring out the direction in which your company is going to grow and learning the technology and related matters that will become the prime areas of activity.

But remember: For many, the urge to surge ahead is a continuing need that satisfies aspirations but also creates crises—everything from how to survive, to success, to learning how to bear up under the loneliness at the top.

7.

The Crisis of Individuality

"My father was a man who went through life selling off little bits of himself until there was nothing left. Then they just threw away the husk. Willy Loman! I told myself I'd never, never get into that spot. And now here I am." Those are the words of a woman in anguish over the realization that ten years has wedged her firmly into a monotonous deadend job that, as she puts it, could be done by a zombie.

Some people do not seem to have an identity apart from their work. "Who are you with?" observes John Kenneth Galbraith. "Until this is known, the individual is a cipher." But you have an individuality that is all your own. Must you have it amputated before you can join the mainstream of economic activity?

This can be one of the most difficult and frightening crises of Stage II. Your individuality is precious to you. But now it is under attack. It seems that to keep your job—or at least to flourish in it—you must accept a little conformity. Is "a little conformity" like "a little pregnancy"? Will it grow until you are an out-and-out hypocrite?

Your feelings of identity and self-worth are deeply challenged by this threat. You will—and should—fight for your individuality throughout your career. During the twenties, the fight is most likely to erupt in flaring crises of anger and disgust.

The issue of conformity can take many guises: the necessity of wearing a tie or dress; the requirement not to say what you fervently believe; the obligation to accept another course of action when you know you are right.

Some years ago, Alan Harrington wrote *The Revelations of Doctor Modesto,* a burlesque of business and success methods. The hero, a lackluster insurance executive, answers an ad and receives the secret of Dr. Modesto. The key is "centralism." Dr. Modesto's pupils always wear neutral shades, speak in neutral voices, walk neither fast nor slow. In a crowd, they always seek the center. (More recently, in *Power,* Michael Korda offered advice on where to stand at an office party in order to achieve control.)

Must one practice centralism to achieve success? No. Is it possible, in pursuing a career, to escape the conflict between the need to remain an individual and the need to conform to the rule? Again, *no,* unless one's "career" is that of a hermit. Even within a monastery or a convent, the conflict exists. The self fights against the obligations imposed by the larger organism.

Peter Drucker cites Kierkegaard's concept of the tension between man's simultaneous life as an individual in the spirit and as a citizen in society. The only true freedom is *freedom within order.* The individual can act voluntarily—but within the framework of the organization. "He has to accept its reality," says Drucker, "has to affirm its objectives and values, has to focus his values, knowledge and efforts on its needs and opportunities."

It's that last part—the focusing of individual values, knowledge, and efforts on the needs of the organization—that is tough. It is always going to be tough. At the core of a career is this dualism that produces a constant tension.

Those who seek to resolve the tension by self-stereotyping are playing a losing game. John Stuart Mill, in *On*

Stage II (20-30): The Learning Decade

Liberty, says, "It is not by wearing down into uniformity all that is individual in themselves, but by cultivating it and calling it forth, within the limits imposed by the rights and interests of others, that human beings become a noble and beautiful object of contemplation. . . . In proportion to the development of his individuality, each person becomes more valuable to himself, and is therefore capable of being more valuable to others."

Social adjustment is adaptation of behavior to societal requirements, society being the environment. When we're young, there is something in us that fights against adaptation. *Any* accommodation of the individual to the social environment, according to this instinct, is *hypocrisy*.

When growing up, it is often possible to shield yourself from the full impact of the claims of the societal environment. But when you go to work, you are fully exposed.

The crisis of self-disgust arising from the self-accusation of hypocrisy is cumulative. Your abhorrence of the perceived phoniness of your business life rises steadily with a series of experiences. The burden of hypocrisy is offset from time to time by the rewards and satisfactions of work. But for some, the level rises until it boils over in a froth of self-hatred. Few people can stand this hypocrisy another minute and will tell off an uncaring boss, or let a colleague have it between the eyes, or stop being pleasant to a loutish customer.

The rebellion against hypocrisy occurs most often in the early years. Sometimes, however, a person in middle age will suddenly erupt in fury and overturn his life and the lives of those around him because he is fed up with being a hypocrite. That's bad. Like measles, excessive reaction against hypocrisy becomes more dangerous with age.

A lot of people don't erupt—ever. They glumly label themselves "phonies" and their whole lives "shams." They continue to live those lives miserably.

Then there are those who brazenly trumpet forth their lack of genuineness. "Sure, I sold out, but so what? I make a damn good living out of it, and what the hell good is a soul, anyway? Yeah, I have to do and say things I don't believe in—but then, we're all hypocrites in a sense, aren't we?" And on and on. In many ways, this poor soul is the most pitiable of all. Certainly he is the most annoying of all, since he insists on proclaiming his shame ad nauseam to anyone within earshot.

What most crises in this area seem to boil down to is that, in business, you have to be nice to people. Instead of saying to a hesitant subordinate, "God! What a pain in the ass you are!" you may feel obliged to speak softly and reasonably to that subordinate and help her or him get straightened out. You are more or less obliged to listen to the boss spout absolute nonsense, and keep your opinions to yourself.

And it's even worse in businesses in which selling is involved. For here, when the salesperson encounters an unpleasant customer, the impulse to let fly with a frank word or to just walk out must be stifled—usually.

Well, yes, the world of work calls for these sacrifices. But then, so does the world at large. What a strange world it would be without hypocrisy.

Tony Zabruski has no doubts about where he would be. Tony is a big bear of a man, a successful salesman, a skillful sales manager, and now a sound and canny marketing vice-president.

"Yeah," he tells you, "I worried about all that when I was—what—twenty-two? How I was debasing my purity by saying good morning to people I didn't like.

"If this went on, I could see where it would begin to hurt my selling effectiveness. So I did a selling job on myself. I *rationalized* it. *Rationalize,* that's another one of those words; one of those things that no decent, honest person does. But what's wrong with making things rational?

"Anyway, I did what I often do with a tough prospect. I get the prospect to consider the alternative. You know, like when you are selling life insurance and the guy says, 'Let me think about it,' and you say, 'Sure.' Then you pause at the door and say, 'By the way, if you're not here next time, whom shall I ask for?'

"The alternative to hypocrisy is not honesty. *It's the*

Stage II (20-30): The Learning Decade

jungle. If we all did exactly what we felt like doing at the moment we felt like doing it, who would be left alive? In other words, hypocrisy is *civilization*.

"Yeah, I sometimes say things just to make other people feel good—or at least not to make them feel bad. Sometimes I do it to make money; sometimes just for a quiet life; sometimes for other reasons. Now and then some of this stuff I say is out-and-out lies.

"This makes me a hypocrite. Okay, I'll try to bear up under the shame."

A lot of people admire the all-out individualist, even though they do not emulate him. They feel a little ashamed of themselves for letting the self/others tension cause them to modify their behavior. Are they right?

Let's try to understand the positive ways in which this self/others tension should be felt, as against the negative ways. Listen to Paul:

"Did you see that meeting? Could you believe what you saw? God, I thought a hundred times, What am I doing here, why am I wasting my time with these clods? That's why I blew my stack. George may mean well, but he's an idiot. If they want the thing done, they'll let me do it. If they don't, then they can do it themselves. But how can anybody keep any self-respect and continually keep trying to explain things to these morons? I am just about ready to tell these people exactly what I think. If they don't like it, they know what they can do."

Not a paragon of pleasant associations. But it seems he is a person who is at least maintaining a good, healthy individualism, right? Paul may not work out in the job, but at least he seems to be fulfilling himself. Or is he?

Not necessarily. The psychologist A. H. Maslow's studies on human needs and organizational behavior form a cornerstone of management-training theory. In his celebrated essay on self-actualization, Maslow has some things to say about the connection between true individualism and the surrounding human network.

In Maslow's formulation, the self-actualizing person maintains a healthy grasp on individuality while achieving success by means of translating ideas into reality. He writes, "Self-actualizing people have the wonderful capacity to appreciate again and again, freshly and naïvely, the basic goods of life, with awe, pleasure, wonder and even ecstasy, however stale these experiences may have been to others. For such people, even the casual workaday, moment-to-moment business of living can be thrilling, exciting and ecstatic."

Maslow goes on to say that truly self-actualizing people often feel what William James called the "mystic experience"—strong and deep emotions aroused by natural and even everyday events.

However, self-actualizing people also "have deeper and more profound interpersonal relations than any other adults," says Maslow. He adds that their "acute richness of subjective experience is an aspect of closeness of relationship to the concrete. . . . " These happy people get that way because they are in close touch with reality, not divorced from it.

And yet they look and act like anyone else. "All these people fall well within the limits of apparent conventionality in choice of clothes, of language, of food, of ways of doing things in our culture. And yet they are not *really* conventional. . . . Hardly any of these people can be called authority rebels. . . . They show no active impatience or moment-to-moment, chronic, long-time discontent with the culture or preoccupation with changing it quickly. . . . "

They work within the system, but they do not permit themselves to be absorbed heart and soul into the system. Those who function within the societal network—and the workplace is a primary part of that network—while retaining their inner detachment, are most likely to find success and, at the same time, contentment.

The tension between individuality and conformity is not in itself a crisis. But it can be a culture for crisis. And its first manifestation is likely to seem very critical indeed.

Best to get used to it. And accommodate to it. If not,

Stage II (20-30): The Learning Decade

then your whole career can be a crisis. Every time you do something that is dictated more by job need than by pure raw preference, you will feel that you are compromising yourself. "God, when I kowtow to those customers, I feel like such a hypocrite!" Well, although nobody has a good word to say for hypocrisy, maybe it can at least be said that we sometimes lump things under the label of "hypocrisy" that woud better be called "courtesy," or "consideration," or "tact," or "commonplace interpersonal behavior."

Torn between the self-you and the job-you? There's something wrong if you're not.

Those who are best at self-actualization understand that they live in a constant state of tense equilibrium between interior and exterior. It comes with the human territory. You do not oscillate between extremes, toadying shamelessly one moment, lashing out viciously the next. You try to maintain an even keel.

8.

The First Crisis of Failure

To every child comes the awful feeling of culpability. You wait fearfully. Mother comes home. She takes off her coat. Now she's in the other room. "Billy! Did you break this dish?"

There may be some blissful states in which you never have to say you're sorry, but not in business. Every now and then you do have to say you're sorry, at least to yourself, because you truly regret something you've done. You regret it because it was a mistake.

The first time you fail, there may be a painful shock. You certainly will have failed many times before your first job. But now, with a new set of judges, with your ambitions clarified, with your hopes crystallizing, your first on-the-job failure can take on soul-shattering proportions. You realize that you're mortal and vulnerable. And the shock of knowing that you are responsible—that a great deal of money or time (not to mention prestige) will be lost as a result—will compound your feeling of remorse.

"When the hum of the machine stopped, I was out of

Stage II (20-30): The Learning Decade

the chair in nothing flat," says Roger Ames. "Today of all days! We had to get the volume out, had to make the run. But when I walked up to Hesburg, the foreman, I kept my cool. If Hesburg had screwed up, I was going to stay calm. After all, he had been around a long time, and nobody's perfect.

"So I asked him nicely what was the matter. He just shrugged. 'Burned out,' he said. 'Shot.'

" 'How long to fix it?'

" 'Well, you got to get a complete new collar and bearing assembly, and I don't know, they're looking at it now, but I bet the regulator is at least damaged. I'd say, even if they have them right in stock and get right out here, two, three days.'

" 'What? You mean we can't get this run finished today?'

" 'Oh, no way we can do it today. No way in the world. Can't you smell that smell? That machine is burned out but good, man.' "

Roger blew his cool at this point: "Well, what the hell happened, Dave? This thing was just overhauled."

"When it's twenty-five hundred rpm for more than ten minutes, you got to expect that something will go wrong. Won't always—it's good gear. But that's way beyond the specs."

"Well, who was on it, Vitali? What was he doing running it at that rate?"

"Following orders."

"Whose orders? My God, Dave, why did you tell him to—"

"I didn't tell him. You did."

Roger just stared. Hesburg, with what seemed to be immense satisfaction, produced a clipboard. The piece of paper on top bore Roger's signature. The words blurred before his eyes. There was a lot of language about the high priority on this run; but there was, undeniably, an authorization to exceed maximum capacity on the machine. And now Roger remembered the talk he had had with the operator when Hesburg was not around.

"My first feeling was, I wished the earth would open up and swallow me. How could I have done such a dumb thing?"

It didn't take long for Roger to start worrying about his job. "Would they fire me? No, they wouldn't fire me. I could see the boss's face in my imagination, looking at me more in pity than in anger. They wouldn't fire me, but this sure as hell would not send my stock zooming up.

"And it was then that I got mad. Mad as hell. I was mad at the operator. How could he have been such an idiot? He's supposed to know the performance characteristics of that equipment. They pay him enough. And the hell of it was, with the damned union, you couldn't touch him.

"But then I really got mad at Hesburg. Standing there smirking at me! He was *enjoying* this. He *liked* seeing me fall on my face. He must have known what was going on, and he could have saved the situation.

"But what could I do? Yell? Get into a shouting match with Hesburg? He'd love that. So all I did was say, 'Get it fixed as quickly as you can,' and walk away. At my desk I started to think about the people I'd have to notify. The boss. The sales manager—God, he would go through the roof! And the customer would have to be notified. Would I have to do that?"

All crises are people crises. Even when their origins are mechanical, the human dimension rapidly takes over. The job of handling the immediate problem has more to do with understanding yourself and other people than with being able to trace wire A to terminal B where it forks off on its way to resistor C.

Roger's reactions were about par for the course. The first time you really fail, you feel ashamed. At the same time, you are angry. But there is something that tries to deflect the anger. So you don't get mad at yourself first; you try to find other people to get mad at.

Now, of course the techniques of crisis management call for objectivity. You're not supposed to be emotional at all.

Stage II (20-30): The Learning Decade

You're not supposed to look for scapegoats. Instead, you are supposed to say, O.K., it happened, too bad, my fault; now let's put our heads together and work out Plan B.

It doesn't usually happen that way. The person who has just made the initial major mistake is shaken by a number of things. The fundamental question underlying many other questions is, What is this going to do to my career? How badly have I damaged my chances for promotion? Am I finished here?

Along with the career doubts may come even more disturbing resonances: Do I really have what it takes? Or am I in over my head?

These are basic questions. But we don't see them right away, because of the anger. That anger is exacerbated when, as is often the case, we realize that there are people who might have helped, but who enjoy seeing us in a bad spot.

It's like falling partway down a steep slope. If you don't handle yourself just right, if you don't manage your delicately balanced position just so, you will fall further. You have only one priority. You have to creep back up to the top, going slowly and carefully. Only when you have gotten back to safety can you enjoy the luxuries of anger and scapegoating.

The first relevant question in a crisis is, How bad is it? A rapid review of the consequences of the mistake should lead to a grasp of the dimensions of the problem. The shipment is going to be delayed; maybe delayed as much as a week. It was promised for tomorrow. Everybody has been assuming that failure to meet the deadline would be catastrophic.

But sometimes such situations are overstated. Maybe there is leeway. Maybe the customer has built in some "give" without telling you.

Of course there may be yelling, screaming, weeping, and gnashing of teeth. You're going to have to take some flak. But keep pushing for a solution, however makeshift, that causes the least amount of harm.

That's not always easy. A person caught in such a bind says, "No way. Do you think I'm crazy? The thing I'm going to do first and foremost is cover myself."

Not possible. You're already exposed. You can't avoid damage to your reputation when you commit a major blunder. But you can minimize and contain it by going into a full-scale damage-control operation. And sometimes you can even enhance your image through the vigor and effectiveness with which you attack the problem. There are major figures in business who have solidified their positions at the pinnacle by this very means. They are very good at handling an emergency. That the emergency may have been caused by their own errors becomes inconsequential.

Victor Hugo wrote, "Be it true or false, what is said about men often has as much influence on their lives, and especially on their destinies, as what they do."

The crisis of the first serious mistake can stretch over decades, because of what it might do to your reputation. The mistake is not the crisis; it's the reverberation and its effect on the career.

Here's an example:

They were sitting around at the agency wondering who could be assigned to the big account. Somebody asked, "What about Larry Holtz?"

"Oh, my God, you can't put Larry on a sensitive account like that. He's a bull in a china shop. He and those people in Cincinnati would be at each other's throat in a month."

A bull in a china shop. This was what everybody said about Holtz. He was tactless, blustering; he might have the right answers, but he would always be sure to alienate the client. Better keep him in a low-visibility job.

Holtz had been suggested by a senior executive who was new to the firm and he was interested in the reaction of his colleagues—interested enough to look into it. Why did Larry have this reputation? Nobody knew; but everybody was sure it was justified. It took a lot of digging to discover that, yes, years ago Holtz had blown up in the middle of a client meeting and stalked out. There had been provocation—the client had been exceptionally disagreeable and stupid—but nevertheless, Larry had committed a cardinal sin.

That one mistake had dogged Larry Holtz for years. To those on the inside, Holtz had never changed. He was still a ticking bomb.

But to the new senior executive, this legend did not conform to reality at all. If anything, Holtz was far too timid about asserting himself with clients. A long conversation with the long-ago culprit elicited the information that Holtz was deliberately holding himself back, consciously stifling first-rate ideas, in an effort to mend his image. He assumed that image counted for a great deal in the company; and obviously he was not mistaken.

So he was paying for one mistake in two ways: Others exaggerated it; and he was trying to minimize by attempting to become something he was not.

This is an example of how the first big mistake can hurt the most. You can skew a whole career in trying to avoid a recurrence. A Persian proverb goes: "He who has been bitten by a snake fears a piece of string." Mistakes are all part of experience—but you can learn the wrong lessons from them.

In the Learning Decade, you are finding yourself, exploring your limits. When you reach the boundary line of your present limits and go beyond, you are apt to get into trouble. Some people take that experience to mean that they should never go near the boundary again. Most rational and perceptive people would accept the notion that if you don't go near it, you will never expand it. However, in the heat (or embarrassment or fear) of failure, this is a difficult dictum to follow.

What the senior executive told Holtz was that the only way he could wipe out the stigma would be by being himself and confronting clients with such persuasive and irrefutable logic that a new reputation would be made, superseding the old.

First failure can be one of the most crucial and determining episodes of your twenties. By responding coolly and logically when it happens—and, much more important, the next time the possibility of failure looms up at you—you can avoid the responses of retrenchment and fear that could well hamstring you for the future.

Simply witnessing examples of how early mistakes have dogged other people is enough to make some people cautious, gun-shy. Whether you're reacting to your own failure or that of another person, don't duck tough decisions and bold moves because you don't want to take the chance of having a bad rep hung on you for the rest of your career. It stultifies creativity. Worse, it sucks the joy out of work. Luckily, it is one of those crises over which you have some control. Nobody can avoid mistakes. But you can avoid the temptation to play it safe because you *might* make a mistake. That's a self-induced crisis. That's slow suicide.

9.

Crises of the Spirit

CRISES of the spirit often involve major shifts in the way you see yourself. When self-image has gotten far out of sync with reality, a psychic earthquake is inevitable. With a terrible shock, you come face-to-face with a limitation in yourself that you had not guessed. You are severely shaken; sometimes shattered. Sometimes the error is yours; sometimes the shock comes from the outside. And when it happens, it seems to come—unwanted, unprovoked, unfairly—out of the blue.

Crises of the spirit take various forms. You find that an idolized boss has feet of clay. You realize that your ambition has dictated an action which you do not feel to be honorable. You choose expediency over friendship in pursuing a certain objective. You find out that some bedrock concepts of ethics, which you thought to be universal, simply do not pertain in the business world.

One way or another, these things involve *betrayal*.

You've been betrayed before. Friends revealed secrets you told them. Parents misled you "for your own good." And so on. You yourself have broken a trust on occasion.

But the extent to which betrayal is the *norm* in the world of work—among perfectly nice people—can come as a critical shock when you're in your twenties.

Emily's first crisis of the spirit was the gift of a loved one.

Emily's first job was not what she had set out to get. She had intended to connect with a big company. It was just a fluke that she found herself being interviewed by Leon Lederer.

Leon was a friend of her parents, a neighbor in their affluent suburb. He had recently to quit his job as administrative vice-president of an insurance company to open a local word-processing center. It was his notion that such an establishment, serving the myriad small businesses and professional offices in the community, would be a success.

Emily took the job. She and Leon worked twelve to fifteen hours a day. The age gap disappeared. They were partners. And they made it happen. The center was making money within a month. This was only the first step; Leon and Emily planned a franchised string of them.

Two months after she took the job, they began sleeping together. The tacit understanding was that, for now, Leon had a responsibility to his somewhat dim wife and children. But after that . . .

Actually, there wasn't all that much time to talk about it. Leon was traveling a lot, setting up the first two branches while Emily ran the flagship operation.

So when Leon broke the news, the words reverberated around inside Emily's head without at first making any sense. "I kept saying, 'You *sold* the business, Leon? You sold *our* business?'"

He explained: A big outfit had made him an offer he couldn't refuse . . . a tremendous offer . . . he would move to Chicago to become vice-president for corporate planning . . . Emily would still run the local office . . . of course it would no longer be headquarters, but . . .

"Would you believe," says Emily now, "that I was wondering what I had done wrong, where I had failed?" It was not until later that she asked, "What the hell does he mean, *his* business?" By then, of course, it was clear. It *was* Leon's business, to do with what he wanted. Emily had been betrayed.

Her mind was a welter of emotions. Shock. Anger. Desolation. Confusion. But one feeling began to predominate: "What I was saying to myself was, 'Somehow it's your fault, Emily, you know.' Where did I go wrong? Either Leon was a rat or he wasn't. If he was a rat, then I must be dumb. If he wasn't a rat, then it must be my fault. I didn't do enough to make him want—well, you get the idea."

From that point, it was just a short step to guilt. "God! How miserable I was! I was to blame, and I didn't even know what I had done wrong so I could fix it."

Guilt has acquired a bad name in our no-fault society. A lot of people want to banish guilt from their lives, and a lot of advisers are telling them how to do it.

But, as Willard Gaylin—clinical professor of psychology at Columbia Medical School—remarks, "Guilt is not only *not* a 'useless' emotion, it is the emotion that shapes so much of our goodness and generosity. It signals us when we have transgressed from codes of behavior which we personally want to sustain."

So guilt is a mainstay of civilization (as is hypocrisy, another word that gets a bum rap). That's fine—if the guilt is sending you the right signal.

Sometimes, though, the shock is so great that the signals get mixed. Neurologists describe a severe brain injury as a "massive insult" to the central nervous system. Betrayal can be a "massive insult" to the psyche. It can make you feel guilty about things you are not responsible for: even about things that did not happen. This kind of "traumatic guilt" can make a person feel utterly inadequate, unworthy, unwanted.

Emily was lucky. She got over it. "I was a basket case. Couldn't look for a job. Couldn't even write a nasty letter to Leon after the first try. And I was loused up so badly at work that the new owners would fire me for sure. But I *deserved* to get fired, right?

"Then one morning I felt something I hadn't felt for

three or four weeks. I was *mad!* It wasn't me. It was Leon, that bastard. Maybe he had his reasons, but I didn't care. I hated his guts. Not that I wanted to see him, or have anything to do with him. I just hated him."

Emily says now she thinks the anger saved her: "Maybe it was no more logical than the guilt—I mean, I was a big girl, and he hadn't made any specific promises, and it *was* his business, and blah blah blah . . . but that didn't really matter. It was healthier to be mad than to go around like a wimp, blaming myself for everything. I guess a lot of us go through something like that, huh? But we get over it."

Not everybody does get over it. Some people never get over the irrational feeling of guilt they get when they have been betrayed. In fact, they seem to go out looking for situations in which they can be screwed again.

Not Emily. In six months she was fine. She even avoided one of the most insidious of the temptations that beset one at a time like this. She managed to stop short of generalizing and laying down rules for herself on the basis of this episode.

"For a time there, I was making up little proverbs. Never trust a man. Never trust a partner. Never trust anybody. But they got boring, so I stopped. I guess I learned something, but you can't wrap it up into words. I matured some, that's for sure. But as for letting it control my life since then—this happened four years ago—I just haven't."

Allen also began saying "You can't trust anybody" after his first betrayal. But unlike Emily, he kept on saying it. He's built a career on it.

He tells you in a jaunty way what happened.

"I was a patsy. Two of us were handling this account, me and my boss. He decided to change a major strategy point. On his own. I wasn't too sure, but he said, 'Trust me.'"

"Trust me!" Allen laughs. He recounts swiftly—like a man who's told it many times—how the plan blew up. Of course, when that happened, it all became Allen's fault. The boss had documentary evidence, witnesses—the works. Allen was out.

He holds no grudge, he'll tell you. It was a good lesson. "Get them before they get you." He has done all right in the ten years since then. He makes a lot of money now, and he has high visibility in his industry.

It's not *pleasant* visibility, however; nor is it complimentary. People don't like Allen. "Who gives a shit? They don't like the rough going. This is not a game. I come to kill you. When you're in there with me, pal, watch your back at all times. Also your coat and pants."

Of course, one event did not turn Allen into a monster. But the first betrayal did trigger his total commitment to a feral way of life. The stab in the back is unlikely to have been all cause, or all pretext. It is both.

These are extremes. Betrayal can strip away all your protective layers—at least temporarily—or it can add so many coatings of armor plate that one becomes an emotional golem. In between, there is a continuum of reactions to the stab in the back. Some people stay hurt. They are emotionally fearful of trusting anyone. They remain tremulously withdrawn, fluttering on the edges of life and work. Others suffer—but come through the experience with a rueful but healthy view of working life that admits people are imperfect creatures. This is the outcome best calculated to avoid severe crisis in the future. The betrayed person does not shrug it off, but neither does he or she resolve never to trust anybody again. Trust is a *risk*. It's a risk that must be taken for a fulfilling life, on the job and off.

Then there are the people who forge a cynical determination to always be the betrayers rather than the betrayed. They use the experience to justify the most outrageous and dishonorable behavior.

There is always a profound reaction to betrayal. This is why it is one of the most potentially dangerous of crises. It's nonsense to say, "Business is business," and shrug off treachery as part of the corporate scene. When it first happens, it is always very *personal*. People whose houses have been broken into and robbed say that the most difficult aftermath is the feeling of violation, the sense that you will always feel not always imperiled but a little unclean in the place. When someone betrays you, you feel personally violated. It's natural to be hurt. It's natural to be suspicious, always asking, "What does he *really* mean by that?"

But in the end, people *must* trust each other. Somehow the crisis of the first betrayal has to be resolved with that principle intact.

One seasoned executive says, "In the end, people must trust each other. Somehow the crisis of betrayal has to be resolved with that principle intact."

There is another point of view, more hard-headed, more difficult to maintain. A company president who herself has experienced the cold steel of deception says, "Be realistic in assessing people's motives. When friends or colleagues are in positions of trust, anticipate how and why they might go astray. To some extent this means probing your own areas of vulnerability. At least you will be somewhat prepared to take remedial action if things start to happen."

10.
Getting a Job Offer: An Early Crisis of Decision

COMPANIES know that there is fierce competition for talent. That's one of the reasons "headhunting"—or, to use its more formal name, "executive search"—has become a thriving industry, riding like a pilot fish on the giant sharks swimming in the murky depths of the corporate sea.

How, top managers asked themselves for a long time, do we keep the headhunters from coming in and robbing us of our brightest young people? (Though the executive-search profession detests it—and though it is unjustified—the words *steal* and *rob* are still used when one company lures a person away from another.)

Once headhunting was confined to the senior echelons. Now a 25-year-old M.B.A. in his or her first job is not unlikely to hear the traditional opening gambit: "We are conducting a search for a *'Fortune* 500' firm and we thought you might help us. . . ."

How can a firm guard against this? You can't abolish the headhunting fraternity. You can't install an alarm system that sounds a warning every time one of your people has lunch with a search professional or with an executive of another company. And you can't chain promising talent. Or—can you?

The manager who first addressed this question forged the first set of "golden handcuffs." While the notion of obtaining present loyalty by promising future reward has prevailed throughout human history, the specific arrangement of compensation plans to bind individual to organization has been operating for just about fifteen years. There are a variety of ploys: the deferred cash bonus, in which "extra" money earned in one year is paid out over three to five years; deferred stock equivalents; variations on retirement benefits; etc.

It quickly became clear to corporate planners that persons in their twenties could not care less about the retirement plan. So the golden handcuffs forged for members of the Learning Decade feature big money, which is dangled before the promising young individual in two ways. There is always a substantial payoff, which the person would lose by leaving the company now. Also, the longer a person stays, the more "equity" he or she accumulates.

If you have anything on the ball, they are very serious about locking you in. Allen Stern, president of Haskell & Stern, a leading search company, says, "For many firms, the loss of a 'high-flyer' today activates a time bomb which will explode later."

Management has become very deft at approaching employees with the precious manacles. One 28-year-old chemical engineer told us, "God, it wasn't just the money! At that time, they were paying me more than enough.

"I didn't need much, thank God. Hiking is not as expensive an interest as skiing or yachting. Once I had the components for a really good sound in my place, what else did I need?

"So when Fred Lamoret started talking to me about this plan, this thing of getting the stock, and the deferred pay, and all the rest of it, I didn't quiver with greed. But I did appreciate what they thought of me. Because, while money was not all that important to me, I knew damn well it was very important to *them*. I liked the place, and of course I took what they were offering me. Why not?"

He scarcely thought about it until a year later. The chance came for a job in San Francisco; not much more salary, but a congenial organization, interesting work, and a different part of the country.

"Why not?" the engineer asked himself. Then his boss started to point out why not. "He did this number on me with the calculator. He was adding it up like a fancy mechanic computing the bill for tuning up your Ferrari. Only he was adding what they'd owe me, not what I'd owe them.

"It was awesome. I mean, the dough that would be in the kitty if I stayed another five years was, to me, boxcar numbers. I tried to tell myself it didn't make any difference, but then, when I thought about it some more, I thought I was being irresponsible. Here they were talking to me in financial terms that indicated a substantial commitment on their part. What was the matter with me that I wasn't willing to make a commitment on my part? I told myself it was time to grow up. This company was as good as another, and I just could not ignore all that dough. Even if it didn't mean too much now, it was bound to mean more later."

So he stayed. The golden handcuffs held. And, as in many other cases, the holding strength did not consist of just the deferred money, but also of the evidence of confidence reposed in him by the organization. In a way, he would have felt disloyal if he had walked out on the plan.

Most young people who have not yet been made such an offer, or who have turned it down, are depressed or disgusted by stories like the above. They feel that the individual who stays with a company for such reasons has sold out or has somehow been bamboozled into servitude. But gold handcuffs are not necessarily bad for everyone, such as the person untouched by wanderlust. Not every career must consist of zigzag moves upward from company to company.

It is certainly possible to stay one's whole life with a single firm, enjoy a satisfactory career, and make sufficient money for one's needs.

The person on whose wrists the gold handcuffs repose has always got the key. You can shed the chains anytime you want. All it takes is the will. Indeed, they are not handcuffs at the point when you are ushered into the plan that involves deferred goodies. (That is, unless they ask you to sign a contract.) They only become handcuffs and begin to bind you when you turn down an opportunity and remain with the company because of the deferred rewards.

The problem with this approach to retaining people is the regret many people feel later. Six years in the future, our hero may wake up one morning full of anger and self-disgust. He will be miserable about his job, and he will be highly conscious that he had a chance to get out. The worse things become at the present job, the better the vanished opportunity will look. And the money will not look good at all.

So it is important to sit down and think hard when you are first approached with the handcuffs—even though you have no other offer at the time.

Here's how one person—a young marketing executive—handled it.

Carly Evans had been pretty easygoing about money: "I was what you might call a cheap date for the company. They were paying me enough, I liked what I was doing. Mostly with me it was ambition. But of course you don't use the word *ambition* with relation to yourself. I wanted to get ahead. I could see myself in a top job, knew how I'd run things. Whether it was with this company or another one didn't matter much."

Carly's boss, Lon McAllister, tried to slip the handcuffs on at the Christmas party. Carly reacted in a way that surprised both of them: "Maybe it was because I'd had a couple of drinks—so had Lon. While I didn't tell him to shove the money or the job, I told him in a nice way that I wasn't that interested in the money."

McAllister tried to argue that the compensation plan

Stage II (20-30): The Learning Decade   97

showed how highly the organization thought of Carly; that it was a sign of commitment to her as part of the company's future.

"For some reason I latched onto that word *commitment*. I said, 'Lon, if you have such high hopes for me, why not make a *real* commitment?' He wanted to know what I meant. I was making it up as I went along. I said I wanted a commitment not in dollars but as to job. I said I wanted to be assured that I would be in charge of a division in five years."

At first McAllister tried to laugh it off. But Carly was stubborn. They ended on a note of somewhat strained amiability, wishing each other Merry Christmas, not really meaning it.

The next day, McAllister talked with Carly again. He assumed the conversation would not take the same direction as that of the night before. (If many conversations begun at Christmas parties were continued in less febrile moments, business would collapse into chaos.) The company never made such commitments, said McAllister. Too many things could happen, etc., etc. But Carly Evans stuck to her point.

It took two months. But at last she and McAllister sat down and drew up a plan of advancement and a timetable. Barring the unforeseen, Evans would move up and be in command of her own operation within a reasonable time. She could not go to court with it—it was not an enforceable commitment in that sense—but once a definite career path for her had been cranked into company planning, she could be fairly sure she would move up at the indicated pace.

It's easy for management to commit future money. It's hard for management to make a commitment to *power*. When an organization offers you the golden handcuffs, it offers to buy an *option* on your availability to fill positions of increasing power. It will make good on the dollars as long as you are there. That's a cost of doing business. The company has the luxury of deciding later how much power you will actually get.

These days, more and more young people are saying that is not enough. They are insisting that the firm agree on the career paths that will put them in commanding positions within a reasonable length of time.

But they run into tremendous opposition. Why is it so hard for senior executives to agree? "Partly," says Kenneth S. Meyers, president of Golightly and Company, an international consulting firm, "it's the us/him mind-set. The president and other top managers do not think of the younger executive as one of them." Their attitude mixes paternalism and fear.

If you have something on the ball, your company will try to lock you in. It's satisfying to be wanted. But should you let yourself be locked in?

For some it's a major crisis: Stay or go? For others, the crisis comes later, in a kind of delayed reaction. They permitted the golden handcuffs to be slipped on while they weren't looking. Now, too late, they feel trapped. "Oh, the money is good, but. . . ."

For some career crises, the single most important rule is to recognize that it is, indeed, a crisis. This is eminently so when you are approached with the golden handcuffs.

And you handle this situation as you would any major decision: evaluate the advantages and disadvantages of the possible choices. The tough part is to be honest and not let biases cause you to underrate or overrate. For example, don't kid yourself in rejecting or exaggerating what the money factor means to you. Then make your decision, knowing it is the best you can make at the time. Now that you've made a choice, don't let yourself be mousetrapped either by your boss or by slipshod thinking.

11.

Relocating

WARREN ADAMS, 27, has been a full-fledged account executive at the Gower & Grove Agency for eighteen months. He handles three brands manufactured by a large consumer-goods client.

One day Adams gets a phone call from a Mr. Wilson of World-Wide Executive Search, Inc. While Warren Adams has of course heard about headhunters, he has never been called by one before.

"Mr. Adams, we are looking for somebody in the twenty-five-to-thirty age range with package-goods experience. Our search is being conducted for a West Coast client who is setting up a new brand group and who wants a young, aggressive product manager. Your name was passed along to me as someone who might be able to help me. Do you know of anyone who might fit into this category?"

Adams thinks for a moment. "Gee, I don't know, Mr. Wilson. What would it pay?"

"Mid-thirties to start, with a good bonus arrangement."

There is a pause.

"I can't say that anybody's name comes to mind offhand, Mr. Wilson, but I'll certainly think about it. It sounds pretty good. As a matter of fact, I'm almost tempted myself."

"Really? Well then, I'd very much like to talk with you some more. Are you free for lunch tomorrow?"

What Warren Adams had gotten was the standard approach of the headhunter. At lunch the next day, he learned the name of the client. Following that, there were meetings with three executives of the package-goods company. Within a month, they had offered Warren Adams the job.

Confronted with the offer, Adams realized that he still didn't know whether he wanted to take the job or not. He decided to have a frank talk with his own boss, Joe Ferguson. When he spoke to him, Ferguson made Warren some very attractive counteroffers.

Warren Adams had to balance the job offer against the lucrative proposals extended by his present employer. He had to consider whether it was wise to go from advertising-agency work over to "the account side."

But there was yet another more difficult question to be resolved: What about his relationship with Sally? They had been living together for two years. Sally was a copywriter for another ad agency. They seemed to harmonize emotionally and complement each other professionally. The new job would mean moving a thousand miles away.

For many young people at the start of a career, the first real job-related personal conflict comes when a job would involve a geographical move. Many long-range relationships simply don't work.

In the old days, the elite corps of the Turkish Army was formed of janissaries. These were strong young men who were captured in the Caucasus and brought to serve the sultan. They were forbidden to marry.

Maybe there should be an updated version of the janissary concept to apply to today's high-rolling manager.

The corporate nomad is a Typhoid Mary of unhappiness. Psychologist Mortimer R. Feinberg points out that the executive who is constantly being transferred never feels the pain; he is always able to plug into a comfortable new working environment wherever he goes. But the 16-year-old who has changed schools and towns eight times—*she* feels pain. And the wife and mother, carted around the world like baggage—she absorbs the most trauma. She is the one who usually goes under first.

All this is changing. Even to use the pronouns *him* and *her* is to misrepresent the situation. Women are living their own lives; working; making their own decisions. Managers, male and female, are resisting the efforts of companies to move them around a global chessboard.

And yet—it still happens.

Hundreds of thousands of executives drift through the American corporate medium. They float from city to city, job to job, industry to industry. At any given time, a considerable part of the management elite is in transit. The essence of business achievement today is wandering, not staying put.

It was not always so. Once, the American go-getter picked the company he wanted to work for, learned the business from the ground up, struggled to the top by means of a vertical climb. If he went into the shoe business, he learned all about making shoes. Then, through hard work, loyalty, competence, and luck, he clambered up the greasy pole. Frederick R. Kappel graduated from the University of Minnesota in 1924 and went to work for Bell Telephone as a groundsman. In 1961 he became chairman of the board. Crawford Greenewalt joined du Pont in 1922, worked his way through a myriad of departments, and was elected chairman forty years later. This was once the very model of a modern management career. It is still the way careers are built in most of the world. In Japan, a young person joins the company for life; it's pretty much the same in Europe.

But not in America. Here, the wandering manager has become the norm. The classic career can no longer be tracked vertically. It resembles the course of a pinball in a machine, bouncing laterally across the board from pin to pin, slot to slot, until it winds up either in the payoff hole or the discard. The big-time manager is a star performer whose services are sought by a wide variety of enterprises. Experience or previous affiliation is no longer important. We can find an analogy in the movie business. Once, actors like Cagney and Bogart became stars by working year after year for the same studio. Now the star is everything; the "studio" no longer exists.

As the concept of executive mobility has grown, there has grown with it a new and comforting philosophy based on the proposition that those who master the science of management can take their kit of tools along wherever they go. They do not have to know how shoes are made or marketed.

The rise of the concept of "pure" management science is frequently attributed in large measure to the writer and philosopher Peter F. Drucker, the progenitor of the theory of "management by objectives." But Drucker never said that you don't have to possess a grasp of the enterprise you are in. He maintains that business has concentrated on objectives and forgotten about management. "Organizational objectives—and their fulfillment—can grow only from a thorough knowledge of what the business is and what it should be."

However, it is far more convenient to assume that the "pure" manager is a completely interchangeable part. Graduate schools of business imbue their students with the idea. The proposition was crystallized by the American Management Association, which declared that the accomplished manager moving into a top policy job need know only four things: the company's legal position; its philosophy; its long-range goals; and its budget.

In the Broadway hit of two decades ago, Professor Harold Hill was the "Music Man." Professor Hill sold outfits for brass bands. What was his grounding in the business? He "don't know nothin' 'bout brass bands." What did he know? "You got to know the *territory*." What if the

Stage II (20-30): The Learning Decade

instruments didn't work and the uniforms didn't fit? Professor Harold Hill could not care less. He would soon be moving on from River City.

The modern manager is told that he don't have to know nothin' about brass bands or chemicals or machine tools. He need only "know the territory" and become "visible" within it, and his territory is the lunch table, the convention hotel, and the business press. He can move from the shoe company, where he knew nothing about shoes, to the turbine company, where his mind will be equally pristine.

The corporation functions as if it feels the same way. Top executives can be shifted from location to location or replaced without much regard for their relationships in a certain locale or their grasp of the fundamentals of the specific operation.

Constant motion has become the essence of the management career. The emphasis has shifted from job doing to job switching and job getting. The ambitious manager is led to develop the qualities of "visibility" rather than accomplishment in the task at hand. This is not to say that these two sets of attributes are invariably antithetical; but they are by no means identical.

Career mobility causes problems; sometimes crises. The difficulties faced by the families of the nomads are apparent, but continual motion takes its toll on the manager as well, in ways that are not always felt right away. The rootlessness and lack of stability of the nomadic corporate life are primary ingredients in the crises of alienation and identity that will be met in the stages to come.

12.
Making Sergeant

IF you do a good job, you'll get promoted. Of course that's what you want. But sometimes, when that first promotion comes, it has some sharp and uncomfortable edges. It's obvious that not everyone will be promoted at the same time. Some of your friends will wind up working for you (or vice versa). Then what?

Many people say, "That won't interfere with our friendship." Or, "It may be tough at times, but there's no reason why we can't keep work things separate from personal things." Or, "If people are real friends, they can handle a difference in rank."

Unfortunately, few of the ideas expressed in these statements, generous as they are, hold true.

It almost invariably interferes with friendship when one party is promoted over the other. A friendship formed with a workmate, even the closest of friendships, cannot be kept separate from work. The fabric of work is woven into it. Friendships need not invariably end when the stripes are pinned on the sleeve of one of the friends, but maintenance of the close relationship is an uphill fight. This kind of crisis will recur. But the first time it happens, it takes on particularly critical magnitude.

Walter's friendship with Harry had survived five years of rough give-and-take as colleagues. They were hired on the same day. They had had lunch together their first day at work. Since then, they had seen each other frequently, on and off the job.

When Walter was suddenly promoted to head the department—replacing a seemingly indestructible veteran who suddenly cracked under the strain and began to denounce the president of the company as the antichrist—Harry offered sincere congratulations. Harry did not have to admit that Walter was smarter, or more skilled. He freely acknowledged that Walter had the kind of personal qualities that won promotions. And as time went on, Harry was equally admiring of Walter's remarkable ability to traverse the rapids of internal politics.

In fact, Harry felt lucky to have Walter as a buffer. "No way would I want to get involved in all that crap. All I want to do is my job, the best way I can." It was good to have a friend in high places.

For his part, Walter found himself becoming more objective about his friend. He liked Harry as much as ever, but he could not blind himself to a certain routine quality about Harry's work. But maybe this was just as well. You could not have a staff consisting entirely of stars. You needed utility infielders, too.

So he tended more and more to rely on Harry for the solid, bread-and-butter stuff. He assumed his friend took kindly to this. Therefore he was surprised when Harry brought up something while they were waiting for a tennis court on a Saturday.

"Somebody's going to have to handle that Balaklava thing," said Harry.

"Yeah. Tricky job."

"By now you must have somebody in mind."

"Not for sure. Dora, maybe. She has a kind of sense of balance in situations like that. She may be worth a shot. Or

Kenny. He's handled something like it before, you remember, on the Benson thing."

"Really? On Balaklava? Gee, I was thinking somebody with more experience . . . "

"Oh, I don't think experience is the big thing so much as—"

"You know, Walt, I wouldn't want you to take this wrong. And I know you won't. Jessica said something the other night, like she wondered if, unconsciously we hadn't gotten into a pattern where being friends made us not always see things clearly. Like I might not look at some career considerations the way I should, and go to bat for myself. And like you might take me for granted a little. Not that she meant anything by it, and you know I don't think for a moment . . . "

Walter was astonished. But just then, the court became vacant.

They talked again in the office on Monday. Harry said that, frankly, he wondered why he didn't get the assignment. He didn't want to rock the boat, but he would not be fair to himself if he didn't, etc., etc.

Walter replied that he had in no way been taking Harry for granted, nor had he overlooked him in his considerations. He tried his best to make assignments objectively. In this case he did not feel Harry was the best person for the job. This did not mean Harry was undervalued, unappreciated, or unimportant. On the contrary, Harry filled a unique place in the operation, etc., etc.

Things returned to normal. Four months later, Harry told Walter he was resigning: "It's time for me to go off in a new direction." The job was to set up a rival department with a direct competitor.

Walter—being as objective as he could be—suspected that this was not the right spot for Harry. He could not envision Harry running such a department successfully. Unfortunately, a little of this feeling came through as he tried to talk Harry out of the move. Furious, Harry stormed out.

The friendship lapsed after Harry left. Then, six

Stage II (20-30): The Learning Decade

months later, Walter got a call. How about lunch? Just because they were competitors didn't mean they couldn't get together now and then.

About two and a half lunches into their resumed relationship, Walter realized that Harry was desperate. He was hanging on to the job by his fingernails. In fact, the next time they met, Harry opened the subject of coming back. "This job has been a challenge. I've learned a lot. I could bring a lot richer experience to the old department. And, let's face it, success isn't everything. Loyalty and old friends mean a lot, too."

It was not easy for Walter to swing it. Organizational policy was against rehiring. But he managed it. He told himself he was doing the best thing, that Harry was a reliable wheelhorse, and would be even more reliable after his fling.

And so it proved. Harry came back, took on the tough, slogging assignments without complaining, ground out the work. Unspectacular but steady. Reliable.

Then one day, Walter, about to round a corner, heard Harry talking with two others. Harry was doing a complete number on him: all his faults, all his ridiculousness, all his vulnerabilities.

Walter strode away, furious. After all I did for that s.o.b., he thought.

This is one example of how the strain between management and friendship exerts its terrible torsion. It is a commonplace of command that the subordinate's job is to take orders from a properly constituted authority, no matter what the personality of the individual vested with that authority. By the same token, people complain about the boss as a *boss,* no matter who the individual wearing the boss's mantle may be. When you first achieve a promotion, this is hard to get used to.

And when your friend has been promoted, it's equally hard to get used to the fact that friendship must inevitably be altered—and perhaps eradicated—by the hard facts of the new relationship.

The problem surfaces in another way when the friend who has been left behind tries to exploit the friendship for career gain. If you're the boss on whom this is being tried, your reaction is likely to be discomfort and then anger. If you are the subordinate who succumbs to the temptation to try this, you are likely to fail in your effort—and to be consumed by self-digust.

By far the best thing is to do what comes naturally. Of course, command takes precedence; that's what career makers are seeking. To pretend anything else is to blind oneself. When all parties accept the fact of promotion with all its ramifications, strain is not eliminated, but it does not grow to crisis proportions.

And, indeed, many friendships that are temporarily interrupted by a promotion are resumed later when the situation has adjusted itself. Other people get promotions, too.

Onward and Upward

As in the first movement of a symphony, the themes of your working life will have been established by the end of the 20–30 decade. The crises you have just been through are, for the most part, "first-time" crises. You have been coping with the strange and new; trying to adjust.

Now you move into a period during which you will gain in knowledge and confidence, acquire power, give hostages to fortune in the emotional relationships you set up.

But the themes of the earlier movements will continue to reappear; much changed, but still profoundly influential in shaping the harmonies and dissonances of your life.

Stage III (30–40): The Power Decade

13.

Thrusting Toward the Summit

THE decade of the thirties is the pivotal period of the working life. It is not the chronological midpoint—there is more to come than has already been lived—but it is the fulcrum. You have worked long enough to be an "insider" rather than a newcomer. You have acquired skills and understand the methods of business. You have moved ahead and have a significant and tangible set of accomplishments. You have encountered shocks and setbacks—but, except in extraordinary cases, you are unlikely to have suffered anything that could be called "serious failure."

Now you are ready to apply leverage to the rest of your life. You must judge the strength of your lever; select the precise spot on which to poise it; choose the direction of thrust that will exert the pressure in the right direction.

And you have to decide how much pressure it is worthwhile to exert. For the fulcrum of the career lever is not inert. It may be living flesh and living soul. The pressure you bring to bear may press cruelly hard on others with whom you work and those with whom you live.

There is also pressure on you; extraordinary pressure. You are no longer dealing with the shock of the unfamiliar. The newness of the twenties has worn off. The crises arising from the bitterness and disillusion of age are still ahead and may yet be tempered or avoided.

In fact, most of those in the Power Decade are strangers to despair. They are in many ways at the top of their form. They've gotten it all together. They have lost none of their youthful vigor and sharpness, and now those qualities are given direction and thrust by experience.

But the rosiness of this picture may heighten into the bright red of danger. One major problem of this decade concerns Crises of *Overreach*.

There is a headiness about this period. You ride the crest, with reality and possibility striking a perfect balance. That this balance may be illusory is not apparent; the illusion is very strong.

When you reach thirty, you are likely to be reaping the fruits of the seeds you've been sowing for ten years or so. Reward and recognition have started to come. Herein lies the seductive danger of overreach.

Climbers experience "rapture of the heights." (With divers, it is "rapture of the depths.") The rarefied atmosphere produces euphoria. The climber becomes light-headed, careless, takes reckless chances. This is the cause of many of the crises of overreach. Success in the twenties has been too rapid. Confidence is supreme. Reach exceeds grasp. The individual plunges boldly into situations that should be approached cautiously.

For some it may be promotion to a job that will brook the Peter Principle hazard: being moved up to a position beyond your true abilities. For others it may be elevation from technician or specialist to manager. You have to be aware that you are in a ballgame with new rules requiring untested skills.

There is a paradox about the Learning Decade that we have just passed. In many cases, unalloyed success is the enemy of learning. If you are good enough or lucky enough to have picked your way unscathed through the minefield

Stage III (30-40): The Power Decade

of the twenties, you may well have formed an exaggerated idea of your own skill and imperviousness. At the same time, you thoroughly underestimate the perils around you, because you were not harmed by any and you didn't know enough to be aware of the close calls. Setbacks are an important part of the learning process. When they are avoided during the time when it is appropriate to learn, they hurt more when they do come.

Some crises of overreach involve failure encountered because the person makes a big mistake due to overconfidence. Another subcategory of crises of overreach involves frustration. In this decade, you meet people who are restless, irritable, champing at the bit. They have had a taste of success and power. They feel at the peak of their capabilities. *But they have not reached the pinnacle of power.*

So they begin to look with resentment and scorn at those who stand in the way. Overreach leads to underrating of superiors. You look down the vista of the years, and you seem to see an appalling assortment of idiots, all sitting there fat and happy and impeding your progress. Why don't they get out of the way?

It is assumed that success in one area must invariably lead to equal success in another. The twenties may have been a time when a person scored one or more magnificent coups by using one particular strength: analytical ability, or the gift of persuasion, or penetrating insight or intuition. This success is sharp, but it is likely to be concentrated in a narrow area. Now, in the thirties, you are given the opportunity to spread horizontally. If you have shown a gift for selling, you try to impart that gift to other salesmen. If you have proven to be highly analytical, you are asked to apply that gift to the improvement of a working unit.

You become a boss. You are expected to get results through other people. And here is where you may run into the most severe crises—because the successes of the twenties do not necessarily make you a good manager. But good management is what is expected of you. Most organizations—though they are unlikely to admit it—still prize promotability as one of the most precious of attributes. You can be brilliant at doing—on your own—a particular important job. But if you don't want to become a boss, or if you're not very good at it, you're a failure.

The successes of the decade of the twenties are different in nature from the successes expected of you in the thirties. At 25, the coups you're able to score are likely to be *problem-solving* successes, in which you go one-on-one with a challenge and master it. As you move up, the challenges become conceptual rather than practical, strategic rather than tactical. You deal with forces and trends rather than with actualities. Some days, you will yearn for the simple time when it was fun; when you could just rip into the situation and solve it yourself instead of going through all this rigmarole.

The thirties is a decade of reassessment. Within these years, you can take a hard look at the means you have been using to pursue your goals, and reexamine the goals themselves.

President Eisenhower's secretary of state, John Foster Dulles, coined the term *agonizing reappraisal*. Reappraisal during this period can be agonizing. One source of agony is the pressure of the clock. When you're 25, you can shift to another job or another career area without feeling that you've made some kind of irrevocable step. At 35, consideration of a shift in career direction is subject to the "last chance" syndrome. "My next move," you tell yourself, "has to be the right one." It is within this decade that you do what climbers of Mt. Everest must do: make the critical decision as to where to site the jump-off point for the assault on the summit.

Crises of redirection revolve around the questioning of youthful goals; the examination of qualifications to achieve goals; and the sense that a mistake at this pivotal point can be permanent.

In *Julius Caesar,* Brutus tells Cassius and the generals:

> There is a tide in the affairs of men,
> Which, taken at the flood, leads on to fortune;

Stage III (30-40): The Power Decade

Omitted, all the voyage of their life
Is bound in shallows and in miseries.

It might be added that Brutus's efforts to ride the flood tide of fortune led to terminal crisis at the Battle of Philippi.

It comes as a shock to many people in their thirties that time is not infinite. This is a matter of wry bemusement to persons of, say, 55, who wish they were 30 again. Nevertheless, the jolt to those in their thirties is real and significant.

Clock-shock puts on the pressure. During this decade, it is an ever-present factor, often combining with other factors, like the need for redirection, to produce critical situations.

One area in which clock-shock has a particularly telling affect is marriage, childbearing, the formation of permanent relationships. For example, many women in their thirties feel they must make it now in terms of career success. But the biological clock is ticking; they must also decide on motherhood. The Power Decade is marked by a number of crises that are precipitated or exacerbated by the uncomfortable awareness of time.

14.

The Crisis of Reassessment

STAGE III people, because they are likely to be at a balance point in their careers, feel a pressing need for reassessment. Three related questions arise: Where am I? Where do I want to be? And how do I get there?

Each element of this three-part question can precipitate a crisis, especially if the answers are unsatisfactory. Those who discover that their status level is lower than they think it should be, who are seized by sudden doubts about goals, may be subject to large doses of soul-searching and anguish: "Should I give up all I worked for and switch to another kind of work?" "Do I really have what it takes to become the head of this division?" "Do I really want to make the rush to the summit that may leave broken bodies, including those of some of my best friends, in my path?"

And the question of how to lay the groundwork to achieve a particular goal also may reveal that one is standing unsuspectingly on the edge of an abyss. Perhaps winning the promotion or getting the size salary increase you want may call for sacrifices of time and energy that may substantially infringe upon a present and pleasant life-

Stage III (30-40): The Power Decade

style. Do you really want to move to Botswana to sharpen your knowledge of overseas operations?

Considerations like these may uncover the promise and hazard of a standard solution to a career problem: a new job. Should you or shouldn't you think in those directions? Could you do better elsewhere? These are only the first of a series of questions you must answer before deciding to place your bets on a new horse.

In the last couple of decades, an answer to job changing has been instituted in the person of the executive headhunter. And one of the important symbolic acts of the power decade may be lunch with the executive-search consultant. It is not that people in their thirties spend all their time listening to the siren song of the headhunter, nor does it mean that all those who hear the headhunter's song are susceptible. But job switching is a very important element of this career stage, whether you engage in it or not. Staying put in the wrong job at the wrong time can have bad consequences. So can moving at the wrong time, into the wrong job.

Back in the 1950s and 1960s, people who moved around a lot were stigmatized as "job-hoppers." If the applicant's résumé showed, say, three moves in five years, the employer was likely to dismiss the person as a bad bet. Nowadays, however, the average career is expected to include several job changes, perhaps half a dozen or more, before age 40. If you look into a glass of cloudy water, you'll see tiny particles zigzagging through the fluid. This constant motion, which continues even though the glass remains perfectly still, is called "Brownian movement." The peregrinations of people in the Power Decade resemble a kind of Brownian movement of career builders.

A number of factors, internal and external, join to trigger the movement that impels Stage III people to switch horses. Sometimes the change is minor, and may take place as a transfer to a related job in the same organization. But in other instances, there is a major alteration: from banker to farmer; from farmer to engineer; engineer to jazz musician.

Stage III is a period when crucial career decisions have

been acted on and can now be reexamined. Did the decision to go with this company prove a wise one? And how about taking a job in Purchasing instead of Personnel?

Various aspects of the job can be looked at with fresh eyes, and the favorable factors of youthfulness and sense of capability suggest that career moves are possible. People feel employable, attractive to skill-hungry employers. All these factors come together to trigger a review of past planning. For this group, any offer of a job is an opportunity to be considered seriously.

"The thirty-to-forties are ripe for picking," says one headhunter. Stage IIIs are red-hot prospects for management consultants who specialize in recruiting. It's unlikely that they'll be looking for presidents in this group—Stage IV people are better for those levels—but the successful thirties are prime for aggressive, growing companies that want fresh young blood to head up departments, and to be the right hands of very top people who use assistants—as both aides and as successors to whom they can pass the baton when they're ready to move into a chairmanship or CEO position.

There is good reason for the many career switches by the Stage III group. It's as though the transition itself, the passage from being 20 to being 30, stimulates reappraisal. And when there are dissatisfactions, it is assumed that a new job or career path will add a magic ingredient to the be-happy potion.

People can change careers at any point. There's an instance of a young woman who started her first job and, before the day was out, concluded that the job was wrong, the industry was wrong, and she was in the wrong city. The next day she resigned and set out for San Francisco, where friends had been urging her to try her luck.

In his fine study *Working*, Studs Terkel explains the lemminglike compulsion that leads people to leave jobs and set out for what is often an unknown career destination: "It isn't the calendar age that determines a man's restlessness. It is the daily circumstance, an awareness of being hurt, an inordinate hunger for 'another way.'"

We have said that this group is at peak energy and

self-confidence. These two factors form a strong support for enterprise, hardheaded reassessments, and considerations for new career moves. Yet you find unexpected attitudes. For example, you find that success doesn't make for contentment. Good enough isn't good enough. Some individuals have a flare-up of aspiration in which they want to shoot for the sky. It's the top in their own organization, or a move to another with an unobstructed path to the executive heights.

You would expect low achievers to be the malcontents. But somewhat the same thing happens on the job that happens in unhappy marriages. Despite all provocations, people hold on to what they've got. Practicing psychiatrists are familiar with the clinging couple that shouldn't, who seem to detest one another and yet remain together. Psychiatrists speak of these star-crossed marrieds as "gruesome twosomes."

On the job, you find the same unexpected death grip. Employees cling to jobs that have brought them little other than a paycheck, and upsets ranging from weekend stomach upsets to headaches, ulcers, and depression.

In between those who are successful and the failures is a vast middle group that adjusts to career imperfections by acceptance and rationalizations—"I'm better off than X, who dislikes his job even more than I detest mine."

People ask themselves a series of questions to probe their job feelings and situations. Some of them ask consciously and some raise the same questions unconsciously.

For example, Grace Ross has a quarrel with her boss and storms back into her office to brood. She hears herself mutter, "That rotten bitch. How come I've put up with her all these years?" And she realizes it's a resentment of long standing that has broken through her awareness for the first time.

In our conversations with Stage III people, we were told some of the queries they use to test their job situations:

- How did I get my job in the first place? Did I fall into it or was it by choice?

- What have I achieved so far, and is it to my satisfaction? What kind of future do I have?
- Am I satisfied with the material returns—salary—or could I do better elsewhere?
- Am I getting what I want out of my work in terms of challenges, successes, self-realization, fulfillment?
- Am I willing to take the risks a change would require? Would I get the emotional support I need from my family—or would that be one more source of pressure and concern?
- Is there some alternative career direction I would prefer? Something I have always been interested in and which would promise more satisfactory employment?

The questions above suggest a tough, hard-beaked approach to oneself and one's affairs. This intellectual gutsiness, a willingness to move in unorthodox directions to attain goals that are individual and may be unique, is typical of this free-swinging group.

The moment does come when you know that the job switching is at an end. You say to yourself, as Brigham Young said upon seeing the Great Salt Lake, *"This is the place!"* This is the place in which you must establish a solid base for your assault on the summit.

But before that moment of certainty is reached, there can be agonizingly critical hours, days, and weeks.

For some, there is the critical decision "Go or stay?" One more move has become a possibility. The new job offers distinct advantages. But you're really becoming established in your present job. Is the move worth it?

In Stage III, it is no longer quite so easy to pull up stakes and decamp. The nomadic instinct of youth is cooling down. You have surrounded yourself with reasons to stay where you are. If the new job calls for geographic relocation, you may by now have formed close associations that make going to another community seem unutterably difficult.

Love can be the primary restraining element. Jeff and

Stage III (30-40): The Power Decade

Celia played out an agonizing comedy-drama over a period of six weeks when Celia got a fantastic offer that would take her to the Bay area, leaving Jeff behind in St. Louis. Jeff proposed marriage four times. Celia rejected him four times, but proposed on her own three times, with equal results. They parted forever a dozen times. Their "discussions" of the alternatives were tumultuous, bizarre, and often highly public. Their friends still remember the party at which Jeff arrived a little late to find Celia—drunk—draped all over a delighted young man.

"Sam's from Oakland," Celia announced to Jeff. "He's going to take care of me when I go out there." There was a near fistfight, a volcanic argument and renunciation, a tearful reconciliation, and an exhausted discussion on pillows in a corner, with Celia saying for the umpteenth time, "Why, dear, dear, dear, dear, do you want to stay here in this shit job? Come to the Coast! God, can't you take the chance for me?"

And Jeff, torn, ready to pack it all in and go with Celia, because he loves her more than anything in this world, but a little later thinking that he's got to stay, because this job is *the* job, what he has been planning for, the job that will serve as his springboard.

Celia went. Jeff took a week off and visited her three months later. It was strained and unsatisfactory. They parted full of assurances that they'd be getting together soon, that Celia would stop off in St. Louis on an upcoming trip to Atlanta, etc., etc. They pretty much knew they would never see each other again.

Jeff is doing all right in the company with which he stayed. He's 35 now, and he figures to be number three man in the organization by the time he's 40. He's thinking that maybe it's time he got married.

Celia has not been quite the spectacular success that she had hoped or envisioned. For a while she considered a job offer that would have brought her back to St. Louis, but decided there was no way she was going to go back and have people think she was a flop and have Jeff think she was throwing herself at his feet. So she sticks it out. The job may not be as satisfying at it once was, but there's plenty of partying. Celia still can't help feeling a sense of loss about the whole thing. Neither can Jeff.

Whether you go or stay, that's often the thing that gives the crisis its exquisitely agonizing twists. Regret.

However, in many cases the problem doesn't boil down to a simple "go" or "stay." There are moves that can modify either the stay choice or the go choice, and even reveal possibilities that enlarge your career horizon.

One possibility that does the latter, for example, is going into business for yourself. Another choice that many people have made, a major change in direction that puts you in a new ball game, is going from the private sector into a government job, or vice versa. Still another switch involves going from teaching to doing: getting an operating job in industry involving the specialty you taught. And for some people, both the atmosphere and the career possibilities change drastically when going from a profit to a nonprofit type of operation, or the reverse.

The world out there, as some people say, is a big place in terms of career development. Your imagination is capable of producing possibilities that are beyond the scope of the best career counselors.

15

When Faults in Planning Appear: A Crisis of Redirection

STAGE III is the period in which the imperfections and failures of career planning tend to surface.

For example, Harley Medson had it made—his opinion as well as that of his colleagues. Most important, it was the conviction of Sam Ericson, his boss and mentor. Ericson was the executive vice-president of A. J. Container Corporation, a bustling, profitable two-plant company that made food containers and disposable dishes of both paper and plastic.

Three years before, Ericson had proposed that M.B.A.s be brought into the company to beef up managerial ranks and leaven the group of homegrown managers with some of the force-fed and presumably more sophisticated academics. Harley Medson was one of the four M.B.A.s who were recruited, and it was he who became the beneficiary of Ericson's special interest.

"He'll be running the plant in five or six years," the executive VP told Al Jewett, the president.

"I don't know whether that's good or bad," Jewett

said. "He doesn't have the education—and I don't mean just school credits, but the ways of thinking—that these university brains have."

And that's the way things shaped up until, after three years of working in Production Control and then Engineering, Ericson decided that Medson was ready and put him in charge of a small quality-control unit. A few months later, Ericson decided that Harley Medson had gotten the feel of production and the protégé was made manager of Forming, one of the larger plastic-materials departments.

Performance nose-dived. It was not only that production sagged and reject percentages mounted. Ericson did a bit of judicious snooping, and in conversations with old-timers got the impression that Harley was a standoffish boss. One veteran told him, "Medson is friendly enough, but that only means saying 'Good morning' and 'Have a nice weekend.' He tells his assistant, Joey Dee, what to tell us. I haven't ever heard him give a direct order."

Ericson put the facts together. He figured Medson avoided working directly with the rank and file not because it was his style of managing but because he didn't feel comfortable with them. He was O.K. at his desk. Working with the people, listening to them—he wasn't emotionally equipped for that.

Ericson was honest enough to accept the blame for the failure. "I never gave the man the chance to get the feel of the grass-roots operation. He certainly wasn't going to get it at Harvard."

After some conversations between Ericson and Medson, it was decided that the latter would go back to the production-control unit, on special assignment to review and reorganize basic operations. What happened after would depend on opportunities at the time, but it was unlikely that he'd be given line responsibility. His difficulty in dealing with people suggested that a staff job would best avoid his weak area.

The Japanese, now envied for their traditions, have a tradition that applies to the Ericson-Medson case. The companies that take on business-school graduates start them off at entry-level jobs—clerks, machine operators, helpers. This gives them firsthand understanding of life in the front lines. Medson lacked this experience.

In an interview with David Rockefeller just before he relinquished the posts of chairman and CEO of Chase Manhattan Bank, the executive said, "I'm very grateful that I started in basic operations at the bank. It gave me an understanding that helped considerably when I got to the higher echelons. I knew not only what the employees were doing at their jobs, but their values, attitudes, and capabilities. I doubt that I could have done my higher-echelon job effectively without that exposure. The people who supervised my training deserve credit for their foresight."

The slow-to-build crisis that eventually roadblocked Harley Medson, in retrospect might be described as "What does a person do when a basic job qualification is lacking?"

"He just doesn't have it" is the way Sam Ericson might have put it. The *it* in Medson's case was the touch needed to deal with people. A gap in education, training, or experience may precipitate a career crisis.

Other areas in which past errors in planning tend to appear: insufficient education, or education in areas of little value in the individual's job or career; inadequate training, including that gotten at below-standard schools or training institutions; or, despite a passing grade, failure of the individual to really master courses taken. Another error is dependence on others that doesn't prove out. For example, "My uncle took me into his business, but when he sold it, that pulled the plug for me." Hitching one's wagon to a star is O.K.—as long as the star continues to shine. When it stops, plans will fall—baby, cradle and all.

Another planning failure represents a poor career decision of the most destructive kind. The case of Lou Kalo lays it out: Lou Kalo suffered from that ailment known as "controlling mother." Liz Kalo overprotected him as a child, fussed over his adolescence, and took over in his early manhood, prescribing for everything from acne to girlfriends.

Her guidance reached top form and vehemence when it came to career choice: "Your Uncle Dexter invested your dear father's estate for me, so there is money for college—and more. Of course you want to be a doctor like your father. You'll be out of high school in two years. It's not too early to start thinking about a college that will make it easy to get into medical school."

Lou Kalo went through medical school. It was even more of an ordeal for him than for the average student. He developed more hypochondriacal symptoms than his peers, he threw up more violently on first working with cadavers, he went into deeper depression when patients he treated in his internship died.

The day he opened his own office—a part-time subrental from an established internist—was the happiest day in his mother's life, his worst. He had the skills, the equipment, the experience to practice successfully. All he lacked was the desire. He went along, month after month, doing his best to maintain his professional equilibrium. Patients who liked him, despite his aloof manner, said, "He's very thorough." Those who didn't like him didn't come back.

Finally, it was his mother, who had gotten him into the situation, who got him out. She died of a severe heart attack. Three months later, Dr. Lou Kalo gave up his practice and disappeared. A friend told another, "You won't believe this but I saw Lou Kalo last week. In Washington. And he was driving a taxicab."

It was the ex–Dr. Kalo, all right. The career plan that had called for him to enter a profession for which he had neither the mind nor the stomach had been set aside. He had made a miserable doctor. He became a happy taxicab driver.

Of all the delayed complications of career planning, the one Dr. Lou Kalo's history represents is the most drastic. It cuts across the lines of sex, occupation, and age. Although Stage III is most likely to be the time the consequences show up in their most hurtful form, it may strike at 39 as well as 30. The crisis can be devastating, and damage both a career and one's off-the-job life.

Stage III (30-40): The Power Decade

The groundwork for this debacle is a decision, usually made in Stage I, between the ideal and the practical, between "I would like to be a . . . " and "I'd better be a . . . "

Some of the alternatives are classic: Be an artist rather than an art teacher; be an actor—or singer, or dancer—rather than go into business.

And the problem is, *either* choice can lead to crisis or disillusionment. In Dr. Kalo's case, the decision to go into medical practice ended in failure. Although becoming a hackie wasn't an actual alternative at the planning stage—his early college years—it was the kind of unpretentious vocation that brought him the relaxation and freedom that he desired.

The revulsion of feeling, the awareness that a terrible career misjudgment has been made, might for someone else have been exactly the opposite. How often do you hear from cabdrivers, elevator operators, unskilled or semiskilled low-pay people, "I should have gone to school and learned a trade"—studied to become an engineer, lawyer, pilot, and so on.

The fault, as Shakespeare might have said, is not in our stars but in ourselves for failing to anticipate the long-range results of a decision that was either impractical or short-sightedly idealistic.

For Stage II people, there is still time to recoup; to reformulate goals and to get the additional training and experience needed to reach those goals. But in Stage III that is often hard to do. You're fully involved with the headiness of the Power Decade. You realize that there are serious flaws in your equipment, but since the flaws are not hurting right now, you delay doing something about them . . . and delay . . . and delay. . . . You're like the guy falling past the fiftieth floor of the Empire State Building and exclaiming, "All right so far!"

Take Beth Garrett. She had the advantage of knowing what she needed to resolve her crisis of redirection. But knowing and acting are two different things.

One day the boss said to Garrett, "Hey, what about

those engineering courses? Remember we agreed some updating would help. . . ?" Garrett had been asking herself the same question without quite pinning herself down to an answer. She was as aware as her boss that some professional training would improve her prospects. There was every reason to go back to school for some gap-filling studies. The company was a major producer of computer parts. For her to move out of a production department into a management job required more technical background than she had. Her husband had urged her along the same course. But each time Beth got her toe in the water, she yanked it out quickly.

She resisted the idea of the three or four years of night school. Part of the reason was that things were pretty good as they were. She had a good job. Double paychecks made their home one of the more expensive, their car always a couple of years newer in their social circle. She sensed the cold she'd feel giving up the amenities in favor of study.

Many Stage III people face Beth Garrett's dilemma. They know they can do better with more education, more training, going off in another career direction. But no matter how attractive the change, the satisfactions of the current job situation suddenly strengthen in the mind.

Beth Garrett finally decided not to go back to school, to do the best she could with what she had. At worst, it wouldn't be too bad. . . .

There are tens of thousands of thirties-to-forties who choose the long, hard path rather than the short, easy one. They go back to school, undertake home study, do the moonlighting that will help broaden their experiences.

Watch out for the Beth Garretts in Stages IV and V. In ten or twenty years, their self-indulgent decisions may come back to haunt them. In their forties and fifties, they will realize that their working lives haven't been the bowl of cherries they hoped for. The honest ones think back to the might-have-beens. And among these, the failure to commit oneself to additional effort to improve qualifications and capabilities turns out to be a permanent obstacle to advancement.

16.

The Crisis of Responsibility

PEOPLE who move from job to job in their twenties are naturally anxious to look good and learn all they can in the new job—but they don't feel that they are under terrific scrutiny.

However, when you've accumulated a little weight on your résumé, coming into a new job can involve pressures approaching those recorded in the awesome ocean depths of the Mindanao Trench.

"Maybe I was a jackass," says Steve, "but it came to me quite suddenly. My first day on the new job I seemed to myself to be looking for something. I realized I was looking for the instruction book . . . the kit . . . the role model . . . something that would tell me how to act.

"Then I saw that everybody was looking at *me*. No more role models. I was the role model. The people I had been brought in to supervise were now going to adjust their behavior according to me, or what they thought I wanted. Their thinking, too."

Along with the shock of realization that you are now in

the spotlight rather than in the chorus, there comes the strong feeling that your time is limited. For the first time in your career, you are expected to produce results. In fact, it is demanded that you produce.

"I didn't know how much time I had exactly," says Wendy, who went from an assistant's job with a frozen-food company to a spot as brand manager for a soft-drink firm. "But I had the feeling that one day it would run out, and nobody would say anything to me, but I would know I had had it, just by the way they looked at me."

The difference is power. When you're out of the learning stage, you're expected to bring it with you.

During the first months on the job, there are three general challenges that the new young manager faces. The first is to find the pivotal point on which the unit swings. When you first move into a job in which you're expected to produce results, you're confronted with a range of options. There's no shortage of things on which you can spend time and energy. But just a few of those things can have any real impact on the bottom line.

You are under pressure to locate that facet of the business which has the greatest effect on results. Otherwise you'll waste time and energy. In previous jobs, you were more likely to be judged on form. Now, it doesn't matter how you do it; *just do it.*

In moving into the first job that involves responsibility for results, you must take advantage of your "clean slate." You may see flaws which are so obvious that you conclude your predecessor must have been blind or incompetent. Not necessarily so. The previous incumbent may have been well aware of the problems but have been hampered by politics, inertia, or long-standing relationships.

Knowing this, management probably made allowances for your predecessor. You will not get the same break.

The first job involving responsibility for measurable performance is likely to be one that requires you to get things done through others, rather than on your own. Your grasp of management technique may not yet be fully developed, but you are apt to have a pretty good instinct for

Stage III (30-40): The Power Decade

people. You can observe others and gauge whether or not they are the people you want.

And then you have to act decisively. This means firing people if necessary. Just moving into a new job does not bring on crisis. But the first *performance-intensive job* precipitates a highly critical situation for many people: They are being *judged* again: perhaps they haven't been judged and made to measure up to standards since school days. Maybe they have never faced this requirement.

Along with this comes the necessity to do uncongenial and distasteful things in order to produce the required results. Today there is talk about the "pressure to perform," meaning the traumatic stress felt by men who must struggle to "get it up" sexually. But pressure to perform—and its attendant crises—is by no means confined to males or to bed. The first time you come up against it, it can be very rough.

If you want to stay with your job, you must make a crucial move: clarify the basis on which you are being judged, and shape your efforts towards excellence by those yardsticks.

17.

Depression: A Complication of the Power Crisis

THE first severe setback—if it comes in State III following years of easy success—can stun the individual into depression.

You're in the conference room, brimful of confidence and fight. You're presenting your approach to a problem. There's no question in your mind that they'll buy your idea. After all, they've always bought your ideas. And afterwards they've patted you on the head because the ideas worked out so well.

But suddenly out of left field comes a rival. This greenhorn, a wimp if you ever saw one, has the nerve to present an idea of his own. Furthermore, he doesn't even tip his hat to the merits of your proposal. He attacks it.

Confidently you rebut. You expect the boss to see things your way. Suddenly it's very important that he see things your way.

He doesn't. The wimp wins the day.

Half an hour later, you're sitting behind your desk like a stunned ox. Not only has a neophyte gotten his proposal

Stage III (30-40): The Power Decade

accepted, but he has been placed in charge of a high-powered task force to execute the plan. You're going to be under his command.

You're no longer upset, or dumbfounded, or angry, or shocked. You're nothing. Who gives a damn?

As the days go on, you continue not to give a damn about anything. You go through the motions, but you don't care. You don't care about people around you. At the desk, you're apathetic. In the conference room, you're silent. And inside, you loathe yourself. You're a failure. Somewhere, you went wrong, and you don't even have the brains to see where. What difference does it make anyway?

You're in a *depression*.

Only a few years ago, you would have been dismissed as sulking, or in a snit, or as a sore loser, or just a gloomy person. People would say that you had better snap out of it. The assumption was that depression was self-willed. Now depression is a star in the pantheon of psychiatric ailments. It is spoken of with gravity, a sickness that, if it goes on too long, can have severe consequences.

Depression is more than just glumness and lack of interest in the external world. Its destructive and malignant feature is an aggressive assault against the self. People see themselves as guilty and punish themselves.

Psychologists have now identified various kinds of depression according to the cause of the condition. *Reactive* depression is caused by overt situations: death, rejection, failure in business. Usually the depression is mild. You're listless and pessimistic. If you slip into *deep* depression, everything about you sags, including your facial muscles. You can no longer keep up the pretense of caring about anything. You may become suicidal.

Now, of course, psychoanalysts ascribe the fundamental causes of the neurotic symptom called "depression" to early childhood. The individual has suffered a deprivation. He or she has been unable to prevent the loss of a "love object," which can be a person, a promotion, a product, anything on which one fixes.

Whatever the genesis of depression induced by a job

setback, its consequences can be quite severe. Some people remain in a state of depression following a setback for a long time—so long that their colleagues and their superiors come to take the depressed bearing as normal. Once, a manager whose euphoric view of his future had been struck a heavy blow by failure to receive a coveted assignment, sat silent in his office for three months during the lunch hours while others chatted and laughed at the desks in the middle of the big room. One day his door opened and he issued forth, smiling and making conversation. People edged away from him warily. One muttered to another, "My God! He's in a manic state!" The explanation was simpler: He had made peace with himself, saw the "failure" in reasonable perspective.

18.

The Crisis of Management

THE saying "it's lonely at the top" has long since become a truism. But some things become truisms because they are very true.

During the Learning Decade of the twenties, the young person who "makes sergeant" often finds that former friends feel differently. The "making sergeant" syndrome sets in with full force in the Power Decade. As you move up, there are more people below you looking up at you. They may not regard what they see with favor.

The picture of the alienated, disillusioned, successful businessperson has become a cliché. This is one of the prime crises of command. The trimmings that come with command may be unappetizing.

The disillusionment of command results only partly from the fact that fewer people like you when you are the boss. It also comes from the empty feeling when illusions fade into thin air. The person who has established a good track record in the twenties must succeed in quite different ways as power accumulates. Now the key is *management*.

And it is at this point that some of the cherished myths about management and success in business—if they have lasted till now—disintegrate.

As you make your way into the world of management, your path leads you past the bodies of sundry sacred cows. For example, you may have bought the proposition that apple polishing never pays; that promotion to the high echelons is based on merit. You will witness brown-nosing so blatant that you're embarrassed. You will assume that the recipient of the arrant flattery will see through it and be altogether unaffected by it. And then you will see that, in many cases, buttering up the boss really does pay off.

Another myth you may have cherished—because so many organizations proclaim their devotion to it—is the idea that top management welcomes creative dissent and imaginative troublemaking when it is for the good of the company. Alas, this is not so. For the most part, the boss who tells you "My door is always open" means that it is open to admit people who will agree with him and make him look good. Whatever he must say in the speeches and articles ghostwritten by the PR department, he does not welcome aggravation.

You will come upon other myths: for example, that which holds that looks and manner don't count; it's what's inside the head that makes the difference. You will see that the primary criterion for promotion is often the "look" of promotability, a complex of cosmetic qualities that have little to do with the person's actual performance on the present job.

There are a lot of other myths. Some of them are shared in toto by all of the members of the old guard. Still clear-eyed, you may look at these assumptions and find them wanting. But try telling that to the boss. You'll be in the unfortunate position of the child who tried to tell people that the emperor was wearing no clothes.

Such a myth, for instance, is the touching faith held by so many business people in the efficacy of consultants. This is not to say that consultants are not often helpful; but you will find that representatives of prestigious consulting firms are regarded with awe equaling that of the aboriginal native for the witch doctor.

To make your involvement with such myths even more poignant, you may have the fleeting insight that in time you, too, will come to share the assumptions.

Add to your disillusionment the renewed discovery that a boss has to do unpleasant things. Pile on top of that the realization that making lieutenant is worse than making sergeant; people are suspicious and resentful even if you do backbends in an effort to be a nice guy—or especially so.

Very simply, being part of management can be unpleasant. When you are placed above your peers, a whole new set of relationships and tensions is created. New managers are especially sensitive to the alterations. Consider Rex Kilby, just promoted from packer to head of the mail room. His entry into the department the first day of the new regime was spectacular. At the threshold, he banged the door with a broom handle to attract all eyes and announced to his ex-peers, "All friendships end here."

What was he saying? That he had to give up the patterns of closeness with friends and aloofness from the unfavored, possible when he was one of the group. That his friends could not expect special treatment; they would have to shape up like everybody else. And simply but forcefully he was serving notice that he was boss. As of that moment, he was assuming the authority that went with the job.

Entering the ranks of management forces you into situations that demand new roles. You have to play God and the devil in turn. The symbolic multiple "hats" that managers must wear involve everything from the judge's wig to the devil's horns. Managers may have to enforce policies with which they are personally in disagreement. They may have to make unfavorable judgments involving people they regard as longtime friends. Despite their own authority, they must accept the higher authority of those on the upper rungs.

Management is hierarchical, and the company must suffer the personal strains as well as the organizational benefits of that structure. One executive says, "An organization chart usually hides as much heartache as it reveals who gives orders to whom."

There is a saying that power has its price. When you are a manager, there are times when you must pay it. But be even-minded about it. Power has its rewards and gratifications as well.

19.
Cutting Corners

THERE is a particularly prevalent crisis that lies at the confluence of clock-shock and overreach. The individual is in a tremendous hurry, will do just about anything to reach the destination, and thinks that he or she can get away with just about any tactic.

In the mid-1970s, Bruce Caputo was one of the bright shining stars of Republican politics in New York State. He was wealthy, attractive, well educated, bright, articulate. As a freshman congressman, he achieved quick prominence by exposing what the newspapers began to call the "Koreagate" connection: a flood tide of money streaming from Korean business interests to American lawmakers. Congressman Caputo could be seen frequently on the news broadcasts and talk shows. He was refreshing. As he talked of these seamy matters, he projected a sense of dismay and disgust that said to the world, "This is an honest man."

Although there were Republican pros who felt that Mr. Caputo ought to remain in Congress for several terms—he was in his mid-thirties and had the boyish looks of 25—he decided to run for lieutenant governor of New York. This meant giving up a relatively safe congressional seat. However, Mr. Caputo evidently had decided that his career—which he saw as unlimited in potential—would move faster and better if he established himself in administrative and state politics. From lieutenant governor, he could step up to governor.

Of course, it would be necessary to be *elected* lieutenant governor. But this was not supposed to be a problem. The Republican candidate for governor was Perry Duryea, a potent and personable veteran of the state legislature. Their opponent was incumbent Democratic Governor Hugh Carey, whose allegedly poor term as governor was assumed to have doomed his chances for reelection.

But Carey's "gift of gab" made Duryea look sick in debate after debate. Duryea's campaign was leaden. Mr. Caputo, of course, was not a candidate on his own; he was linked with Duryea, as the vice-presidential candidate is linked with the candidate for president on the national scene. Caputo and his team looked on helplessly as Duryea put audiences to sleep and Carey projected a vibrancy and a grasp of business that his critics said did not mark his actual work as governor.

Carey won. Caputo was out of a political job.

Here we see a couple of aspects of the problems of the ambitious person in the 30–40 decade. You're in a hurry. You tend to reject counsels of caution and advice to sit tight and wait. But, irritating as it may be, in your push upward, you are all too often tied to someone else. You share the other person's fate, even though you know damn well you would do better on your own.

Bruce Caputo's next move was to run for the U.S. Senate in 1982, rather than try to return to Congress. In your thirties, you want to keep pushing upward.

Mr. Caputo's campaign for the Republican nomination was going along nicely—until some unkind soul disclosed that his claims to have been an army officer during the Vietnam War were slightly askew. As a matter of fact, he had had a civilian job in the Pentagon. Then it was revealed that, while he had certainly graduated from the

Stage III (30-40): The Power Decade

Harvard Graduate School of Business Administration, he had not graduated, as he claimed, "with distinction." The Republican leaders deserted him in droves. He was political anathema.

Needlessly. Why not stick to the truth? The fact is that Mr. Caputo's "misspeaking" had not made any difference. His image was not that of a John Wayne Green Beret; what difference did it make whether he had been in the army or not? As for the graduation business, one would have been hard pressed to find a voter to whom it would make a particle of difference whether or not he had graduated "with distinction."

Clock-shock puts on terrific pressure. You feel that you must rush, must get there by the fastest possible route, whatever corners you cut. So you take chances. When you take a big risk that doesn't pan out, you may be devastated; it may be the first severe setback you've ever run into. And when the risk has been compounded by doing something you know to be dishonest or unethical, your discomfiture is all the greater.

People who are in a big hurry become very self-absorbed. Here is Paul, about to make his bid to become group chief. To do this, he will have to unseat Arthur, a genial veteran who has been around a long time but who does not—at least to Paul—project an image of tremendous dynamism.

Paul had made no secret of his opinion that Arthur is no electric circus of energy. "This guy is instant Sominex," Paul tells his lunch companions. "Jesus, you doze off just hearing him on the phone. The restful life is fine, but what we need around here is a little excitement."

Paul aims to provide the excitement. He has been saying things and writing memos that emphasize what he sees as Arthur's cardinal weakness. Typically, he comes back from an industry conference and writes a report that starts: "Vitality and innovation! Those are the words I heard most often at the Annual Convention. This industry is pulsing with life. When pressed to talk about what our organization is doing to maintain itself on the cutting edge, I had a hard time. . . ."

Although Paul thinks his campaign is subtle, everybody knows what he is doing. Paul is not blind. He just has blinders on. So single-mindedly is he pursuing his goal, he is scarcely aware of the reactions of those around him.

When you're in a hurry and cutting corners, you see things in black and white, missing the shadings of gray. All of Arthur's faults are magnified. From a slow-talking and fairly complacent but knowledgeable executive, Paul has constructed an image of the boss as an inert moron.

Clock-shock tends to dull critical faculties. Every nod and acknowledgment Paul gets from top management is taken as tacit approval of what he is saying and as tacit disapproval of Arthur. And of course Paul hasn't got the faintest idea that poor Arthur knows what's going on.

Poor Arthur knows exactly what's going on. He has seen hurrying hotshots before. And Arthur's bosses are no strangers to the phenomenon either. Furthermore, there is not the slightest chance that Paul can unhorse Arthur. Indeed, Arthur, in an informal lunchtime chat, tries to get this point across. He emphasizes to Paul that top management is reasonably happy with things as they are. Paul comes back from lunch ecstatic. He's got Arthur on the run, he figures.

Arthur's advice has not been altogether altruistic. Paul is a valuable performer. He has a future, although probably in another division. Arthur and the company would hate to lose him. But it is impossible to transfer him now, and he does not seem to be able to take the hint to slow down his guerrilla campaign.

At last Paul makes his overt bid. He goes to the top with a detailed memorandum that, if accepted, would leave the company no choice but to dismiss Arthur and put Paul in his place.

The company has no intention of doing that. Unfortunately, Paul is so extreme in his efforts that he has to be transferred to the equivalent of Siberia. His career in the organization is over.

This is not to say that it is wrong to bid for power during the decade of the thirties. After all, this is the time

Stage III (30-40): The Power Decade

when you have it all together. By and large, corporate philosophy no longer dictates that people wait patiently, well into grizzled middle age, before they accede to command. Furthermore, there is no reason whatsoever why the individual who has spent a fruitful Learning Decade cannot reach the top during the Power Decade.

The trouble comes when clock-shock impels the person to move too fast and to ignore too many warning signals. In the grip of impatience, brilliant people can act very foolishly. They blunder ahead into the minefield of tradition and entrenched relationships. They utterly minimize the qualities possessed by their competitors, and they place much too high a value on their own strengths.

The saying has it that when one strikes at a king, one had better kill him—anything short of that is disaster. When a premature ill-considered bid for power falls short, the future of the individual within that particular organization is likely to be dealt a severe and perhaps deadly blow.

But this is far from being the worst crisis that one can meet. There is still plenty of time. The usual recovery route is to move to another area as fast as possible and to benefit from the lessons just learned to make the next bid for power a more rational and better-prepared one.

The factor that makes this crisis worse than it needs to be is limited vision. In Paul's case, his failure was brought to his attention forcibly. He was transferred. But often nothing appears to have happened. Life goes on as it always did. The would-be king-killer thinks that he has not been harmed. He may even think that the fight is still going on and that he has a chance of winning it. Such lack of perception can cause the person to keep on trying or to stay in the same place until it is much too late to recover.

There's nothing wrong with ambition. And it is not uncommon for ambition to cause people to cut corners and try to move too fast. The resulting setback is critical and somewhat traumatic, no doubt about that, but it need not be catastrophic—if the person sees in time what has happened.

While it is nonsense that one can learn from all adversity, this particular crisis of clock-shock can provide a learning experience; kind of a postgraduate follow-up on the Learning Decade. Benjamin Franklin said, "Experience keeps a hard school, but fools will learn in no other." However, there are certain things that can be learned only by experience. Perhaps this is one.

20.

Workaholism

A physician who is also the head of a thriving family of businesses says that he gives certain standard psychological tests to job applicants. He was asked about the psychological profile of his ideal employee: Did he look for the well-balanced, rational, all-around human being?

"Oh, no," he replied. "My ideal employee is an extreme compulsive personality. I screen for that."

This was refreshing. All employers tend to enunciate certain pious standards when they describe their hiring practices. "We look for the 'whole person,'" one told us jovially. I almost said, "'The Whole Man,' but that's against the law, isn't it?"

Yesterday and today, the kind of individual who is frequently prized as a real "comer" is the driven character who puts work ahead of all else. They may shake their heads and click their tongues and lament the fact that Jack doesn't know how to relax. They may beam upon Mark, who goes home at a decent hour, spends time with his family, does not utterly immerse himself in the job twenty-four hours a day. "All work and no play makes Jack a dull boy" is one we've all heard. But don't kid yourself. Jack may be turning himself into a dull boy, but he may have a big "promotable" sticker on his personnel jacket.

The workaholic, like the alcoholic, becomes something between a figure of tragedy and comedy in the general folklore. Alcoholism is an insidious and destructive disease, but a lot of people still roar with mirth as the big-time comedian does his lush act. The workaholic may indeed be destroying his life and the lives of his loved ones, but to many he is just a comical nut. A nut, that is, until he gets the big promotion one fine day.

During the thirties, work becomes an increasingly powerful magnet. People who are by no means classic compulsives find themselves pulled toward the pulsing core of the job. Some do it out of fear; they see their rivals putting in longer hours and getting more deeply involved, so they follow suit. But with many, the motivation changes as the involvement with work becomes more intense. The individual may start by devoting more time and energy to the job because of fear. Frequently the competitive urge takes over, and the involvement becomes more than just a defense tactic.

The phrase "competitive urge" rather than "competitive instinct" is used because in our culture, we take competition as a given. In other cultures, the impulse to compete is practically nonexistent. Ruth Benedict, in *Patterns of Culture,* contrasted the behavior of two Indian tribes. One tribe featured the "potlatch," a ceremonial feast in which men try to outdo each other in giving things away. The competition continues until one man is driven to destitution, sometimes to suicide.

In another tribe, competition does not exist. The norm is to help those in need. On the basis of anthropological observations like these, along with other research, sociologists and psychologists have come increasingly to consider that the competitive drive is not inborn but learned.

When you are in the grip of the competitive urge, it may not matter much. And the competitive urge pushes one into deeper work involvement.

Stage III (30-40): The Power Decade

Take the case of Janice. No one could have been cooler about what she wanted from life: enough money to live well; personal relationships that gave a maximum of pleasure and a minimum of pain; work that was interesting, absorbing, and satisfying because it contributed to the well-being of the world.

The particular career path Janice chose was the law. She liked the work and she looked forward to the challenge. She saw herself as a public advocate, taking up the torch for the downtrodden of the world and for the benefit of mankind.

Since Janice graduated from a good school with high marks, she was courted by eminent law firms. Advised that she would do well to learn her craft and earn her spurs with a big Establishment law outfit, she chose an old-line Baltimore firm.

At first she was bored. Seeing this, her seniors stepped up her pace, began to give her more responsible work on more significant briefs. She looked at the other young lawyers around her with amusement. The competition was ferocious. The fledglings vied with each other to see who could stay latest, boning up on the cases.

Janice would have none of it—at first. But then, annoyed at the pretension of one of her principal rivals, she decided to go all out—as if she were indeed set upon an Establishment legal career—just to show it could be done. She began to work until close to midnight. Her competitiveness became ferocious.

Today, Janice is well on her way to becoming the youngest associate the firm has ever had. Does she want it? She would tear human flesh to get at it.

The man she had lived with for three years, easygoing Jeff, has long since been discarded. *Too* easygoing. It looks as if Janice will move in with Harry, one of her colleagues. They like to talk shop, and they can help each other on the briefs.

Workaholism is one of the most common crises of overreach during the Power Decade. But it is often not easy to perceive as a crisis, at least not by the person to whom it is happening. (The nature and depth of the problem is all too apparent to others.) The disguise worn by this crisis is that of success. The work-obsessed compulsive tends to get ahead, at least in the short run. And for many, the run is not that short. At the end of the run, however, perhaps two decades hence—some may find severe and devastating crises of loneliness, alienation, and despair.

21.

Love Among the Laborers

TOTAL absorption in work makes everything—and everybody—encountered off the job seem dim and insubstantial. This applies across the emotional board—so it is to be expected that people who work together will become attracted to each other.

This may not in itself be a crisis, but, because of the inevitable conflicts, it is a situation fraught with potential crisis. Sometimes this is because of the disparity between what people like to pretend is happening and what is actually going on. Sometimes it is because of the strain between career ambition and sexual/emotional attraction.

Some workplaces are more susceptible and open about work-sex involvement than others. However, while it is understandable that people who work together are attracted to each other, liaisons between colleagues often clash with the job and career considerations of one or both of the parties. And that leads to crisis.

Eileen Gray, 31, was a rising star, recently promoted from associate to full-fledged group manager. Eileen's affair with the department head—of three years' standing now—still seemed in full flower. Seemingly his promotion two years ago had made no difference. They still talked shop in the most intimate way. Eileen maintained what she considered to be perfect discretion. And although everyone in the department knew of the clandestine affair, there was apparently no resentment, because, in Eileen's view, nobody could possibly think she was sleeping her way to anything.

The fact that the affair did not seem to be going anywhere was not, on that day, Eileen's major concern. It was the job of assistant department head, which did not yet exist. Her boss and lover had told her he was instituting the position. And, yes, though she was the person best suited for it, she was not going to get it. That he had made clear to her just last night.

"Sure," he had said, "it's a pretty easygoing place, and maybe it would be O.K. down here, but no way would the big chiefs sit still for it."

Eileen's disappointment had turned into rage as the night and the following day wore on. Now she was feeling something like shame; unclean; she was being had. She quit, went to another house, carved out a fine career. Her bitterness never really faded.

Like many things in life, romance on the job can bring both good and bad. And sometimes a mixture can create a career-rending as well as a heartrending crisis. Doubtless there are possible enrichments from romance. But the aftermaths make an arresting list:

• *End of romance—disillusionment.* This can mean the embarrassment of chance encounters in the corridor; still worse, the difficulties of having to work together. There is a high separation rate of secretaries after an affair with the boss.

• *Limitation on other possible relations.* The man who gets a reputation of executive-suite Casanova may find present relations with others strained and the opportunity for future relationships thwarted.

Stage III (30-40): The Power Decade 151

- *Jaundicing of assessment by higher management.* Among the group of top executives, there's likely to be at least one and maybe more individuals who consider job romance and job capability mutually exclusive.

It's a tough choice people have to make when they see a friendship beginning to glow with amorous elements. Different individuals and different organizations create their own microcosms in which the consequences may vary. But if you are the person beginning to feel the silken coils of romantic entrapment, you surely won't be the first who may have to choose between love and duty.

22.
Biology vs. Economics

A recent phenomenon, sufficiently marked to be featured in newspapers and magazines, reflects a special problem for Stage III women. Basically what's involved is a conflict between biology and economics, although sociologists might claim that their field rather than biology is the antagonist.

Simply put, many 30-to-40-year-old women, particularly those at the younger end of the group, feel the desire for motherhood. And this natural yearning can be a threat to their careers.

Three aspects of this problem reveal some of the critical pressures that arise: the childless wife who feels the end of her childbearing years approaching; the young careerist who wants a child enough to bear one out of wedlock; and the working mother who finds the double role more than she can easily handle. First consider the young wife caught in the conflict between the urge to motherhood and the possibility of damage to career aspirations.

Stage III (30-40): The Power Decade

There is considerable controversy about the point at which a fetus becomes a human being. For a working couple, even a child that hasn't yet been conceived can become a problem, convulsing husband and wife and even drawing the parents of the couple into the crisis.

"Should I give up my job to have a baby?" Or, less drastic but also thorny, "Am I willing to put up with the inconvenience and rearranging of our life-style that childbearing will bring?"

For young married women, whether or not to have a first child is a consideration with a lit fuse. The further past 30 a woman becomes, the greater the problems of not only conception and childbirth itself but also the chores of motherhood. Child psychologists say a woman of 30 generally makes a more relaxed parent than one past 35, particularly of a first child. Despite the problems, the satisfactions of parenting are surely there, because many women in their thirties cancel out the negatives and take the fruitful step.

These days, the working mother has become more in evidence—and better accepted on the work scene. Employers are both more flexible and more generous in maternity-leave benefits, and most mothers are back in their jobs three or four months after birth. Although there has been a lot of talk about paternity leaves, only a small percentage of new fathers take time off to help at home, and the time off is usually one or two weeks.

The calendar is a relentless enemy. Career complications as well as medical ones tend to increase with the years past 30. For one thing, the older woman has probably moved higher up the ladder if she is in management, or has taken on more responsibilities, so that the job is less easily set aside for motherhood. And there is another deterrent: The woman happy in her work must pit the possible watering down of that satisfaction against the uncertain pleasures of motherhood.

Consider Beth Kane. Her profession is exotic—she is a modern dancer. At 32, she is a member of one of the most outstanding groups in the United States and ranks among the top fifty dancers in the country. Her husband, Calvin, is a lawyer.

Perhaps a dancer is not quite in the same category as a production executive or computer specialist. But while the work may differ, other elements—job satisfaction, pay, job responsibilities—are not too dissimilar. We could get involved in the distinction between a calling—and for many performers their art may be so described—and a job. But in the crisis we're discussing here, the urge to motherhood, Beth Kane's conflict is like that of other employees except for the presence of a single intensifying factor: The physical consequences of childbearing are a serious practical consideration.

To have or not to have a child, for Kane, is a critical choice. While many female dancers have children and return to the stage, they usually have them earlier. The general feeling in the profession is that motherhood tends to interfere with, if not completely end, a performer's career. The body changes. Muscles lose their tone, joints swell, breasts swell. The first three months after childbirth are a total loss. Postnatal fatigue and recurring nausea are not uncommon. And physically, dance is a relentless taskmaster. It is not unusual for dancers to practice eight or nine hours a day.

"Having a baby after thirty," Beth Kane says, "takes about two years out of one's professional life." And since 35 is generally the age at which performing ends, motherhood is a difficult role for the dedicated performer to accept.

"And," adds Kane, "when you're out, another dancer takes over. If she is any good, when you come back you are at a disadvantage. There are instances when motherhood has cost a performer her job."

At least in this last respect, a dancer may not be too different from any other worker. And certainly all the domestic aspects of becoming a mother—child care, the shrinking of available housekeeping time, and the increase that a tiny infant adds to the chores—are factors shared by all new working mothers.

Stage III (30-40): The Power Decade

The Beth Kanes and would-be mothers among the Stage III group have both a personal and professional problem that is not unique—Stage II women face the same situation. But the crux of the problem for the older women is the closing of the time door, the difficulties of deferring the decision, and the diminished resilience to changes in living pattern that parenthood may bring.

Calvin Kane is a loving husband, proud of his beautiful and accomplished wife. But he is eager to have children, or at least one. And his mother, an admiring mother-in-law—rare category—said to Beth one day, "Dear, I don't know whether grandmotherhood generates the same juices as motherhood, but I want a grandchild so much I can taste it. However, I really understand the dilemma you and Cal face. . . ."

Despite their caring attitudes, Cal and his mother add to the difficulties of Beth's decision. Her problem is that her eagerness to have a child is exactly matched by her desire to maintain her identity as an artist. Certainly, as a way of life, the rewards of performing reflect youth, challenge, self-fulfillment in a way motherhood might match in other ways. But becoming a mother cannot help but be an obstacle to Beth Kane's life in art.

Women who may not suffer physical changes that interfere with their jobs must still weigh the possible consequences in job terms. For example, many feel that, regardless of intentions to continue a career, the problems of childbearing and child raising may diminish energy and increase time pressure so as to make returning to work impossible. Another, and possibly happier, outcome has surprised some women, who discover that the joys of motherhood are sufficiently fulfilling to cancel out the drive to participate in the world of business.

For women experiencing this shift of what's important in their lives, a crisis of decision will have to be thought through: There's an important social change they must confront.

An executive well on her way toward the upper echelons in a brilliant career in retailing says: "After little Lila was born, I had every intention of going back to the store. But I became so involved with that lovely creature, I certainly wasn't going to short-change her with substitute mothers who might stunt her emotionally. It's a decision I never regretted even though the title 'mother' has much less appeal these days than president of—and you can add the name of any well-known, successful, big-city department store."

But many make the choice of *both* childbearing and continuing their careers. And they try to make the double burden as bearable as possible by judicious planning—with the husband's participation—of child care, housekeeping, and the rest of the activities that make family life viable.

Even the most involved professionals can take motherhood in stride, but they must be good planners who make the effort to touch all the bases on child care and rearing, and to integrate working and living patterns.

Catalyst, a national organization that seeks to foster increased participation of women in corporate and professional life, recently conducted a study of two-career families. Included in the findings were some statistics that show how age influences attitudes toward having children.

"The period of greatest conflict between spouses over the decision," the Catalyst study reports, occurs when wives are 21–25, while the period of greatest indecision for women was between the ages of 26 and 30. Women were likely to wait until over the age of thirty to decide definitely not to have children."

The last statement suggests that Beth Kane is hooked on a most painful dilemma. Her decision is no longer what it might have been in her twenties: *when* to have a child. Now the more anguish-producing question is *whether* to have a child.

As you will soon see, there is considerably more to be said about the mix of job and motherhood, since continuing the race is such a potent motivator.

23.

The Motherhood Decision

A successful and perceptive young woman told us, "I work with half a dozen women in their late twenties or early thirties. I don't know of a topic we discuss more than the question of whether—and when—to have a baby."

Once, the accepted wisdom was "You'd better have it by the time you're thirty." While the optimum ages are still seen by the medical profession as 25 to 29, the "maternity window" remains open until the late thirties; sometimes beyond.

One of the most stressful situations confronted by women during the Power Decade is the consciousness of the slow, inexorable closing of that window. The constellation of crises evolving out of the motherhood decision presents a number of variations.

- *Will it hurt my career?* There's a law against penalizing a woman for having a baby. Maternity leave is generally accepted. It would be a die-hard organization indeed that would be so foolhardy as to fire or blatantly punish a person for motherhood.

But there are subtleties. A purchasing agent for an office-supply company said, "Around the seventh month, there wasn't anything more that cleverly cut dresses could do. Boy, was I pregnant! I gloried in it. I felt great. But I could feel them edging away from me in the elevator. I noticed nobody sat next to me at meetings. These guys acted as if I had a fatal disease that wasn't to be mentioned. Did it hold me back? Listen, I loved every minute of it, and little Penny is the light of my life, but I don't kid myself that it was a big career plus. It wasn't, at least not in the short run. And in my business, the long run is made up of a lot of short runs."

- *"What's the matter with me?"* The balancing of motherhood vs. career is a major decision, requiring cool assessment and a high degree of objectivity.

But the act of applying so much objectivity can cause severe problems. "God, what am I, a monster?" asks a woman in the anguish of the dilemma. "How can I be so laid back about this? This is a baby I'm thinking about, not a new briefcase!"

This is one of the Catch-22 aspects of the situation. If you don't think logically about the decision, you compound the crisis. If you do think logically about it, you may perceive yourself as cold-blooded. "I'm too analytical," laments a victim. "Real mothers are gushy."

- *"Can I handle it?"* The *it* usually refers to the heavy load that would be imposed by the simultaneous raising of an infant and pursuit of a career.

Here is the point at which some women begin to think of themselves as inadequate. What they feel inadequate about depends on which side of *it* they come down on. Some envision mostly career damage: coming unprepared to the big conference because you ran out of Pampers; embarrassing phone calls from the sitter; etc. Others foresee their problems in terms of flaws in motherhood: neglect of the spiritual nurturing of the child because of ignoble concentration on advancement.

"I was really surprised at myself," said a media buyer.

"My mother and I were friends, but nothing she ever told me seemed to have all that much zip in it after I was grown up. Along comes this thing. A friend and I talked about it endlessly. I knew all the buzzwords, like 'It's not the time, it's the *quality* of time.' Neat. But I was resisting it. When I thought about it, it came to me that, on the subject of motherhood, I had bought everything my mother said. Without realizing it."

Other women speak of similar things. In effect, they carry along with them a set of attitudes given to them by their mothers. They had not examined these attitudes; in fact, they had not known they possessed them. They were there, like mother's china in a crate in the attic. When the question of being a working mother came up, the parental viewpoints weighed in heavily.

"The toughest thing for me when I finally went ahead and had the baby and went back to the job was my mom. Not that she ever said anything. Not a thing. She didn't even look at me funny. But sometimes I thought it was like a betrayal of her. Pretty nutty, but I still thought it."

• *"What do I really want?"* Having a baby is serious enough. But inevitably it gets mixed up with other serious subjects. Some women go through considerable anguish because they feel that their decisions about working and mothering will somehow make a profound statement about their lives. Sometimes they suspect that the longing to have a baby is really a cop-out—an excuse to drop out of the career race, or a handy alibi for not going farther and faster. Others find that the decision leads to soul-searching that probes into the dark corners of the self. "What am I trying to prove? . . . Do I have the right to do this? . . . Is it selfishness or mother love?" And so on.

In fact, there are few career crises so riddled with big questions that can't be answered. Waiting until all the questions are answered before making a decision is in itself a decision. The answers do not come. The window closes.

One woman, a unit manager for a giant communications firm, was—at age 36—deeply involved in the process of sorting out these knotty questions when a surprising thing happened. "I was embarrassed! I plan everything! How could I have forgotten? Anyway, there I was. Pregnant."

Presented with the obvious conclusion that she must really have wanted the baby, she laughs and brushes it aside. "Well, I thought about an abortion—but then I thought, The hell with it."

She says people thought her pregnancy was funny. "You have to understand that they had me pegged as the original PB (pushy broad). Maybe they were right. Do you know something, I think even the fact that I could be a mother knocked some of them on their ear. They didn't think I was that human."

It wasn't just the image of humanity. She found, to her astonishment, that "it really did change me!" She felt being a mother had made her more human. This was a case in which having a baby was a definite career plus. "I lucked out," she says.

You don't always luck out. Motherhood profoundly changes one's life. It certainly has a tremendous effect on routine. But this is not the same as saying it is a career drawback.

However, the difficulty of being both a good mother and a good business person cannot be ignored. The seriousness—sometimes to the point of anguish—of the thought that leads to the decision is justified.

And yet—it may be that many of the most profound aspects of the predecision deliberations don't matter. There are people who ask themselves all the prescribed questions, seek all the indicated help, adopt all of the most enlightened attitudes—and then mismanage motherhood and career. Others ignore the difficulty—"I don't see why I can't be the best damn mother in the world and still make it to CEO of this outfit"—and somehow get away with it.

The most difficult crises may be the ones associated with the making of the decision. After the baby is born, things tend to sort themselves out. It's hard—but there are far fewer questions with no decent answers.

Mother Courage

Jenny Fields, mother of the protagonist in *The World According to Garp,* John Irving's popular novel, is a prototype of the woman eager to have a child all her own. The indifferent way she chooses the father illustrates her single-parent-mindedness. Garp is a badly wounded tailgunner, chopped up by flak in the ball turret of a B-17 over Germany in World War II. For Jenny, his imminent demise is a plus—no strings. That their mating will be his final meaningful act is accepted by Jenny and counted on to remove the possible complications of double-parenting.

The union is accomplished in a hospital bed—Jenny is head nurse—and is antiseptic and matter-of-fact. The man expires a few weeks later, and Jenny is free to go on to have her nine-pound boy and to enjoy the concerns and pleasures of motherhood without conflicting marital ties.

Here is the lead paragraph in a recent article by feature writer Georgia Dullea in the *New York Times:*

"Even in the age of the so-called super mother there are examples of the breed: Secure, self-sufficient women in the 30s who are choosing to become unwed mothers, to combine careers with child rearing in a home where there is no father and no serious talk of marriage."

Dullea is reporting on a trend that, according to Dr. Patricia Conrad, a Manhattan gynecologist, was "almost unheard of five years ago." She is talking about single women whose urge for motherhood is strong enough to overcome the social taboos and the practical inconveniences for unwed mothers. Don't let the phrase *unwed mother* summon up an incorrect picture. The phrase traditionally applied to the usually young, often teen-age, and mostly naïve women to whom motherhood came unwanted and imposed an immediate social and economic burden. Dr. Conrad describes this new group as unmarried, financially secure, career-oriented, and age 35 to 42.

What is the motivation for the act of conception and childbearing for these women? In Dr. Conrad's opinion, "They hit the panic button," by which she means that they fear passing the childbearing age. By the late thirties, it is the most resolute segment of the group that persists in the desire to have a child, and the decision is made with full knowledge of the difficulties, even hardships, that may be involved.

But to get the full impact of this situation, you have to imagine the agonizing and soul-searching that precedes the decision. Most of these women, being highly intelligent, examine their motives carefully. Although there is no husband, the biological father is likely to be a lover or friend. And a marriage may or may not have been desired.

Various reasons may explain the situation.

Legal: The man may have a wife, and divorce is not in the cards.

Economic: The man may feel he can't afford to get married, because he's not earning enough; or he refuses to marry a woman who may outrank him in job status.

Emotional: The woman may be fond of the man but be aware that a permanent and stable relationship would be impossible.

It's likely that the final decision was made only after all other possible choices failed. The man may have tried to get a divorce and finally given up. The woman and her lover may discover that they are emotionally incompatible. The woman may have spent many years hoping to meet a desirable mate and failed. As the years continue to recede, the biological window for motherhood becomes threateningly smaller until the woman makes a choice on a now-or-never basis.

The single-parent choice is a precedent-shattering one, yet an increasingly large number of women are adopting this unusual life-style. Being the kind of women they are, they make it despite the possibility of handicapping consequences.

Among the people interviewed in this group, one woman says: "I worked in a small office; all the people were my friends and I didn't expect any damage to these relationships. But there was one result I didn't anticipate. I actually found my status raised because I had become someone special. I felt, particularly among the women, an increased respect. And as far as the occasional conflicts between child care and job, I found my boss being particularly generous in agreeing to somewhat flexible hours and time off for emergencies."

Of course, an unwed mother's problems involving child care are substantially the same as those of the married woman. The only amelioration for the latter is the possibility of the husband solving some of the time problems that arise when a baby-sitter has to cancel out, play school unexpectedly closes for the day, and so on. The husbandless mother tries to have hired help with time flexible enough to come in on short notice. Friends, neighbors, relatives also have a chance to shine in emergencies.

The Consolidation of Power

By the end of Stage III, you're likely to have reached the jumping-off point for the rest of your career. For better or for worse, you're on a particular track and you are rolling with certain impetus. From here on, changing tracks would take an extraordinary effort.

You've developed your muscles to maximum power; and if you're lucky, you've learned how to use them. Your crises of redirection are behind you—or at least they should be. The individual who emerges into the forties still seeking an answer to "What will I be when I grow up?" faces some feckless fun—but some very severe jolts as well.

The efficacy with which you've managed to come through clock-shock will stand you in good stead; there are severer time crises to come. By now you should be past most of the temptations to overreach; the decade of the thirties teaches us to bring reach into conformity with grasp.

In short, you came into this decade a rookie. You emerge a veteran, still vigorous, still surging upward, but now seasoned by the crises you've come through. You're ready to sit on the high-stakes games of working life. That's what they're playing in the decade you're about to enter.

Stage IV (40–50): The Win/Lose Decade

24.

Time's Winged Chariot Keeps Rollin' Along

In the years between 40 and 50, the tiny ball clicks into one of the slots on the roulette wheel. Efforts begun twenty years earlier reach their fruition—or fall short.

Many of the crises during this stage are functions of success or failure. Losers—or those who perceive themselves as losers—face a whole set of difficulties: "Where do I go from here, now that I'm over forty?" "Is there anything I can do in my job to regain status and improve my prospects?"

But the winners are by no means home free. The act of winning creates pressure and vulnerability. It is in this decade that people must struggle to keep what has been won. And it is now, also, that people wonder just what their success adds up to.

The import of time changes; it becomes more of a threat than a promise. Some begin to flirt with the melancholy adjective *last* as in *last chance* or *last time.*

In championship chess matches, you hear the term *moving under time pressure.* Each player is allowed a total amount of time—say two hours—to make a certain number of moves. If the player spends too much time on early moves, there is a sense of rush and pressure later in the game.

Something similar happens during this decade. The individual in midlife seems to hear, in Marvell's words, "time's winged chariot hurrying near." There's a sense that the years are running out; that one is now face-to-face with one's *last chance* to make it to the top, to strike off on one's own, or just to become safely established on the job and in personal life. For some, time has run out.

In 1953 a massive expedition led by Sir John Hunt set out to climb Mt. Everest. It was to culminate on May 28. Evans and Bourdillon were the climbers who were selected to be the first to reach the summit. They were chosen the night before to make the final assault on the summit.

They fell short. Hillary and Tenzing made it the next day.

What about Evans and Bourdillon?

Some of the most significant Stage IV crises involve what we might call the "Evans/Bourdillon syndrome." We may have no idea what went through the minds of these two climbers when they stopped a little way short of the summit, but disappointment, frustration, anger, and despair are likely feelings.

Those who *have* made it can be in deep trouble, too, however. There are crises of the heights, in which winning makes you a loser. And there are those who, win or lose, are beginning to suspect that it was not worthwhile to run the race.

For most of these, the point of no return was passed some time back. That fact can make crisis in the Win/Lose Decade a matter of deep desperation. But it's desperation with a difference: The victims must face the crisis without the benefit of youthful resilience. In the stages before this one, there were more options, more freedom to act. Many who see themselves in a dead-end situation feel they're not going to get another shot.

When companies offer employees major-medical plans

that include psychiatric help, an interesting thing happens. Plot the usage of psychiatric help according to position in the company and you find the line is swaybacked: high for the lower echelons, high among senior executives—but quite low among middle managers.

It would be a Pollyanna indeed who would conclude that this means middle managers are less in need of psychiatric help than others. No. Investigation shows that middle managers are *afraid* to avail themselves of this help under the company plan. They fear that the news will get out and that their careers will be blighted.

Rank-and-file workers—who, because of cultural hang-ups, would be expected by some to ignore the opportunity to consult psychiatrists—are quite willing to admit that they have emotional problems and to seek help. The high-level executives don't give a damn who knows they are seeing a "shrink." Indeed, at their level, it might seem like a deficiency if one did *not* suffer from stress.

Gradually, middle managers have begun to seek help openly. And with the opportunity to observe people in a full range of occupations, psychologists and psychiatrists note a paradoxical situation. At the very point when individuals seem to be reaching the peak of maturity and success, they are assailed by ferocious self-doubts.

There is a Catch-22 element to this situation. The more one achieves, the more one is aware of what will never be achieved. As soon as goals are attained, they are questioned; then discounted. "I won this prize," says one careerist, "but it's worthless, junk."

In *Career Success/Personal Failure,* Abraham K. Korman and Rhoda W. Korman identified the symptoms of this prime-of-life alienation as follows:

- heightened sense of getting old
- awareness that others are getting old, too
- realization that many goals cannot be attained
- dwelling on past aspirations
- fear of obsolescence
- increased worry about the future

One reaction to prime-of-life alienation is *flight*. The individual thinks about going somewhere else, occupationally and geographically. He or she dreams of making a major change in status—as impractical as that may be.

In a prominent manifestation of what Dr. Mortimer R. Feinberg has called "middle-aged megrims," there is often a yearning to go into business for oneself. This is particularly unfortunate and critical when the person who does it has been sheltered within the corporate cocoon for many years. Those who work in organizations get used to relying on others for research, for advice, for help . . . even to turn out the lights when they leave at night. But that's not the way it is when you go into business for yourself. You are truly—sometimes devastatingly—on your own. Even if you boasted tremendous entrepreneurial strengths some years back, they may well have atrophied.

For a while, one of the opportunities most favored by executives who wanted to do their own thing was the restaurant business. It was commonplace for a couple of big-time advertising luminaries to pool their savings and open a steakhouse in the suburbs. Their sole qualification for the restaurant business usually was that they had eaten a lot of lunches in such places. This would be akin to becoming an airline pilot because you'd racked up a lot of air miles. Many stars of the corporate world lost their shirts as would-be restaurateurs and then fled back to the shelter of the executive suite.

The yearning for change often goes beyond just the job. People really want to "get away from it all." They want to change occupation, location, even time. They strive to go back in time to a point when life was less complicated.

Ruminations of this kind usually are some version of the "tropical paradise" dream. Here you loll on a sunny, flower-strewn beach surrounded by attractive members of the opposite sex, your needs and wishes readily satisfied. Hungry? The sea abounds in exotic delicacies. Thirsty? You say, "Bring me a coconut," and a dozen eager hands thrust liquid-laden shells at you.

Some of the musings about escape from the unsatisfac-

Stage IV (40-50): The Win/Lose Decade

tory present are more practical. Every need, if strong enough, engenders an enterprise to fill it. As the old-time immigrants, accustomed to the less entrepreneurial ways of the old country, used to say, "In America, everything is a business."

Midlife yearning for a simpler existence can be satisfied through the services of the omnipresent middle-person. Country Business Services of Brattleboro, Vermont, is a brokerage specializing in finding small businesses in New England and upstate New York that can be taken over by disillusioned executives.

Country Business Services itself was started by a onetime high-rolling public-relations counsel named James Howard who worked for Richard Nixon in the 1968 campaign and then became a White House adviser, whereupon he had a nervous breakdown (making him one of the early victims of a nervousness that became endemic among Nixon aides when Watergate reached full flood).

According to the *New York Times* of November 27, 1981, Country Business had flourished, with more than twenty branches and independent brokers in the East. The average client is 35–55 years old; in middle to upper corporate management; and makes $50,000–$100,000.

"They have no seeming reason to be dissatisfied," says Mr. Howard, "but they're very unhappy. They've accomplished everything they set out to do. They belong to the country club. They've made vice-president. They're invited to all the cocktail parties. And none of it has any meaning."

Of course, the disaffected middle-life executive has become a cliché; a truism. But things become truisms because they're true.

Many of Country Business's clients buy rustic inns, thus running true to the pattern followed by executives who go into the restaurant business.

But if you can't open an inn or a general store in Vermont—and God knows the supply of locations must be finite—you can always just stick around and burn out.

25.

Some Inner Consequences of Leadership

THE ways people think about you when you are at the top have little or nothing to do with you personally and everything to do with your position. Take it that way. Often, there's nothing else you *can* do.

However, insight into your own feelings may ease some of the discomfort. Being aware of the consequences *on your sense of self* can alleviate some of the pangs. The following four methods of adapting to leadership may shed some light on your behavior.

• *The Trade-off.* A newly promoted boss tries to counter the loss of the warmth of old friendships by dealing with his people in peremptory fashion. He's saying, "Okay, if you're telling me our friendship is over, I'll play it the same way." Further, by putting on the screws he is telling himself, "Since they think I'm a louse anyhow, I might as well behave like one." But he suffers from their dislikes, decides it is the price he has to pay for power. Perceiving the nature of the trade-off and really accepting it can diminish the tension.

• *The psychic callus.* This is an adaptation made by

some doctors, prison guards, and executives. They harden themselves. For them, it has become professionally inadvisable to empathize with the discomforts of their patients, wards, subordinates. One of the physical signs of this self-protection is the rigid mouth line, the compression of lips to block out feelings that might interfere with their objectivity. In effect they develop an armor that protects them from self-damaging sensitivity.

• *Tentative leadership.* Some managers let themselves be intimidated by the thought of subordinate displeasure. And so they seldom use their authority, try not to be "bossy," and even cringe when the word is applied to them. Their entire leadership style is largely shaped by their inability to accept their own dominance. They try to show subordinates that they are to behave as though they were on equal terms with the boss. But that can create difficulties.

Dick Deadeye, the maverick seaman aboard Gilbert and Sullivan's H.M.S. *Pinafore,* has it exactly right when he says, "When some people have to take orders from other people, equality is out of the question." (His messmates, outraged by such revolutionary sentiments, dunk him in the harbor.)

Some egalitarian-minded managers reject the idea of the superior-subordinate relationship—to the detriment of their effectiveness. In some instances, an attempt is made to resolve the leadership problem by adopting a democratic style. But it is frequently misused. The purpose seems to be for the boss to be indistinguishable from one of the crew, but this is a distortion of the democratic-leader concept. While the democratic approach does give subordinates the opportunity to participate in decisions and increases the level of self-management, ultimately the responsibilities and crucial decision making are functions of the boss. Any efforts to avoid this fact usually result in managerial confusion and failure.

• *The reality cure.* Finally, there is a strategy that diminishes inner turmoil and creates calm. Here, the manager does two things:

1. He or she plays it straight, matter-of-factly accepts the realities of the situation. The basic premise is simple: "I'm being paid to be boss, I try to be the most effective boss I can be."

2. He or she facilitates the activities of people in their job roles, assuming that they are as accepting of the subordinate position as leaders are of theirs.

Mary Parker Follett, a leading business philosopher of the early twentieth century, developed the idea of the "Law of the Situation." This principle proposes that, in given work matters, the *situation* determines what is to be done and who is to do it. By this rule, managers act to do the things their role demands—determining objectives, directing employees in the procedures that will achieve them, and so on. And employees are similarly obliged to turn their skills to the tasks to be done, as directed by their manager.

The crisis of being boss, of wielding power and relating to those who are subject to that power, demands a combination of perceptiveness and realism. Just as the integrity and persons of subordinates must be respected, so should the boss. The difference is that, in the latter case, the standards of acceptability and approval tend to be higher.

One executive, the head of a management firm, says, "*Boss* is not a dirty word. When an individual fills the role well, he or she has the respect, even the admiration, of the bossed. And when the manager has charisma, and is a leader as well as a boss, employees outdo themselves to perform, and look up to him or her as to demigods."

26.

The Great Disillusionment— a/k/a/Burnout

SOMETIMES it seems that illness is, for many people, the most precious possession. Certain kinds of illness, of course; nobody cherishes cancer—too lethal—and nobody boasts of psoriasis or athlete's foot.

But certain disorders that are generally thought to be induced by stress are often flaunted as badges of accomplishment. High-powered executives used to joke proudly about their ulcers. For various reasons, the ulcer went out of style. For one thing, it became evident that anyone, even a ditchdigger or a housewife, could get an ulcer. For another, treatments were developed so that people who suffered from a severe stomach ulcer seem stupid rather than important.

More recently we have seen a great fad for "burnout." It began with teachers, who submitted "burnout" as their reason for requesting longer holidays and higher pay. Now the word is a commonplace of the executive suite.

Managers who attend meetings can almost be sure that at some point on the agenda there will appear a discussion of burnout. And it seems to have been co-opted, at least for the time, by middle-management people who have reached the middle years.

The symptoms of burnout are diminishing interest in the tasks of the day; loss of motivation; feelings of futility; anger, frustration, and listlessness.

It must be noted that "burnout" has not been isolated and identified with pinpoint accuracy. The symptoms certainly resemble those encountered among all kinds of people. The housewife who is bored, frustrated, etc., is told that she doesn't have enough to do; that she should go out and find herself a job. In the bad old days in the armed forces, sergeants used to provide treatment for similar symptoms with a kick in the ass.

Nowadays it's burnout. It seems to us to be another name that is applied to the combination of attitudes and insights that often coalesce during the middle years. Nothing seems as much fun as everything did two decades before. The end of the rainbow is in sight and there's no pot of gold, and a closer examination shows that it wasn't really a rainbow anyway—or at least that there were other rainbows that *might* have led to the gold. Yours doesn't.

Burnout is a culmination. It begins early. It is a reaction to the disintegration of the hopes of many years before.

Burnout is *reality* shock. The individual can no longer delay or avoid moment-of-truth time. The truth about the person, the job, and actual achievement induces the shock, whose reverberations go beyond job-related needs to affect the whole personality. An expert sums it up this way: "*Shock,* as used in the construct of *reality shock,* means the total social, physical, and emotional response of a person to the unexpected, unwanted, or undesired, and in the most severe degree to the intolerable. It is the startling discovery and reaction to the discovery that school-bred values conflict with work-world values. In some instances, reaction to the disparity between expectations and reality is so strong that the individual literally cannot persevere in the situation."

Stage IV (40-50): The Win/Lose Decade

The first stage of burnout comes as a vague feeling of malaise, uncertainty, unfocused unhappiness. The person has a feeling something is wrong but can't figure out what. At this stage, just sitting down and talking with somebody can be helpful. The professionals call it "ventilation."

Often some kind of change can be beneficial. A lot of people are able to give themselves new interest by simply rearranging their working routine: handling the correspondence in the afternoon rather than the morning, taking a long walk at lunchtime, starting an hour earlier, etc.

When burnout reaches full force, it brings with it a long list of symptoms:

- the feeling of lack of control of events
- growing suspicions about unfairness of treatment
- questioning of the goals that one has spent one's life pursuing
- other pessimisms about the future
- the conviction that everyone looks at you and knows you are a failure

By this time, burnout is serious enough so that competent professional advice is needed.

When the condition is unchecked, people do *burn out* altogether. They become unable to work and have enormous difficulty in relating to others about anything.

This is a very common crisis of the Win/Lose Decade. It is insidious because it comes whether one wins or loses; and indeed is more likely to come to winners.

27.

The Crisis of Frustration

WHEN you're young, anything seems possible. But in the 40–50 decade, it is realized that, with regard to certain goals, "You just can't get there from here."

That's coming to grips with reality—and that's good. But it's also frustrating—and the ramifications can be devastating.

When people are frustrated, psychologists tell us, they may react in four ways:

One type of frustration behavior is *aggression*. Most of us are familiar with the impulse toward physical violence engendered by extreme frustration; those atavistic flashes of the urge to kill.

You sit in a meeting, having just described a bold, imaginative plan. You look at the blank faces in front of you, and *you know nothing is going to get done.* Your hominid ancestor might have seized a tree limb and slain the whole lot of them. Civilization or refinement—or something—has deprived us of that outlet. But there is still the urge to do *something*.

Stage IV (40-50): The Win/Lose Decade

Usually we direct the reaction into somewhat less self-destructive channels: slam a door; go for a long, hard walk; swim a few laps.

On the work scene, the impulse to aggression may manifest itself in verbal assault—snapping back directly; or indirect assault, on the reputation of someone at hand.

Daria Williams just seemed "to start in on" Fred Hanley. Why? Nobody could figure it out. Fred was one of the best of the younger generation in the department. Daria had wholeheartedly endorsed his hiring, and she had been enthusiastic about his work.

Now, however, Daria was showing a flair for cutting sarcasm. Most of it was directed at Fred Hanley. Fred himself was at a loss. "Out of a clear blue sky, she shoots me down. Just shoots me down. What the hell did I ever do to her?"

"Maybe it's what you *didn't* do to her," says a sexist colleague.

"Bull," says Fred. But in the absence of any other cause, he begins to wonder. That just makes things worse.

The industrial psychologist Norman R. F. Maier, in his book *Frustration,* writes that "aggression may appear in a disguised form . . . the source of the frustration might not be readily apparent from the behavior."

Frustration that has been building for years can boil over during the years from 40 to 50. The result is destructive behavior, and the problem is that nobody—including the target and the originator of the aggression—knows what's really the matter.

Another form of reaction to frustration is *fixation.* One of the most lethal examples of fixation in history occurred during World War I. Maddened by their inability to break through the German trench lines, the Allies decided to try something new: surprise. Instead of preceding the attack with a long artillery bombardment, they would just attack with practically no artillery preparation, overwhelming the surprised enemy.

The important thing about this plan was that the Germans really had to be surprised. Otherwise it would be a slaughter.

A few days before the scheduled advance, the English commander, General Haig, received undeniable proof that the Germans were totally aware of the plan and ready for it. They had withdrawn a few hundred yards from their previous front line and set up machine guns to mow down the advancing troops.

So, knowing that the essential element of surprise was no longer there, Haig called off the attack, right? Wrong. At the appointed moment—July 1, 1916—the British armies went over the top. They plodded ahead to certain death on the bullet-swept fields near the banks of the River Somme. The attack failed utterly, with an unprecedented loss of life even for that bloody war.

General Haig was disgraced and demoted for his idiotic reaction to frustration, right? Wrong. He was left in command, promoted to field marshal, and given a rainbow of decorations. After the war, a grateful nation presented him with £200,000 (though since Haig was a scion of the whiskey family, he was already a rich man) and a castle in Scotland.

But Haig was a general. The person in business who reacts to frustration by developing a fixation is not likely to kill so many people; nor to be so handsomely rewarded.

Jim Schooler, a marketing VP—45, good track record, excellent reputation—is in the process of seeing a pet project go sour. The product introduction has gone wrong. Sales are lagging, and the market-research reports give practically no hope.

One of the cornerstones of Schooler's success is his ability to know when he is licked on a particular project and to move on to something else. He has every intention of doing that in this case. But at the crucial meeting, he looks around at what seem to him the glittering eyes of younger competitors. He listens to overt criticism and veiled questioning of his continued ability to cut the mustard. He has not realized his increasing frustration—after all, he never used to have a short fuse—but suddenly it gets to him.

"No!" He slams his palm on the table. "This concept is

Stage IV (40-50): The Win/Lose Decade

a winner! I don't give a damn what the numbers say! We're going to stick with it!"

Incredulity and vicious pleasure mingle in the minds of those observing this irrational decision. But the executive sticks with it—and he's stuck with it.

Fixation can be "pure": The individual becomes a "true believer" and insists on pursuing the goal in spite of all objective evidence that the goal is unattainable. Or it can be more cynical: Up to the eyeballs in frustration, and unable to get a word through to the boss, a person will continue to follow—to the letter—procedures and policies that obviously will not work.

Frustrated people who develop a fixation may be said to be "butting their heads against a stone wall." It's a figure of speech that exactly describes the behavior of laboratory rats who bang their heads against a blank wall instead of taking another path that will lead to food.

Another kind of reaction to frustration is also seen in the 40–50 decade.

Artie Leeper has been wrestling for months with an assignment that at the beginning looked like it might be the culminating triumph of his career. Surely when he brought this one off, his path would be clear to the executive vice-presidency, and even beyond to the top spot.

But it hasn't worked out. One damn thing after another has gone wrong. Leeper has coped with amazing patience, good humor, and optimism. There comes a day, however, when a subordinate enters Leeper's office to discuss the urgent need to hire temporaries to complete a crucial project, only to be told, "I don't have time for that now."

What could be so important as to supersede this vital topic? Leeper waves his hand at the pile of papers. "Annual merit review forms. Got to get them filled out and into the house mail."

Now, as in a great many companies, the merit review system is honored in Leeper's firm more in the breach than in the observance. It gets lip service, but people don't take it seriously. Perhaps they should; but that is not the point.

The point is that Artie Leeper has unaccountably

turned his back on momentous affairs to bury himself in what he has always dismissed as trivial.

Beset by frustration, Leeper is *regressing*. People do that. They revert to modes of behavior that are virtually childish. They go on meaningless trips. They play games with papers. They become deeply absorbed in every rumor flashed along the grapevine. They cannot distinguish between the important and the unimportant; and they cannot make mature decisions.

One may hear it said: "He's in his second childhood." Frustration may have made him that way.

Yet another reaction to the frustrations that pile up at this stage of working life is *boredom*.

Once vibrant, the person becomes apathetic. Instead of butting against a stone wall—as in the fixation reaction—the person says, "Why butt your head against a stone wall?" The trouble with this is that many of the obstacles are not stone walls at all; merely paper partitions. In the resignation induced by frustration, the person does not care. Unmotivated, he allows listlessness to become a way of life.

This individual is numb; oblivious not only to pain but to feeling of just about any kind. At home he is a zombie—but then, maybe he has not been much of a factor around the house for some time.

At work, however, his zero-ness is bound to arouse comment. People look at the apathetic man or woman and say that he or she "is getting old."

Of course, that is what's happening. People used to comment in some surprise to the late William Holden, the actor, that he seemed to be getting old. He would reply, "I'm delighted to hear that you have found a way to arrest the process."

Frustration is part and parcel of Stage IV. It is practically impossible to escape it. One avoids frustration only if all of one's plans go 100 percent right. Were that to be the case, there would probably be psychological problems of a different sort.

When people react to frustration in one or another of

Stage IV (40-50): The Win/Lose Decade

the ways we've mentioned here—with aggression, fixation, regression, apathy—they bring upon themselves many of the other problems that are most identified with this stage of the career. A lot of the Stage IV crises are shoots that grow from the basic rootstock of frustration. The frustration cannot be eliminated. It is always there. The idea is to understand that it is there, and cope with the various guises in which it surfaces.

And this stage is the one in which the theme of frustration is dominant. When it comes earlier, it seems temporary. When it comes later, it seems invariable, and must be accepted, sadly or otherwise. But during the years when the individual feels that he or she should have "gotten it all together," signs that this has not happened are bad news indeed. Perhaps the obstacles are no greater than obstacles encountered twenty years before, but the stakes are higher—and there is less time to break through.

That, indeed, is perhaps the great key to the frustration that engenders so much crisis during this decade. Time—and the consciousness that one may be running out of it.

28.

Falling Through the Status Gap

How absurd the whole notion of status is—when you're 24. How important status becomes—when you're 40.

If you've reached the fearful forties, you're ready for one more problem that you never knew existed: *status imbalance.* It's a gap between your standing in the community of work—as you see it—and the kind of work you're being asked to do. If the balance gets out of whack on either side, you're in trouble.

Tom Farrington is 47. He went to St. Paul's, Yale, Harvard Graduate School of Business Administration. He has twenty-five years of marketing with *Fortune* 500 companies in a series of jobs with increasingly impressive titles. And he is very *unhappy.*

"At the meeting I said to them, 'Hey, you guys, let me sit with you and kick this project around some. I've got package-goods savvy in my head that you won't find in a memory bank.' But they go right ahead. Experience doesn't count for all that much anymore. All right, my position in

Stage IV (40-50): The Win/Lose Decade

the firm is certainly secure—I've got nothing to prove and, God knows, Charley Peters, the CEO, knows what I can do, but sometimes it gets on your nerves, sitting around when you know you could be making more of a contribution."

Along with Tom's feeling that he is being underutilized, as he puts it, is a nagging worry about physical condition. Recently, for example, he felt pain in his chest. Just sore muscles, as it turned out, but Tom is not used to sore muscles in the chest. It's all right for your leg muscles to be sore after three tough sets of tennis, but the chest? No.

He's having trouble sleeping. He gets mad at little things, things that never used to bother him. And—though it's tough for him to admit it—he is even having trouble with his vaunted memory. The other day somebody asked him about the Fort Wayne test on the famous Amalgamated product introduction that he handled ten years ago, and he could not remember the I and R scores. He thinks—though he could be wrong—he heard them snickering about the "human memory bank."

Eleanor Grace is 43. She has never worked for another firm. She was hired twenty years ago as a typist, a position she sought because her two years of college didn't seem to warrant more. She became a secretary, and in the following years her progress was measured in terms of the increasingly awesome titles possessed by the men for whom she worked.

Eleanor is alone; a brief marriage ended in divorce some ten years ago. More than once she has been told she is "married to her work"; and her answer, spoken or not, has always been that there are a lot worse things to be married to. At one time she was courted briefly by a neighbor, a salesman who lived on the floor below. Nothing came of it because she realized that the idea of physical intimacy was unattractive to her.

And then she was made assistant office manager, and she caught fire. The thought of moving up became the single most exciting thing that had ever happened to her. She started taking courses at night in business management and business law. She found the management courses particularly rewarding. The dead-end feeling about her job was replaced by a sense of the challenging echelons above.

Her boss, Connie Berg, praised her newfound dynamism in a performance review and concluded with "Eleanor, just remember that the firm will never let you down." Let her down! Not being let down was not her concern. She was counting on being invited up.

The trouble was that Connie, an attractive blonde and ten years younger than she was, seemed an immovable roadblock to progress.

Eleanor was able to arrange an interview with Connie's boss, Al Rogers, executive vice-president. Early in the meeting, she let Mr. Rogers know of her ambitions and of the courses she was taking to achieve them.

"Fine," the executive said, "fine. But, Eleanor, there's a bit of wisdom I'd like to pass along. You're doing an excellent job where you are, Connie Berg tells me. Don't make the mistake of overreaching yourself, aiming at a goal that I expect you'd find unrewarding if you got to it."

She said she'd like the chance to show what she could do.

"What kind of position are you thinking of?"

She had anticipated the question and had an answer: "I'd like to be in charge of internal services, help make our clerical and word-processing operations more efficient and available to more people in the organization."

Rogers laughed. "I admire your vision, but we're not ready for that kind of function." Then, noting her dismay, he told her she would be getting a sizable raise at the end of the year.

That evening Eleanor went home and brooded. Self-doubts made her miserable. Was she being blocked because she was a woman? Was her entry into the company as a typist a stigma that handicapped her? Maybe she wasn't as good as she had begun to think she was. She had a fierce, short-lived impulse to quit and look for another job. It seemed like an impractical move.

She had always enjoyed a glass of wine before dinner,

Stage IV (40-50): The Win/Lose Decade

which she liked to eat alone ("I'm a great reader and enjoy the company of Dickens or Somerset Maugham at the dinner table more than any other company I can think of"). Now it became a martini, occasionally two. And she started to preface lunch with a regular cocktail, something she used to frown at in other people in the office.

The job continued as before. Everybody, from the highest to the lowest, came to her for help. At one time she had been pleased to be wanted, taken it as a compliment, thought it was rather funny that people seemed to prefer her to Connie Berg, and told her friends about it. Now she tried to avoid those requests. "Just remember, I'm only the assistant manager," she'd say. "See Connie."

She continued with her courses to the end of the semester but didn't reenroll. She had become a member of that unhappy group of people who hate their work with a passion but stick because they see no practical alternative.

For Eleanor, the job had become a dead end. If her boss moved up or out, she might be promoted. If not, she'd stay put. At 49, she began thinking of early retirement.

A paper in the *American Journal of Sociology* (September 1975) by James S. House of Duke University and Elizabeth Bates Harkins of the Battelle Human Affairs Research Centers examined some of the consequences of status. The researchers found that stress caused by "status inconsistency" increases with age: "Younger persons can hope their social situation may change, but by middle age opportunities for social mobility or other means of eliminating inconsistencies diminish, as does the opportunity to believe future rewards will compensate for present stresses."

Typically, when you're young you don't notice the stress. When you're in your thirties and enjoying the exhilaration of achieving mastery, you are willing to endure stress because you can look forward to future goodies that will have been earned by the stress. But when status crystallizes, the stress begins to take its toll because there's less to hope for.

The status inconsistency that causes stress works in

two ways. Tom Farrington is under pressure because he is being treated as beneath his status. His education and his track record have conferred upon him a certain cachet. Maybe he never made it to the top of the mountain, but his triumphs—or at least his experience—should make people defer to him. Or so he figures. When younger colleagues ignore him, he begins to feel psychic and physical pain.

Eleanor Grace's anguish is caused by the realization that she does not have the status to which her brains, her accomplishments, and her abilities entitle her—and she never will. The time to have gone after higher status was twenty years ago. It's too late now. The rewards she once felt in being relied on and complimented by senior executives—almost always men—are now perceived as insulting pats on the head.

In one case, the individual is suffering from *status underload*. His job— and the obligations it places on him—does not measure up to his expectations. The gap may result from doubts by superiors of an individual's ability to succeed with demanding assignments. He or she is viewed as marginal in the job, and others are given the mettle-testing tasks. One's peers may avoid requests for help, guidance, or even the traditional "I've got a problem I'd like to discuss with you. . . . " The reason for the avoidance may range from a lack of trust to low evaluations of the individual's capabilities: "He's the dumbest vice-president I ever knew," an executive told us, referring to a colleague. "He's just a figurehead, must have gotten the job in some kind of political payoff."

In the other case, Eleanor Grace resents the fact that her station in the workplace (and in life) is not commensurate with her capabilities. Result: *status overload*.

Status has gotten a bad name in recent years, almost as bad as "hypocrisy." Books like *The Status Seekers* imply that status is something that one may put on or not, like Gucci loafers. The person who lusts after "status" is a bad person—vain, snobbish, more interested in the appearance of things than the meaningful underlying reality.

But every creature who is involved with a social system

Stage IV (40-50): The Win/Lose Decade

has status. The "pecking order" of the barnyard is the result of chickens sorting themselves out according to their standing. All societies are organized into a series of hierarchies and status systems. And the workplace is—emphatically—a society.

You've probably heard the jokes, seen the cartoons and the advertising-copy lines ("A title on the door rates a Bigelow on the floor"). For those who have never been a part of a certain kind of working society, it probably seems fantastic that persons would seriously count the windows in their offices and resent the possession of an equal number of windows by an individual considered of lower status. Doubt it not. Status concerns are felt everywhere.

In the jungles of New Guinea, there was and perhaps still is a tribe of Pygmies who wore no clothes whatsoever. However, each adult male wore a bright orange sheath, resembling a carrot, on his penis. The higher the standing of the man, the longer the "carrot."

A prominent New York psychoanalyst whose practice consisted largely of high-level executives and entrepreneurs described the troubles of one of his patients as follows: "Every time this man closes a big deal, he adds a quarter of an inch to his penis. But every time he blows a big deal, the opposite effect is felt—*and right now he is in a losing streak and feels castrated.*"

We achieve status in either of two ways: through some fortuitous factor of birth—sex, skin color, bone structure—or by means of accomplishments.

The sociologist Max Weber said that everyone needs *status and function;* the society that does not confer status and function upon its members would fail. Sometimes a plethora of status can, at least for a time, make up for a paucity of function. In Nazi Germany, Hitler never really solved the economic problems left by World War I, but he put a lot of people to work making guns; and he was a master at bestowing status; janitors wore snappy uniforms with shiny boots.

Young people don't care all that much about status. They concentrate on function, assuming that status will come as a natural adjunct of successful contribution. But that does not always happen. The working society sorts itself out in odd and often unfair ways. And during the Win/Lose Decade, that unfairness often begins to hurt.

One reason is that younger people tend not to measure themselves and others by the same standards that society in general applies, and the work society in particular. But as years go on, the general standards are subsumed more and more into one's own measuring apparatus. People start to eye the other person's carrot, become concerned about the length of their own.

Status shock may result from taking seriously the standing imposed by occupation—whimsical and unjust though that may be. The status quirks of the workplace are like the situations of the mortals ruled by the ancient Greek and Roman gods. These gods were by no means all-wise and all-just. They were narrow-minded, petty, and flighty. But they were also all-powerful.

Many a top executive's office has reverberated with the shouted scolding of a subordinate who, one way or another, has failed to meet expectations. If the dressing down has the slightest justification, the subordinate usually stands there and takes it. This is the *boss* speaking. *Boss.* What a word that is. It says it all. The boss has status; the subordinate, at best, has less.

We tend to accept the standards of the workplace because it is convenient. It's a kind of social *fait accompli* that saves the trouble of figuring out what the person really amounts to in the overall scheme of things.

When you realize that, in spite of your ability, you are of low caste and probably always will be, the trauma can be severe. You feel pain you never felt before. You have trouble concentrating and remembering. You nurse grievances, resentments, and hatreds. Maybe you drink. Occasionally, you explode in rage.

When the status imbalance results in serious *material* disadvantage—like the substantially lower wages paid to women, blacks, and Hispanics—the injustice is real. But often the worst status shock is subjective. People suffer

Stage IV (40-50): The Win/Lose Decade

because they think that others do not take them seriously enough or do not accord them the respect due. And if they have older children or a spouse who consciously or unconsciously disparages them, they're getting the message at home also. It takes a strong individual to withstand the double derogation.

When your discontents are centered on status, this doesn't mean you are being silly—status is a part of the human condition. But it does mean that you may be using the wrong set of criteria. If you are paid less for the same work than some fool who has a paler skin or better bone structure, it's the logical and recommended move that you do everything you can to correct that situation. Have a serious talk with your boss, get his agreement on the unfairness of the situation, then ask for a commitment to rectify the matter soon. But you should *not* react as if the imbalance were invested to plague you. It is a by-product of the system.

As long as we function within a human system, we wear a "carrot." This can't be helped. But we hurt ourselves when we begin to think and act as if the carrot were all.

It's all right to maneuver for status because a higher status will bring you more money, or greater security, or other benefits you seek. That's common sense. What is not sensible is to destroy one's emotional security because of inadequacy, real or imagined.

29.
When the Axe Falls

You can get fired at any time—but the jolt is often most severe during the Win/Lose Decade. A young fighter can take a hard punch better than an old one. And in our society, firing may be a knockout blow.

Sure, it's tough to lose your source of income; but for a lot of the Stage IV waifs, that's not the worst part of it. The job has come to symbolize so much more. By now, the workplace may well represent the most important group in the individual's life, more important than family, neighborhood, community, church.

Some people get the threads of personal and work life thoroughly tangled. Pursuit of success on the job is a great tangler. Admittedly, accomplishment is a measurement, and termination is the ultimate negative measure—zero. It provides a simple appraisal to apply to others and to ourselves: *You couldn't cut it; you're no good.* Never mind that the circumstances were scarcely the fault of the person fired. It *happened*.

Stage IV (40-50): The Win/Lose Decade 193

Separating a lower-echelon employee, as difficult as it may be emotionally, tends to be straightforward.

"I'm sorry, Martha, but we're cutting down on services and your section is going to be discontinued. Please report to Personnel. . ."

But when an organization sheds a high-echelon employee, there are some additional wrinkles. For one thing, very few executives are ever fired. One reason: Whereas employees below management level are still, in a sense, "hired hands," executives are "family."

But there are other reasons: "A firm with any sense at all," explains the president of a California engineering firm, "can't see itself putting an executive out on the street. It's bad public relations. And it's hardly a good advertisement for the judgment of the management that hired him."

Such reasons lead to the traditional "executive resignation." Regardless of the "good reason"—better professional opportunity, for example, the real reason may be anything from politics to a merger that kills off the need for the executive's particular skills. The "good" reasons behind executive separation are as many as ingenuity can create. Here are some standard face-savers.

"Our vice-president is leaving to fulfill an old ambition. He has always wanted to go into consulting," reads part of the announcement in a dairy company's house organ.

"J.D.'s wife needs a change of climate because of her health," announces the company president at a staff meeting.

"An opportunity she couldn't afford to pass up was offered to Marie," explains Marie's boss, "and as of the end of the month, she'll be hanging her hat at the XYZ Company." Interpretation: After months of searching, Marie, with her boss's help, finally landed a job at XYZ.

Some executives are subjected to such roundabout firing tactics, report the editors of *Fortune*, that they're not aware of what's happening—until they're out. The head of a department store, for example, told a vice-president, "I think you're the best damned troubleshooter I've seen, and I want you on my personal staff as a consultant." When two weeks passed without the vice-president's having been given anything to do, he asked the president about it. The president suggested he take a month off, to rest and relax. When he returned from vacation, his original job was filled by a new man, the president himself was on vacation, and the executive's consulting office had been turned into a filing room. He did the only thing he could—he resigned, and turned to the executive market for a better answer to his job needs.

Fortune also notes the popularity of the "bypass" technique. For example, the man to be fired finds that his name starts being omitted from important memoranda, or he's excluded from conferences. Or top management uses a personal habit to break an executive. The production manager of a cosmetics firm, for example, made it a rule never to work on Sundays, although some of his colleagues did. The president and general manager deliberately scheduled meetings on Sundays. When the production executive continued to refuse to attend them, he was told that the company had to let him go, because of his lack of interest in his work.

Generally, firings are done verbally because the executive responsible can soften the blow more effectively than in a curt dismissal notice. But not always. One president, embarrassed to fire a subordinate vice-president because she was also a friend, put a dismissal note on her desk without mentioning it. The woman, fully aware of the president's discomfort, retaliated with a brilliant ploy: She never acknowledged receiving the missive, and the president didn't dare write another. She then went on to do a good job for the company. (Few misfirings turn out as happily as this.)

Executives may even resort to downright trickery to remove a subordinate. *Fortune* relates the story of a clothing manufacturer who suspected that his sales head was looking for a better job. He placed a blind ad in the news-

Stage IV (40-50): The Win/Lose Decade

paper for a sales manager, asking for the exact qualifications his man possessed. The latter rose to the bait, answered the ad by letter, and was instantly given the heave-ho for his "disloyalty."

There are many and varied ways of getting rid of top people when management decides they are no longer "right for the team." But from the bluntest to the most kind, no technique can alter the fact—the executive has lost a major prop in his life, and must find another, as rapidly as possible.

Because one comes to depend so much on the job during this decade, the experience of joblessness is almost sure to be critical.

And the mood of those who have been separated, and have then undertaken a late-career job hunt, can be chaotic. Deep levels of emotion have been broached. Here's one view:

"I think it likely," states Dr. Lloyd Hamilton, Hudson Valley psychiatrist, "that executives who suffer most in the jobless situation have undergone some kind of severance from a figure on whom they were emotionally dependent. It may have been an esteemed superior, a mentor within the company; in some cases, perhaps the company itself played the role of protector. With this prop gone, a mixture of emotions, including fear, is mobilized."

The firing crisis takes different forms with different people.

Ben Foster says, "It came like a bolt out of the blue. I didn't have an inkling. . . ." But everybody in Ben's shop realized he'd had it before he did. It's often that way. What's interesting in this case is Ben's reaction to that day when the boss called him in.

"Sit down, Ben. How's Jessica? How are the kids? . . . Good . . . One thing I have been meaning to tell you. When I was on the Coast a week or so ago, Bobby Fellows asked me to give you his regards. Bobby was saying he's heard a lot about some of the great stuff you've pulled off for us over the years. We'll always remember the fine reputation you have in this industry, Ben."

These words, meant to reassure Ben Foster, are having the opposite effect. A welter of emotion is boiling in Foster's brain. The roaring behind his eyeballs is so loud that he can hardly hear what's being said.

". . . so we decided that the best thing would be to bring these operations under one head . . . Jack Hanley from Chicago, with the state-of-the-art knowledge of the technology . . . none of this reflects on you, Ben . . . it's just that we have to make a change. . . . I'm sure you understand, Ben."

As the fired Ben Foster sits behind his desk for the last time, his mind is beginning to thaw. He is shocked . . . he is mad as well . . . he is baffled . . . but mostly he is *ashamed*.

Guilt and shame are often the dominant reactions of people who get fired. There is no logic to it. Getting fired does not make you a bad person. However, the situation resembles that commented on long ago by the American humorist Kin Hubbard: "It's no disgrace to be poor, but it might as well be."

An awful lot of people who have reached the middle years respond to being fired as an end to their hopes and dreams; indeed, an end to life. They sink into apathy. Others do strange things.

When Betty Robertson was fired, she had a limited amount of funds in the bank, substantial debts, one child in college, and one about to begin. Her former husband was no help at all. What could she do? There were a lot of actions she might have taken. What she did do was to blow every last dime on a month in the Caribbean. After the first week, she even stopped using the rationalization that she needed this time away so that she could plunge into an all-out job-hunting effort upon her return. She just said, "The hell with it—I'm going to have all the fun I can until the money runs out." *A la* Scarlett O'Hara, she'd worry about tomorrow tomorrow.

The record shows Robertson and her kind survive. She got another job, and things are going reasonably well for her. What price irresponsibility? Who knows?

Stage IV (40-50): The Win/Lose Decade

Reactions to firing are unpredictable. It is a jolt of such proportions that it can send the needle to one end of the scale—total apathy—or to the other—wild euphoria. The possible family ramifications are profound. In many cases, the job has been a kind of fault line in the family, with uneasy groans and shifts over the years to which the members adjust. When the job tie lets go, there's an earthquake that wounds the ex-wage earner, alienates him or her. Or, everybody gathers round, and the firee gets more attention and solicitude than ever before.

Terminating people to straighten out anomalies in the organization chart or because of "chemistries" is pretty much unique to the American work culture. There are those who say we are a violent society. Maybe one of the reasons some people are not more physically violent is that their most murderous inclinations are played out in the ritual slaying of the firing.

And certainly, people are fired for economic reasons. An organization that sees its cash flow reaching zero, or that must cut back on unprofitable operations, must trim staff. And when companies are forced out of business, the president joins the janitor on the unemployment compensation line.

It happens; people get fired every day; and few of us are ever really ready for it. It becomes a major crisis when it is taken as a rejection of the total person, rather than just the end of the job.

The feeling of guilt that follows a firing is natural. What is unnatural—and damaging—is its persistence. Here's a case that shows how extreme the consequences can be.

Frank Ahlberg, an accountant for a medium-size accounting firm, was fired on Friday morning. It had taken three years for his superiors to decide to take the step. But eventually, Ahlberg's perfectionism, which inflated the time spent on assignments and created billing problems with clients, became intolerable. His boss soothed his conscience by telling a colleague, "He'll do better with an outfit that can afford his nit-picking."

The dismissal shattered Ahlberg. At first he was incredulous. This feeling was replaced in turn by anger, argument, and finally pleading. Eventually he went from office to office, telling co-workers of the injustice to which he had been subjected.

In the days that followed, the real horror began, in full view of everybody on the staff. Frank didn't tell his sickly, worrisome wife about the catastrophe. And so, every day he continued to show up at the office, receiving mail, writing letters, making phone calls, using his old desk. Management, feeling not without guilt, tolerated his presence. Colleagues took turns having him out to lunch and for an occasional after-five drink.

When the talk turned to his job hunting, his invariable statement was "They're looking for younger people." Somewhere along the way, a psychic support had snapped, and the accountant's self-confidence, his ability to initiate, even to think incisively, had collapsed. Months went by and, despite attempts at help from colleagues, Frank Ahlberg continued to be unemployed. Seven months later and fifty pounds lighter, he and his family moved out to Milwaukee and Frank went into his brother's hardware business.

Frank Ahlberg's pattern is not unique. Many people who have been fired continue to leave "for work," come home at the regular time, and never tell anyone, including their spouses, that they have been sacked. They continue to do this until the severance pay runs out. Eventually they grab at any job they can get—taxi driver, waiter, salesclerk—or go to work for a relative. With some cash coming in, the stronger-minded ones succeed in getting back on the career track.

Of course, the logical things for the individual to do are: (1) get as big a severance arrangement as possible; (2) arrange to use the facilities of the company as long as possible; (3) get the word out immediately of one's availability; (4) undertake a systematic search for a job.

But logical procedures aren't always available to the upset and status-bereft individual. You don't expect a bad-

Stage IV (40-50): The Win/Lose Decade

ly shaken victim of a car accident to get right up and resume normal routines.

A healing and reinforcing ministration is necessary. From family, spouse, and friends, the firee needs reassurance and support. Doubts and loss of self-confidence have to be worked on, reminders of skills and past triumphs repeated. Even in a job-tight market, persistence and ingenuity can locate or even create a job opening.

But most of all, the individual must reach deep within himself or herself and find the strength that will restore self-confidence and the drive to undertake a job-finding program or to develop an entrepreneurial venture that will restore earnings, status, and self-esteem.

30.

The Crisis of the Heights

A dominant thread running through American foreign policy after World War II was the notion that it was possible for the United States to be *loved* by a host of countries throughout the world. Not feared; not merely respected; but *loved*.

In our professed idealism, we were using our world leadership to do good for the less fortunate around the globe. And yet, we found that nobody loved us. Even those who were most dependent on us took a periodic bite out of the star-spangled hand that fed them. It was disillusioning to learn that a giant—benevolent though he might be—is feared and disliked.

Career achievement usually means that a growing number of people become your "subordinates." Americans don't care much for "subordination"; it smacks of Old World autocracy. We go for the democratic ideal.

On most work scenes, you don't find people calling each other "sir" or "madam," etc. The language we use on the job is informal—or should be. Peter Drucker once explained that American English is the language of choice in German executive circles; when German managers speak German, they cannot avoid calling each other things like "Herr Doktor" and being overly deferential, to the extent that ideas never cross the lines of rank.

In the United States, the "democratic style" of leadership has reached its pinnacle. Managers are told that the best way to handle people is to be down-to-earth, never pull rank, reason with people rather than give orders, etc. People stick to this concept in spite of data which show that a vast number of workers *prefer* more structure; i.e., they want a boss who *tells* them what to do.

Is the "old shoe" style really best? Or do bosses cling to the illusion that they can be boss and still be loved?

George Davis clung to that illusion for a long time. Davis is one of the world's winners. At 42, he is president of one of the biggest units of a multinational. With his track record and standing in the industry, there's no reason why he shouldn't be chairman of the whole works within ten years.

Davis told us about his day. He was miserable. Things had gone all right until lunch. Lunch had been with Pete Rambeau. Pete had headed up a department eight years back. George Davis had worked for him briefly and they had become friends. Now George was his boss. Pete had called; they hadn't seen each other for a while; George saw no reason not to have lunch.

"I might have known it would be bad," he groaned.

It didn't get bad until Pete began to reminisce: "It's funny how things go, George. Remember when you first came here how we used to talk about the future?"

George remembered the old days only too vividly and a little uncomfortably. It was the same old Pete—a little grayer around the temples, but handsome, deep-voiced, solid. Eight years back, George had thought of Pete Rambeau as having everything. He had to admit that he didn't think that way anymore. Pete was all right where he was—but . . .

Pete moved the conversation into other channels.

"Hey, George, you spend a lot of time around the seats of the mighty. They tell me that old Frank is about ready to retire. What's the dope on that?"

George had been given the dope on "old Frank's" impending retirement. He had also been told that for the time being it was confidential.

"I haven't heard anything about that, Pete."

Rambeau looked at him quizzically. "You haven't heard anything?"

"Oh, some scuttlebutt here and there, but . . . I didn't know anything about it."

Rambeau's eyebrows went up another eighth of an inch. "Are you kidding, George?"

Davis had a flare of resentment at this point: Who the hell is he to imply that I'm lying? A second later he felt ashamed of it, especially since he *was* lying. Switching to another channel, he asked Pete about a project that was supposedly about to be completed.

"Meant to bring that up. I need a little more time."

"A little more time? As I recall, we said—"

"Yeah, well, things have come up. I wonder if you could give me, say, three weeks—a month."

"God, Pete, I don't know. Corporate is looking over my shoulder on this. We had agreed—"

"Oh, come on, you can give me a break. A month or so isn't going to make any difference, is it?"

"I'll see what I can do."

"Thanks, pal."

Now George was definitely looking forward to the lunch check, which finally came.

"Thanks a lot, George. Oh—listen. Harry Salisbury is going to be in town tomorrow night. What do you say you and Harry and I get together for a drink and kick things around like we used to in the old days?"

George had left the tip and risen. "I'd love to see Harry, but I don't think I can make it tomorrow night, Pete. Some other time, maybe."

"Sure, some other time. Well, thanks for the lunch."

These were the high spots of Davis's day after lunch:

- He chewed out a department head.
- He pressured a longtime employee to take early retirement.
- He ran a meeting at which he presented an unpopular corporate decision to a sullen group.
- He listened while his top technology expert—who scarcely bothered to conceal his contempt—outlined a list of reasons why a particular directive could not be carried out with the present equipment.

What stuck with George at the end of the day were the faces; the eyes. "They all hate my guts," he said.

We like to be liked. In general, we know that bosses are not usually loved by subordinates, but we usually think that providence will make an exception in our case, because we are nice people.

During the Win/Lose Decade, one of the unpleasant side effects of winning is the deterioration of friendships and the isolation that comes with being more successful than the others.

Of course, the answer is acceptance of the fact of life that it *is* lonely at the top; that's another of those sayings that did not become false just because it is a cliché. It's what goes along with that acceptance that can be very critical.

For example, overcompensation. George Davis did a little of that when he gave Pete Rambeau "a month or so" on something that should already have been delivered. Davis acknowledges that he did not do this out of love ("Right at that moment I was thinking of Pete as one of the world's number one assholes"), but out of a mixture of motives: shame at being the boss, sadness at losing a friend, etc. Davis knew perfectly well that he had bought absolutely nothing; the next time they talked, Rambeau seemed a little contemptuous, which did not surprise Davis a bit: "I asked for it."

Some people swing pretty far toward the other extreme. They grow armor plate that is impervious to almost any feeling. One highly successful woman—who had made the transition from designer to senior executive—says, "When we were all sitting there in the big room with the drawing boards, there was always a lot of horsing around. You could say anything. But let's face it: Most of the really bitchy things were said about the people we were working for. That's the way it goes. Why should I think that when I moved up and out, they would be any different about me?"

So far so good; acceptance. But then she goes on: "Since I know there isn't a goddamned thing I can do to make these people like me, I turn it around. If I'm going to be an ogre to them, then I am every bit the ogre they fantasize—and more. I use sarcasm and fear. They don't bake me cookies, but, by God I get results."

Subordinates are no longer close companions. Of course, there are bosses who remain on cordial terms with the people who report to them, and manage at the same time to be good bosses.

The crisis comes when you try too hard to be a human being—or when you don't try at all. Currying favor with subordinates ultimately ruins you as a boss. But so does the development of animosity toward subordinates *because* of what you know they feel: "They're just waiting for me to fall on my face." Of course they are. It's always funnier when the guy who slips on the banana peel is wearing a high hat.

31.

The Crisis of Authority

In *Henry IV,* the ignorant and boastful Welsh chieftain Owen Glendower proclaims: "I can call spirits from the vasty deep."

And the cynical Hotspur replies: "Why so can I, and so can any man; but will they come when you do call to them?"

There was a time, in what are said to be the good old days, when people knew their place. They did what they were told. Alas, no more. One of the shocks encountered by people in the 40–50 decade is the unwillingness of members of the younger generation to pay unquestioning heed to authority.

Donald Smylie has never considered himself stuffy. Far from it. He is an informal guy: He doesn't "pull rank"; he doesn't put on airs; he gets along with everybody—young, old, black, white, etc. Smylie describes himself as a frontline kind of guy. He's basically an entrepreneur. With success, his business has grown. He never took any highpowered management courses, but he figures if you talk civilly to people, treat them like grown-ups, tell them why you want them to do something, they'll do it.

But there seems to be a new breed of young people. Smylie doesn't mind if they wear jeans and if the guys have longer hair than used to be the case—if they're clean. He insists that nobody use pot on the premises—he figures he's entitled to that, and nobody gives him an argument.

He does expect, though—when all is said and done—that people will acknowledge that he is the boss. So what is he going to think when he says to one of his people, "Cindy, this rack should be replaced immediately from stock so there's a full selection of merchandise. Otherwise we fall behind and look sloppy. So send each ticket to stock when you make a sale, huh?"

And Cindy says, very politely, "No, this time of year that takes too long. Besides, there's a better customer psychology when you have half-empty shelves. They want to grab the rest of the merchandise before it's all gone."

Since Smylie is not the kind of person who says "Do it!," he explains again that he wants the stock replaced as it's sold. And, astoundingly, Cindy just shakes her head. She thinks this section is hers! She thinks she knows better than the boss.

"Cindy," says Donald, very nicely, "you know I never pull rank. . . ."

"Yes, Donald, I know that, and that's why it's such a ball to work here. A person gets to use her brains. Thank you."

And there is Donald, wondering how—short of threatening to fire her—he can get Cindy to do it his way.

He never gets Cindy to do it his way. And this is just the beginning of what Smylie sees as pleasant but stubborn resistance. More and more, Cindy takes to doing things her own way. She just assumes that it is all right. Smylie feels trapped by his often-proclaimed policy of never "pulling rank." He is learning that, whether or not you pull it, the rank usually works. It's like a gun in a holster.

But Cindy . . . "God damn it," Smylie laments,

Stage IV (40-50): The Win/Lose Decade

"maybe I ought to just tell her to do it my way or get the hell out of here!"

The reason he does not do that is that Cindy is very good at her job and would be hard to replace. So Donald Smylie continues to try to impose his procedures by argument and debate. Some he wins, some he loses. And to tell the truth, it gripes him to have to kowtow like this to a kid who is younger than his own daughter.

Nor is that all. Across the board, Donald Smylie finds that the concept of the "boss" has less and less meaning to the kids who work in his store. For some, it seems to have no meaning at all. Just last week he had been talking to a youngster who'd been on the payroll ten whole days, explaining the inventory procedure. The boy had looked at Smylie gravely, taking it all in and seeming to *judge* what he was being told, seeming to *decide* whether or not he would do it that way.

Finally he nodded: "Makes sense. O.K., I'll take it from here."

Now, while Donald Smylie is sometimes bemused, sometimes amused, and sometimes outraged by all this, he is coping. The slackened tendency of young people today to respond automatically to authority is not a crisis for him.

But it is for others in the 40–50 decade.

Jerry Daugherty can get positively violent about it, particularly when his anger at the arrogance of the rising generation has driven him to have an ill-advised second Rob Roy.

"Maybe I just don't understand the world today. You know? In my day, they paid some attention to what was right. I listened to my boss. Christ! How else would I ever learn anything?" And on and on. It is getting harder for Jerry to find luncheon partners who will sit still for his diatribes when he gets into a mood like this.

The latest problem is that Sheila Cohen—whom Jerry has stopped calling a "cute little broad"—has out-and-out refused to follow a direct order. "Jerry," she said, "I appreciate the fact that we have to have a chain of command. But

I wouldn't feel right if I did this in what I think is exactly the wrong way. Now, can I just go through it again and show you where I think we have been a little off in making these calculations?"

Daugherty has looked at Sheila's explanation. "I don't understand it," he says. And he doesn't. He is not seeing it clearly. His eyes are clouded with rage.

A lot of people who are thrown by this particular crisis feel cheated. Authority has always been a big thing with them. For years they have worked hard for a lot of reasons, but one big reason has been the ambition to have authority. Not so much to use authority to achieve specific ends; just to *have* it.

And now the rules have been changed in the middle of the game. At one time, you never questioned the boss. It just was not done. Now these people *do* question the boss, *and nothing happens to them.* You try to discipline them—or fire them—and you get a lecture from your own boss: "Times are changing, Jerry, and we have to change with them. Our human resources are the most precious asset we have for the future. You'll just have to find a way to handle this. After all, these kids are well trained. We spend a lot of time and money to recruit the best. So we should be willing to listen to their ideas. Now, how about rethinking . . ."

This is a very real crisis for the person susceptible to it. That person is likely to be one whose resources are somewhat limited; who is rather rigid; and who is essentially afraid of change.

If the critical situation goes on for too long, the outcome can be extremely melancholy, and often tragic. There are a lot of people whose later lives have been consumed with malignant hatred of the young people who they feel have destroyed them.

Consciousness of the generation gap may have a number of critical results. Some people try to stay young. Through some magic process, they try to shed twenty years and talk, act, and think just like the members of the younger generation. This in itself is not an actual crisis, but it is certainly an incipient one. The greater the extent to which

Stage IV (40-50): The Win/Lose Decade

the individual tries to maintain an extreme simulacrum of youth, the greater the ultimate shock.

That there will be an ultimate shock cannot be doubted. For one manager, it came when she realized that the kids in the place were laughing at her—the way she talked, the way she dressed, the way she did her hair. For George Milton, the shock was caused by a physical reaction. Milton is a senior supervisor for a big utility. He has always liked working outdoors and being "in the front lines with the troops." He loves the camaraderie of concerted male effort under difficult conditions.

And that was why it was so shocking to fall five feet from the scaffolding on that rainy day. To the guys who clustered round, he said, "God damn it, I slipped." He knew that his strength had failed—he simply had not been able to hold on. And when the others said, "Sure, George, you slipped—that's all it was," Milton knew that they knew.

Critical situations are set up for Stage IV people when they reject the advantages which age has brought them and try to cling to a style that is increasingly difficult to maintain. To avoid this kind of crisis, we have to understand that the cards in our hand have changed. We hold winning cards. We have to be willing to play them.

In the early 1970s, Craig C. Pinder and Patrick R. Pinto of the University of Minnesota conducted an "in-basket" study to determine behavior patterns among various groups of executives. They found interesting differences in style according to age.

Managers in their twenties tended to be impulsive, autocratic, and not particularly adept at human relations. Those in the 30-40 groups were more courteous with subordinates than the younger group; more willing to consult with others and to collect information before making a decision.

Managers between the ages of 40 and 55, said the researchers, were the most efficient. They acted as decisively as their juniors, but in addition they based their decisions on a firmer foundation of information. Furthermore, the older managers had better interpersonal skills than their younger colleagues.

The middle-life individual may have "lost a step," as they say in the sports pages, but he more than makes up for any diminution in zip with a lot of experience, common sense, savvy, and ability to get along with people. He or she had better use these strengths. Otherwise, the growing indifference to authority by younger people is going to hurt.

For the person who must supervise younger workers, it is best to overlook rank. Don't just give lip service to the proposition that "I don't pull rank." Forget about it. Persuade people to do things by making sure that they understand; that they see the purpose of the instruction; and that they comprehend the benefit to them in carrying it out.

If they don't go along? Objectively as you can, stack up their idea against yours. If theirs is better, say so and use it. But if yours is superior, compliment them for trying, tell them the advantages of your way, and pleasantly but firmly insist on compliance. The next move is up to them.

32.

Quitting

IT's a vision that flits through the mind of many a frustrated worker. The individual walks into the boss's office and announces, "I quit." The boss is stunned, horrified, and desperate. The resigner is beseeched to recant: "The firm can't get along without you. We'll take care of whatever is bothering you. Perhaps we have not adequately acknowledged your contribution—what do you want?"

Dreamers of this pleasant dream frequently don't bring it to an end. They just let it hang there, savoring the delicious taste of indispensability.

The vision comes at any time. Young people will resign impulsively. Usually there is no vast amount of damage. They are at the start of their careers. They simply go elsewhere. That kind of resignation is the one often looked back upon with the comfortable thought, It's the best move I ever made.

The impulsive resignation by the person in middle life is quite another matter. This move, caused by a welling up of frustration, can be catastrophic.

There is a tendency at any age to overestimate one's value. Arnie Ross worked for an elderly gentleman who, after many years as a professor at the Harvard Business School, started a small consulting firm. Arnie, young and eager, had plunged into his work with the firm. It was emphatically a "lean" organization: Two or three people did everything. After six months Ross felt he was carrying the business on his shoulders.

He was glad to do this. He had the highest regard for the president. Moreover, he felt protective about the old guy. So when an attractive job offer came along, he agonized for weeks before taking it—and then had to make a desperate effort to nerve himself up in order to break the news.

At last it could wait no longer. He went in to see the old professor, beat around the bush for twenty minutes—and then blurted out the awful news. He was prepared for the older man to beg him to stay; to comment bitterly about disloyalty; to withdraw into somber mournfulness. What he was not prepared for was the boss's jaunty response. Without batting an eye, the supposedly bereaved senior commented, "Well, there's a lot of moving around in this business." And that was it.

Careers have come to a sudden halt when a person has presented a resignation that he or she assumed could not possibly be accepted. Winston Churchill's father, Lord Randolph Churchill, was one of the shining lights of British politics in the late nineteenth century. His cockiness was matched by his intelligence, ability, and drive—though not by his popularity. Annoyed at something done by Lord Salisbury, the stodgy but unflappable prime minister, Lord Randolph presented his resignation. To his consternation, it was accepted instantly. Furthermore, God did not strike Lord Salisbury dead on the spot. The citizenry did not rise en masse to insist that Churchill be restored to a position of power. The influential persons of the Establishment did not go in a body to the leaders and say, "Our country cannot be without the services of this great man."

In fact, not much of anything happened. Randolph

Stage IV (40-50): The Win/Lose Decade

Churchill waited; then tried to recoup; then sank into bitterness, melancholia, and, at last, they say, insanity.

It happens today. Sandra Stamm, 46-year-old account executive for a public-relations company has been under more and more pressure, from inside herself and from outside. Her clients seem pickier and more obtuse than usual. Her colleagues seem to be deliberately lousing her up. And her boss, who is supposed to keep things running smoothly in the office, listens to her complaints, nods his head—and then does nothing.

Stamm becomes convinced that she is getting a very raw deal. She thinks about it for three or four days. Then she heads for the boss's office.

Most days, the boss—an executive used to dealing with creative and volatile people during their ups and downs—could handle this. He has heard people resign before. He knows when it's a phony resignation. And he has developed a technique for cajoling, mollifying, soothing, and talking the person out of his office as if the resignation had never been mentioned.

Most days, the boss can do that. But this is not most days. The boss himself has been getting considerable flak from *his* boss and from one of the firm's oldest and most lucrative accounts. It's a bad day to hear the account executive coldly say, "Jerry, all this crap around here has finally gotten to me. I've talked to you about it, but you're not really helping. So I have to think my contribution doesn't count for much anymore. And I guess that means the only thing I can really do is pack it in. This is it. Three weeks' notice."

Instead of doing what he would do under other circumstances—and what a voice inside tells him he ought to do—the boss just stares at her. She is good; she is one of his best people; she has a future at the firm, has been counted on to move to bigger things. But, for God's sake, is anybody absolutely essential? Must he take all this other stuff and play mother to these babies besides? He says, "All right, Sandra. Sorry it didn't work out. Three weeks is fine. I'll talk to you tomorrow about shifting your accounts."

Sandra Stamm is back at her desk, wondering what hit her. Because she didn't *really* mean . . .

The boss sits immobile behind his desk—he shouldn't *really* have . . .

But they both did it. And it sticks.

Some resignations are bluffs that are not that well thought out—that is, the resigner has not thought through the result if the bluff is called. The 1981 air controllers' strike turned into a mass resignation.

A good many resignations are offered because the individual is asking, "Do you really love me?" The question—expressed in terms of a resignation—comes out of feelings of frustration, uncertainty, and possibly failure, real or imagined. The person wants to know that there *is* a place for him or her; that he or she is *wanted*; that there is still a distinct role on the work scene. For a lot of people who do this, work means life.

Frequently, this sort of gambit is not accepted. The boss who values the person, particularly a boss sensitive enough to anticipate that some such thing is coming—handles it.

But that's easier to do when the resignation is tentative. They are given, in effect, with a question mark: "If there's no real future for me here, I might as well quit. Tell me. . . ."

The crunch comes when a person has done such a self-psyching job—or is so mad—that the resignation is presented truculently or with an air of flat finality. If there seems to be no way out without humiliation, the boss may be bound to accept.

The impulsive resignation is childish behavior: "I'll eat worms and die and *then* you'll be sorry."

But then, whoever said that everybody in the 40–50 decade was all grown up?

Stage V (50–60): The Consummation Decade

33.

Frosting on the Cake

THIS is when you get it all together. Or this is when it comes together, whether you like it or not. The fifties are the decade of completion. A lot of things end, for good and all. A lot of the subplots of our lives, developing for thirty years, reach what the playwright John Howard Lawson called "the obligatory scene." There are many consummations in the fifties, not all devoutly to be wished.

Within each decade of life, we age exactly the same—ten years. That's what the calendar says. But of course we know better. The sands run a lot faster during some stages than others.

It is probably during the fifties that most of us age the most. "Until I was well into my fifties," says Dave, "I thought of myself as being in the mid- to late forties. I mean, what was the difference? I looked like a man in his forties, acted like a man in his forties. Then one day I woke up and I was fifty-seven. My God, I was practically *sixty!*"

During the consummation decade, we come in like lions and go out like lambs.

The years between 50 and 60 contain the greatest dangers, the deepest chasms. But paradoxically these same years give us the chance for the most solid contentment of our working lives.

The crises during these middle years are formidable. But they are also fixed, and therefore foreseeable to a greater extent than the crises of any of the earlier periods. Everything in life, on the job and off it, is pretty much in place by now. The foundation is solid. While you are unlikely to be able to build a complete new edifice on it, you can remodel the present one or add to it. That is, if you think it worthwhile.

For a lot of people, it just does not seem that way. As they move into the decade of the fifties, they are overcome with melancholy. For some, it starts earlier. "After thirty," said Emerson, "a man wakes up sad every morning, excepting five or six, until the day of his death."

In that line, Emerson violated a taboo. As pundits wrestle with the phenomena of midlife crisis in a variety of ways, it is amazing how often they leave out the word *death*. After all, death is a lot of what the crises of this period are all about. An underlying consciousness of the approaching end gives a special resonance to things that we used to take for granted. We suffer the "last time" syndrome. Or we are goaded into spasmodic efforts to seize the brass ring of thirty years before. We can't reach it anymore. Goethe remarked, "Whoever, in middle age, attempts to realize the wishes and realms of his youth, invariably deceives himself. Each ten years of a man's life has its own fortunes, its own hopes, its own desires."

There is the key. The period from 50 to 60 can truly be a time of consummation—for those able to focus on goals that are appropriate to this stage of working life, and who can bring to bear the faculties which experience has sharpened.

Too often wisdom is overwhelmed by weariness. The opportunities for satisfaction, renewal, and resurgence are missed because one's eyes are fixed on the end. That the end is no more precisely predictable in time than it was before is no help. It is just statistically closer.

In trying to devise a workable psychology of aging,

Stage V (50-60): The Consummation Decade

psychologists argue about whether people age because of "nature" or "nurture." At 50, is the greatest impact on the psyche caused by the biological changes brought by the years, or by the social context surrounding the *fact* of midlife? Both factors, of course, are at work. They interact. It is not as important to assign relative weights to "nature" and "nurture" as it is to develop a coherent picture of midlife and its total effect.

Fifty is a fact; in the cells of the body, in the mind of the individual, in the eyes of those with whom the individual comes in contact.

Many psychologists discern a basic rhythm to adult life. Charlotte Buhler, writing in the journal *Personality* (1951), indicated that a study of biographical information led to the division of life into phases of construction, combination, and reduction. Applying this formulation, we might infer that a working life is likely to reach its climax of combination during the decade of the fifties. From that point, the tide begins to ebb. There is a reduction in activity.

Is this reduction primarily a function of biochemical change or of social role? Is there any point in fighting to change the pattern?

Different answers will be right for different people. It's enough for us here to try to understand a little more about the nature of the Consummation Decade.

Things gel when you're in your fifties. There are few shoes left to drop. There is likely to be plenty more to your life—but its course is pretty well set. You have a diminution of options—which, as we shall see, is by no means a bad thing. But there are not that many new directions for you to take.

At times in this section we will take the utterly heretical tack of talking of 50 as old. It is commonplace—in fact, it is practically mandatory—to insist that people are not old at *any* age, let alone such an early one as 50. "You're as old as you feel," and so forth.

It is true that age is partly a function of how you feel about it. It is also true that age is a matter of how old others feel you are—particularly if they feel you're getting too old for the métier and life-style you follow. The 75-year-old lady wearing fringes and beads and dancing at the disco may be applauded for spunkiness and appreciated as a character, but there are few who would not say she was behaving inappropriately for her years.

And then there is the fact that the years do have their effect; and that if the individual does not adjust, age invariably wins the battle. Readers of the sports page have seen the interview with the veteran star in which the player says, "What difference does age make? I'm as good as I ever was," etc., etc. Sports reporters and over-the-hill athletes seem to be in a conspiracy to pretend that this is true. If it were, Willie Mays would still be in center field for the Giants.

But of course the field you're in may have nothing to do with the Giants ball team. It's a fact of working life that you can be a has-been at 10 or 12 if you are a child performer; at 25 if you are a poet or a theoretical physicist; and so on. Different fields of endeavor have their laborers-in-the-vineyard peak in capability at different times.

In careers that do not require youthful muscle, looks, stamina, or other youth-related strengths—remember the poets and theoretical physicists—Stage V can still be one of enterprise and aspiration. Many people in their fifties still have plenty of headroom and upward mobility. Turn to the business section of any newspaper and, in a feature on recent promotions, you'll see that, along with the Stage II whiz kids and the Stage III powerhouses, there will be a good number of people in their fifties and sixties who have just been put in charge of major corporate branches or made it to a vice-presidency or to the very top of the hierarchy—president, or chairman of the board.

The fact of 50 doesn't mean you're less valuable as a person or as an employee. It certainly doesn't mean you get less joy out of life. But it does bring with it a set of perceptions by others, which cannot help but influence you. You can flout these perceptions as you choose. But you cannot expect that, because you prefer to act as if you were 30, people will think of you as 30. They will think of you as somebody who is trying to act young.

Herein lies the cause of many of the crises to be found in this decade.

34.

Obsolescence and Push-out: A Climactic Crisis of Competition

"I feel pushed," we keep hearing from people in their midyears. They're not imagining it; they *are* being pushed. The young push the old. That's the way of the world. You can go to the beaches along Baja California and watch old elephant seals being driven out of the herd by young bulls. You can journey back in time in the pages of Frazer's *Golden Bough* to witness the ancient custom of killing the king when his strength began to fail.

Or you can visit almost any workplace.

"Nothing I can put my finger on," says Genevieve. "Nobody says I'm slowing down, or my work is bad. But maybe that's just it. They seem to go out of their way to try to make me feel good about my output, or to humor me. There is one person who, I swear, talks louder to me, as if I were deaf."

That's one way they push you. Here's another: "They're making me the point man. Every real rough assignment I get. If I bitch about it, what do I hear? 'If you don't feel up to it. . . .' "

Inner crisis is always real. The causes may be more or

less "real" in objective terms. The individual may assume that colleagues are plotting against him. In actuality, there may be no plotting going on at all. No matter; the crisis is no less painful.

Examine a job-related crisis and you often find a mismatch between cause and effect. Getting fired is a crisis; no question about it. And the consequences to the person can be shattering. But making a mistake on the job need not in itself constitute a crisis—unless the individual makes it one.

Not every difficulty entails crisis. If your department is hit with an avalanche of work at the same time various machines have broken down and lines of supply have been severed, the task of keeping the operation going is a hand-to-hand battle. You and those who work with you may do an outstanding job or a poor one. Most likely, the group will do a job that is somewhere in the middle, with some people distinguishing themselves, others doing good but not spectacular work, others just getting by, and still others doing a lousy job.

All of this is challenge. None of it—of itself—is crisis. The crisis emerges from people's reactions. The guy who doesn't do well—or who thinks he does not do well—worries. The person who distinguishes herself/himself may run into a crisis of estrangement from resentful and envious friends.

However, when you reach the fifties, you encounter at least one crisis that is not of your own making. The crisis of obsolescence emphatically does not reside mainly in the mind. American business displays a lust for obsolescence, seeks to outgrow its technology, ideas, and people. In some cases, this is termed "progress."

The first manifestation is age discrimination. There is a law against it, and the law has some teeth. There have been successful suits for age discrimination. But they take a long time and they are profoundly wearying and humiliating.

Furthermore, there are clear signs that age discrimination is on the increase. One indication: The Equal Employment Opportunity Commission has reported that in the two-year period from 1979 to 1981, formal charges that employers have discharged and demoted workers solely on the basis of their age have jumped 75 percent.

Congressman Claude Pepper, chairman of the House Select Committee on Aging, which monitors age-related trends, says, "Age discrimination has oozed into every pore of the workplace. It stalks mature workers and severs them from their livelihoods, often at the peak of their careers."

The EEOC survey indicates that old-age discrimination runs across the board, affecting all types of employment and involving people from 30 years of age up, although it is most common among those in their fifties.

The unfortunate fact is that in most of American business, you are old when you reach 50. You're not necessarily old in terms of mental agility or physical vigor—unless you're a linebacker or an astronaut, a slackening of muscle tone doesn't make that much difference—but you are old simply because you went to business school before they started to teach the latest theory about the decision tree or whatever, and you are likely to have become too cynical about faddish panaceas to buy the latest nostrum that has been dressed up in academic language by the latest savior of business. (We no longer stick to the homegrown variety; now we venture to Japan for "Theory Z" and other trendy ways of saying "work harder and better.")

If you're the boss, your worries about obsolescence are likely to be somewhat less acute. Many years ago, a Hollywood director was about to shoot a spectacular climactic scene in a western, with thousands of extras. Suddenly he spotted a little man passing along the forefront of the phalanx of extras and bellowed through his megaphone, "You don't look like an Indian! Get out of there!" The little man shouted back, "I don't have to look like an Indian! I'm Harry Cohen, the producer!"

Even so, the boss is apt to feel put down when he attends conclaves at which he is told by professors that nobody who received a master's degree in business administration before 1980 has any conception of how to run a business today; and that the only decent thing for older management to do is get out of the way and let the younger generation take charge.

However, the top bosses are unlikely to be stampeded by these arguments. The crunch comes for the middle-echelon person who reaches 50.

Fifty is the bad year. Employees who are 60 are usually given a free pass. They are close to retirement anyway, and so what is seen as their doddering is looked upon indulgently by the young tigers around them.

But in a lot of jobs in a lot of companies, you become a target just *because* you are 50. Just as the mountain climber Mallory wanted to scale Everest "because it is there," young competitors go after a middle-aged rival simply because age seems to make that person a prime target. Indeed, to many newcomers—cruel and impatient as young people often are—the very idea of a 55-year-old individual pretending to be a performer is an affront. Nobody that old can be any good. So they take out after you.

In *Decades—Lifestyle Changes in Career Expectations,* Edith M. Lynch describes her interviews with people in the 50–60 age group. Education was much on their minds. They were keenly aware of what they considered to be the shortcomings of their own educations, and they were at pains to see that their children did better. The irony is that those children, in turn, are likely to feel in middle age that their own educations have become passé, and that they are surrounded by younger people who, armed to the teeth with the latest academic theories of business success, are prepared to hunt them down.

An appropriate parable for this crisis might be called "Swinging Out of the Fast Lane." You've driving at the speed limit, maybe a little more. Someone is tailgating you, riding your rear bumper so close you can count the fillings in his grinning mouth in your rearview mirror. If you're like a lot of people, you clench your teeth and say, "I'll be damned if I'm getting out of the way for that idiot!"

But what if it were a matter of survival? It's all very well to get mad at the guy who pushes hard from behind, but the time comes when common sense tells you —not

Stage V (50-60): The Consummation Decade

necessarily pull off the road—but at least to drive in another lane.

At 50-plus, you may find that you're being tailgated. Ask yourself three questions:

- Where am I going?
- Do I have to go this fast?
- Will I be more comfortable in another lane?

Midlife crisis, on and off the job, is frequently caused by continued striving toward goals that are no longer worth the strife. Those in their fifties who seemed to us to be getting maximum fulfillment at work were people who, deliberately or otherwise, had readjusted their sights. *Not lowered.* Readjusted.

Marcie Kampner, for example. She had been the company's first saleswoman, and she had surprised everyone by *succeeding* in a rough, tough business—wholesale electrical supplies. At 53 she was a regional manager. She certainly felt no diminution of energy or savvy, but sometimes she got bored. She'd seen and heard it all.

So she made another job for herself. Seeing that the business was about to undergo a minirevolution caused by the onset of computerization and word processing, she took some courses, became the company's resident expert on new technology, and now holds a unique position as she presides happily over the firm's technological updating.

Ben Greer didn't create an entirely new job for himself, but by swinging out of the fast lane, he found he was able to do better work in his existing job. It wasn't until he stopped scrambling for promotions that he realized how much energy it took. Now, while he'll never be chairman of the board, he is well-nigh indispensable because he stands out from the crowds. He stands out because he keeps finding ways to do his present job better.

Some people obsolesce most when they stay in the fast lane, fighting the one battle they cannot win. You can be smarter than your younger competitors, more resourceful, more tenacious, more courageous. The one thing you cannot do is be younger, or as young.

By "letting down your buckets where you are," you

move into a line in which your ability, not your age, is the salient factor.

At 50, you are probably either in the takeoff pattern that will automatically launch you to the top, or you have gone as far as you are going to go. The competition with others should be over, or at least should have entered a different phase. For while you may still be polished in the cosmetic values of aggressiveness and personal ability which add up to promotability—that touchstone of corporation success—you are *still* 50 years old. That does not make it impossible for you to be promoted or to get another job—after all, there are laws, aren't there?—but, truth to tell, it cuts down on your chances.

So, in the Consummation Decade, you had better find some other way to get kicks than from the constant battle to win out against competitors, unless you are able to develop a taste for losing.

Your safe plateau, at its best, should be defended by an impregnable bastion of competence. By now, there should be something essential that you can do better than anyone else. If, when you reach 50, you have not yet prepared such a position, it's time to do so. Three things are essential:

First is the accomplishment itself. What is it that you do better than anyone else? Solve problems? Troubleshoot? Reclaim lost accounts? Train people? Make speeches? Whatever it may be, start building it into your function in more and more substantial doses. When you were 30, perhaps the idea was to go head-to-head with a competitor, doing the same things but doing them better. At 50, the idea is to differentiate—and distance—yourself as much as possible from younger associates. You are *not* just another competitor—only older. You are different—unique. You have a value that nobody else has, a value that exists not in spite of your age but *because* of your age.

The second element of the plan is to let the proper people know that you possess a unique and essential ability. One way to call attention to your difference is by eschewing the usual blue-smoke-and-mirror act that is part and parcel of the paraphernalia of the on-the-make career climber.

"Internal public relations was always the key in my shop," says Edith Ryerson. "Or in any shop I worked in before. But I was always trying to project the same image—vibrant, eager, hot for the roughest assignments, the biggest accounts. Big game.

"But you look in the mirror one day and that seems ridiculous. Or people tell you. Not directly. By the way they look, or what they don't say.

"Anyhow, I was desolate. But then I wondered. If I had been so good at projecting a winning image for so long—and I *was* good—why couldn't I project a new image? So I got one. A kind of dynamic elder stateswoman image, experienced, reliable, but still tough. A cross between Betty Crocker and Gloria Steinem. Everybody else was still trying to be at least ten years younger. By playing it my age—or even a little *older,* which was an incredible thing to do in this shop—I became the unique, the absolutely irreplaceable. And, by God, with my experience, I *am* irreplaceable. But that wouldn't stop them if I didn't play it right."

Honing a new image, one that makes you important and needed—that's the third element for echelon security.

35.
Midlife Anger: A Crisis of Success/Failure

It's been said here earlier, but let's repeat it for emphasis: age need not incapacity make. There are people in their fifties, sixties, seventies and eighties who are capable of doing one hell of a job, and do so. As a matter of fact, our time has seen a new phenomenon: a group of people who, because of modern health care and a conducive social climate, are seen as the "Young Old," getting on in years but vital, fun- and life-loving, and physically and mentally superior. The other, less attractive side of the coin is that some individuals do age less well. And this fact creates a problem for others and for themselves.

You can find a lot of anger among those over 50; more than the literature had led us to expect. Over and over again, the years past 50 are said to be characterized by an autumnal ruefulness, a bittersweet nostalgia. One concept has it that midlife crisis is a kind of quiet, despairing submergence into hopelessness and bitterness.

In books and articles written about these years, we read of how people are finding it harder to cope with the

Stage V (50-60): The Consummation Decade

increasing complexity of work and life: "The damn job is running me. Once, I could handle innumerable options, suspend them in my head like a colloid. But now I can't keep things straight. One thing blends into another, and the inside of my head is one great big undifferentiated mass. That's no way to run a railroad."

The feeling that age is eroding mental capabilities that you thought were yours forever is stark and terrifying. To the victim, often caught in what is hoped to be the peak achieving years, these self-doubts come like a January blast in September. One executive gouged a hole in a $2,000 mahogany desk with a metal letter opener in a rage at his inability to recall the name of a longtime customer.

One asks: Is it for real? Is it really happening? Is my brain developing rotten spots? Are decisions—tough ones that I used to make off the cuff—now causing me to hesitate and agonize? And what about that run-in with young Sid Bradley, the new sales-promotion man? Was I as far off base as it seemed when I argued against his ideas and the others all went along with the program he suggested?

A common reaction to these doubts is self-testing. One gives oneself little quizzes, tests of everything from memory to problem solving: What was the name of the man who gave that talk on executive computerization two years ago? In my talk to Milt Welsh yesterday, was my presentation of the quarterly performance report as sharp as usual? Would I handle that cost situation I was the hero of last year as well today?

Mostly, the fears are exaggerated. Doctors tell you that some memory loss is as natural as graying hair, and go on to talk about your need to lose weight. "I just make more reminder notes, and double-check key reports my department puts out," one executive says in giving his personal hold-the-line recipe. "And I use my dictionary more."

In some cases, the higher echelons seem to want to rub salt into the raw spots. Some common practices:

Giving the tough but attractive assignments to younger people. "We want these youngsters to feel the fire. . . ."

Omitting the older people from key counsels: "We

didn't want to take you away from that Acme problem. . . ."

Pitting the Old-timers against the Young Turks: "The task force will be made up of a good mix of experience and fresh minds, to get the best thinking of both. . . ." The older people invariably become defensive and feel they must come off looking good. They are sure Big Brother is making comparisons.

Many Stage V people tend toward passivity. When you're past 50, things happen *to* you. Your freedom of action is shut down. Your crises are internal. You wish things had been otherwise; you resent the way they are now. But you admit your helplessness to change them. The fire is dying down; that's the picture. To some extent, this is true. But it leaves out something very important.

When we talked with people in the 50–60 decade about work, we heard things like:

"What pisses me off is that experience is just ignored. They laugh at what you've learned."

"I worked my ass off for everything I got. Now these kids come along and expect it to be handed to them on a silver platter. They haven't got the faintest idea what anybody else went through."

"You'd think after you give your life to an outfit they'd treat you with a little consideration. They treat you like dirt. Dirt! God, how I wish I could tell them off, let them know just what scum they are!"

"Well, I let them have it today. All of them, sitting there fat and smug. If they don't like it, the hell with them."

What are all these people angry about? They are angry about getting old. When they reach 50, a lot of people are mad all the time. Rage seethes inside them. They try to bottle it up. They find scapegoats, preferably young scapegoats. A wild tempest blew up in an office in Chicago because one of the vice-presidents happened to go into the mail room and found a mailboy and a typist behind the shelves in fairly close proximity. Once he would have stolen away quietly and laughed his head off. But now . . . loud

Stage V (50-60): The Consummation Decade

denunciations ("Slut! Punk! Pigs!"). Official complaints. Attempts to cool it. Self-righteous insistence ("Are we running a brokerage house or a massage parlor?"). And throughout, the amused and scornful reactions of the younger generation to the follies of their elders.

What was he so angry at? Being over 50.

Not every angry midlife person looks for a scapegoat. You can try to keep your cool. But often anger that can't get out does a lot of interior damage. Otto Fenichel notes in *The Psychoanalytic Theory of Neurosis* that if rage is deflected inward to the ego, the person may develop an abnormal fear of death. Partial repression of rage may translate anger into fantasy; one dreams of terrible things happening to one's enemies.

Well, obviously this is dangerous. Anger does not have to become pathological to make us very unhappy. Moreover, too much rage can precipitate crisis upon crisis. You get so mad—at somebody else or at things in general—that you jeopardize your job. Tony Blanton recalls, "There was no reason. No reason at all. I just blew up. Unfortunately for me, all the brass was there, plus our second biggest account. Later, everybody was very understanding. But I could see it in their eyes: I was on very thin ice."

The worst part of it for Blanton was that a similar display of anger by a younger colleague a few days before had been treated quite differently. "They gave him hell, but they put it down to youthful spirits. Actually, they felt like patting him on the back, like losing his temper was a good thing. But when I did it, they acted as though I couldn't control myself, was getting senile."

In Stage V, what you do is perceived differently. If you are doing things that are very much like the things done by 30-year-olds, you'll be seen as acting inappropriately.

Whose fault is that? Well, it's *somebody's* fault.

A department head says, "We don't have any policy here that discriminates against middle-aged people. God Almighty, I'd be discriminating against myself. And anyway, it's just not that kind of place."

It's not. This department—Accounts Receivable in an

office-equipment supply house—is not populated by hotshots. And that is why the boss could not explain why one of his most dependable and even-tempered subordinates started acting out of character.

"Alice just took this dislike to Ruth. Just hates her. Doesn't even take that much trouble to hide it. This is a close-knit shop. We can't afford this kind of thing. And I can't figure what Ruth could have done. . . . The only reason I can see is that Ruth is the youngest one of the group and Alice turned fifty. Could that be it?"

Anger is often expressed in terms of hatred. The psychoanalyst novelist Ernest Jones observes that "hatred for someone implies that the other person, through his cruelty or unkindness, is the cause of one's sufferings, that the latter are not self-imposed or in any way one's own fault."

It's a form of scapegoating. Unhappy people direct their anger against a likely object. When the unhappiness is connected with age, the likely object is someone young.

One particular object of anger is something that concerns few people young enough to do something about it. But during the fifties, physical attractiveness—magnetism, sexiness—can take on unexplained importance. Because they are things that are considered to be the peculiar province of the young. And while the diminution of sexual appetite and allure is not primarily a job-related problem, it is unrealistic to say that it has nothing to do with the work scene.

"Once I could kid with them, and have the hope of even scoring once in a while, although it only happened once or twice. But the idea was that it *could* happen. Now they treat me like their father. If I say anything that's even a little suggestive, they get embarrassed."

A salesman. Once he was, in his own mind, a dashing figure, a knight-errant who would come in from the dangers of the territory to flutter the hearts of the admiring young girls in the office. Of course, it was pretty much all playacting—he knows that—but that didn't make it unimportant.

The workplace is not a sexual herring barrel. But, says

Stage V (50-60): The Consummation Decade

the director of the mental-health program in a large corporation, this is not to say that there is no sexual dimension to work. "You have more interplay between men and women in the office than outside it," she observes. "No, I don't mean they're involved in overt seduction. But a lot that happens on the job is a laboratory of the self. You're being tested—by yourself. 'Am I good enough?' . . . 'Did I handle that right?' It's only natural that you ask, 'Does he or she like me?' And maybe there is a way to compartmentalize the idea of sexual attractiveness from the concept of ego strength or weakness, but few do so."

There are varying opinions about the prevalence of sex in business. Neil Simon in his play *Plaza Suite* has his character, the wife of an unfaithful executive, scold her husband for the target of his affections: "Your secretary! *Everyone* cheats with their secretary. I expected more from *my* husband!"

While things are changing, the workplace has been and still is a hunting ground, if only in fantasy. A man builds the friendly kiss of a woman colleague whom he hasn't seen for a long time into a stupendous mental adventure. A woman notes the surreptitious glances of a man and utterly dismisses the idea of seeing him outside work, but is nevertheless a little flattered.

Meanwhile, the ego shoring and libidinous game playing come to be taken for granted. So for some, when the nature of it changes, the result can be a crisis. It is a crisis that may be part of an all-consuming personality crisis. But as the years go on, work becomes an integral part of your life.

"I remember exactly the moment when I let it all go," a man about 57 says. "I was getting ready to go to work, just like I always do, and I was taking a last look at myself in the mirror on my closet door. I started to comb my hair so that it came down a little more over the bald spot.

"And then I said, 'The hell with it.' I combed it neatly, but without doing a camouflage job. *And I relaxed my gut.* You would not believe the relief! I can't count the years I was walking around with my stomach sucked in, practically suffocating myself with the effort to make me look like Robert Redford. Now I just relaxed. It was a spare tire, no denying it, but at least it was real. The real me."

Jerome Ellison, founder of the Phoenix Society—a think tank for the study of the dynamics of aging—observes that midlife anger shifts from object to object, and is triggered by a wide range of stimuli, many of which are inappropriate to the ferocious rage they engender.

Says a 50-year-old architect: "I realized that I was getting to be really funny, like one of those wild *New Yorker* cartoons by Koren, a kind of hairy curmudgeon. Grumpy. The terrible-tempered Mr. Bang. They would kind of nudge each other when I got going, and I knew it, but I couldn't help myself."

He's reasonably secure in life, about as secure as any of us get, a principal in a prosperous and esteemed firm, with a high place in his profession. Then what was he mad about?

"A lot of the time it was myself. Partly that was because I knew damn well it was not fair to get mad at other people—juniors, secretaries, the guy who shines the shoes and parks the cars. So instead of anything that went wrong being somebody else's fault, I made it my fault. Didn't make me feel any better, I'll guarantee you that."
It's still scapegoating, only now the scapegoat is the nearest possible target—oneself.

The architect had enough perspective to look for help. "My job enforces objectivity even when I'm fully involved. You conceive something that is breathtaking, something that will knock your world on its ear, you think, but then that voice from way down below says, 'Look it over again. It may not work.' And a lot of the time it *won't* work in terms of the client's needs, the environment, the purpose. You think the same way if you're renovating an old building. Considering myself as old, badly in need of something, I took the problem to an expert, somebody who gets paid for it. Deep down, I have always been a guy who thought, as in the old joke, anybody who goes to a shrink needs to have his head examined. But what the hell. I don't do the plumbing in my buildings. So I went."

Working with the analyst helped the architect to understand—if only because "she helped me to see it was by no means unique. I got so that instead of saying to myself—so mad I could hardly see straight—'What's the matter, are you getting old?' I could accept that. Well, of course I was getting older—nobody gets younger—but that didn't necessarily make me old unless I allowed it to."

He found a channel for his anger: "Getting mad is not a bad thing, if you get mad at the right things. I had never been much involved in community activities [he lives in an affluent suburb]. To tell the truth, I didn't even know the names of the people in Town Hall. But I latched on to a cause that was particularly suited to me."

The "cause" was the effort of an entrepreneur to build a gigantic electronic-games emporium that would entice the young people of the community. The architect brought to the fight a considerable ability at sarcasm and derision, as well as the special knowledge to pinpoint the least desirable effects of the proposed structure. The entrepreneur was a battler, and the architect found this good: "It was exhilarating. Let's face it, I was still as angry as hell. But now I had something really worth getting mad at. This fellow was really a loathsome guy, the building he wanted to put up was monstrous, and the campaign he conducted was disgusting."

Finally the fight was won. The developer took his electronic one-armed bandits elsewhere. "In a way I was sorry. If he had won, I could have stayed furious at the son of a bitch and his appalling project. Now I will just have to find something else. But there are plenty of things around that are worth getting mad at, and that getting mad about will make a difference."

36.
The Crisis of Identity

IDENTITY CRISIS is a term applied to the anguish of people who do not know who they really are, and it is discussed several times in this book. By and large identity crisis is associated with the young. Erik Erikson tells us that the primary task of the adolescent is to resolve the confusion of roles imposed during childhood and forge a strong sense of identity.

But the sense of identity does not remain fixed, and consequently crises occur at all ages. Frequently the question of identity is assumed to apply across a broad range of persons who fall into a certain class. A speaker urging the adoption of the Equal Rights Amendment says that "women today are undergoing a crisis of identity."

In *Women of a Certain Age,* Lillian B. Rubin says that "the issue of identity—a troubling one for women at any age—is brought to center stage at midlife." She describes women as a powerless group who have "learned well how to please, how to ingratiate, how to present themselves in accordance with the definitions and expectations of the

Stage V (50-60): The Consummation Decade

powerful." When one has played a certain role for a long time, goes the argument, one becomes that role. Marilyn French, in *The Women's Room,* declares, "When your body has to deal all day with shit and string beans, your mind does too."

The subject of identity crisis is being preempted. The territory is staked out—for polemical purposes—as belonging to middle-aged women. They are seen as prime sufferers because of the roles they have been forced into by men. Thus identity confusion is assumed to set in automatically as a function of age and sex. It is, of course, assumed to be a bad thing; and yet feminists seem to cherish it as proof of their arguments that women have been forced into subordinate roles in and out of the workplace. But just as Clemenceau said that war was too important to be left to the generals, the identity crisis is too important and too universal to be arrogated to support a cause and to be inferred to afflict only people of a certain age and sex.

Other commentators acknowledge that men past 50 face similar problems. Eda LeShan writes in *The Wonderful Crisis of Middle Age* that the "task of the middle-aged man is, first of all, to face his own aging and to begin the hardest challenge he has ever faced—to get in touch with who he is and what he really feels—why he behaves in the way that he does."

The 52-year-old woman—marriage crumbling, children gone, life dissolving—asks herself if all she has become is shit and string beans. This is a real and agonizing crisis, but not sexually exclusive. The 51-year-old man sees his power waning, his world changing to his disadvantage, his values demolished—and he wonders who he is, and who he is becoming.

The self-appraisal that is the core of identity questioning is usually triggered by a setback or a failure. When you are sailing triumphantly along, you *know* who you are—you're the successful Mr. or Ms. XYZ—who, it is hoped, will continue those winning ways.

However, objective success is not the same as subjective success. Many an individual, at the height of triumph, may abruptly feel let down. When you are alone and the applause has stopped and the applauders have gone, doubts set in: Was the accomplishment so great? Did I pay too much—for example, trample on others, creating victims—to win?

At this point also, people who don't realistically appraise their situations may flounder both in their efforts to mount higher in the echelons and also in their efforts to clarify their self-images.

Jennifer Peterson was such a person. Moved along both by ability and her organization's awareness of the need to enlarge opportunities for women, she had converted the librarian she had been when she joined the company to Vice-President, Information Services.

Although she sometimes spoke scoffingly of herself as a Betty Friedan VP—that is, a beneficiary of tokenism because of the women's liberation movement—she did aspire to acquiring more power and a larger constituency under the VP title. For example, a computerized information system that she felt logically should have been her domain was headed up by a computer-oriented manager. The situation was not an oversight: Top management had made this organizational decision knowingly. Jenny Peterson, they felt, had reached the end of the line as far as her abilities were concerned. Perhaps wrongly; the facts were never made plain to her. At any rate, Peterson's attempts to take over the computerized information unit led to nothing but frustration and a simmering resentment that accomplished nothing except to interfere with her work relationships and her effectiveness.

Misdirected aspirations will always intensify efforts to position oneself more advantageously in the job hierarchy. And this exaggerated picture of one's potential also makes the question of identity more difficult to resolve. The two elements of identity resolution—seeing oneself clearly and accepting the validity of that image—are impossible to achieve when self-appraisal is unrealistic.

Remember, too, that identity—in midlife or at any age—is not an unchanging part of consciousness. When correct answers are not forthcoming, identity questioning

Stage V (50-60): The Consummation Decade

becomes identity crisis. When we assume that to ask "Who am I" is a terrible thing, we are certain to bring on crisis. The question itself is taken by the individual as proof that the self is seriously flawed—that there is no self at all.

In this sense the crisis is self-feeding. One knows from what one reads and hears that identity confusion is commonplace at a certain age. Indeed, the person who does *not* have doubts about identity may be led to ask, "Why not? What's wrong with me?"

"Who am I?" is, after all, a broad question. Who, one might ask, am I in terms of my work, my family, my hopes, my fears, my loves? When told that the question is more fundamental than that, the individual has trouble reformulating it. Roles are usually defined in terms of behavior. Much behavior has to do with work. While certain people deride those who define themselves and others in terms of work ("This is Jim Brown. He's with Continental Can"), there may be more validity in that way of doing it than in trying to draw a map of the psyche. Who can ever really know the true, the all-encompassing answer to the question "Who am I?" But there is a need to know and people continue to seek.

You can be impelled into anguished self-examination by pressure from others. A world-renowned industrial psychologist once described a prototypical instance of nudging from without:

"A few years after I began teaching industrial psychology at college, I had the good and deserved fortune to get a promotion. I rushed to the phone to announce the event to the one who would relish it most. 'Ma,' I said, 'great news! I've just been made associate professor.' There was a moment of silence, then came the cool words, 'Why not full?'"

Our idea of who we are is influenced by ideas others have of who we should be. The other may be a parent who is ambitious—or overambitious—for us. It can be a spouse, friend, relative, who says, "I hoped you'd be a . . ." Their disappointment makes us feel inadequate, builds a sense of failure and guilt that may wither a previously acceptable self-image. And approval boosts us skyward.

It is during the fifties, when people are assailed by doubts as to their goals and their achievements, that they are susceptible to those who may praise: "You've really made a name for yourself in [company or profession]." On the other hand, they may register disappointment.

Consider the case of Angela Truex. Angela's husband, Larry, celebrated her forty-eighth birthday by telling her that he was leaving her. "If this were a novel," Angela told herself, looking across the kitchen to where Larry was casually drinking from a trembling coffee cup, "I would be numb." But she wasn't. She had never felt sharper. So the stories she had heard were true. He had been having an affair with Stacey Kern.

"There's no one else," Larry said, his voice unnaturally high-pitched. "We're no longer any good for each other. I know you've felt it. . . ."

She heard herself saying, "But I thought we had a good marriage. . . ."

"Maybe good for you, not good enough for me."

Three or four months after he had moved out—and Angela learned that he and Stacey were living together on the other side of town—he phoned to ask for a divorce. She was too proud to cling, or implore, or show her anger. She did permit herself one self-pitying arrow: "Is good riddance acceptable grounds for divorce these days?"

"I'm sorry," Larry said, "really sorry. . . ."

She hung up.

Time passed. The divorce finally came through. She felt that her life was just one big loose end. "Get moving," she finally told herself.

Not another man but a job was her prescription for recovery. She looked up employment agencies in the phone book and as a start picked the one easiest to get to.

Three days later, she started as a receptionist in the showroom of Goldart, Inc., a costume-jewelry manufacturer. Her problem, she quickly realized, was not inability to do the work but staving off death by boredom. One device was to become interested in the factory operation on the two floors below that endlessly produced rings, pins, pendants, charms that filled the display cases in the showroom.

Stage V (50-60): The Consummation Decade

Mr. L.—for Lavery—did most of the selling, except during the Christmas and Valentine's Day buying seasons, when everyone was pressed into service.

One day Angela was at her desk when Mr. L. escorted a buyer out to the elevators. "Come back in a week," Mr. L. was saying, "after you've had a chance to see other lines, and I'm sure you'll beef up the order considerably."

The buyer, a graceful brunette, laughed and said, "Everybody's showing plenty of cake, Mr. L. I'm looking for the raisins."

The woman got on the elevator and Mr. L. went back to the showroom. But in a minute she was back. "Can I use your washroom?" she asked, and Angela directed her down the hall. A few minutes later, on the way out again, she smiled and thanked the receptionist.

"May I ask you a question?" Angela said. "What do you call 'raisins' in this business?"

"A natural, a grabber, something that is unusual enough to attract a shopper's attention, and pretty enough to make her buy."

The receptionist said, "I've only worked here a few months so I don't really know this business, but I once had an idea that I thought was pretty good. Can I try it out on you?" Her art course at school came in handy. She quickly sketched an ear wire and three separate pendants. "The basic idea is an earring with three interchangeable stones, to match different costumes."

"Looks interesting," the buyer said. Sketch in hand, she went back into the showroom, and shortly returned, trailed by the boss. "We'll have the samples for you by next Monday," Mr. L. was saying. "Fine idea, Angela." It worked out and they produced her earrings.

It was a beginning. Angela went to night school to take classes in design, read up on merchandising and retailing. Mr. L. encouraged her. "Your brain is a goldmine," he told her.

In the months that followed, Angela Truex learned things about herself she had forgotten or never knew. The main thing was that she produced sketches for jewelry that ended her receptionist days and made her assistant designer. So when her old college friend Tina Marlowe called to say she was in town and could they have lunch, Angela was pleased at the opportunity, not only to see her friend, but to be able to tell of her professional triumph.

To her surprise, Tina didn't jump up and pound her on the back. Instead she put down her dessert fork and said, "Angie, you forget. You're talking to someone who knows you very well. Don't tell me this nonsense as though it's a big success story. I remember at school you were always the brightest and most creative. With what you've got on the ball, you should be head designer of a national firm, not assistant in a back-street outfit."

Angela went home that night with a splitting headache. Tina Marlowe's blast had laid bare a whole new question about her self-image. She had weathered the transition from contented middle-class housewife to working divorcée. But her classmate had talked of talents, abilities, latent skills that might have made her into a success of much greater dimension. Suddenly she felt guilty, guilty for her waste of capability and her willingness to be so easily satisfied. She realized that her feelings about Larry and her marriage had reflected this same easy-to-please attitude. What she was not was what she could have been.

But at her age the drive was weak. She didn't see herself, even goaded by Tina's accusation, setting out for new heights. Goldart, Inc., she knew, was the small pond in which she would try to be a reasonably-sized frog.

Identity questioning can never stop with the simple question "Who am I?" Inevitably it gets into the question "Why am I that person?" . . . "Who should I be?" . . . "How can I become the person I ought to be?" The *"ought"* in that last question is, lamentably, often defined by peers and principles and platitudes rather than by the individual.

Let's look at the identity question another way. Since "Who am I?" is so universally asked, why should we not assume that it is a normal and healthy thing; part of the growth and change of the psyche, like the shedding of an

Stage V (50-60): The Consummation Decade

outgrown skin? The body is said to recreate itself 100 percent every seven years. Why not the self?

"Act your age" may not be bad advice. In the fifties, you just can't be a boy or girl wonder anymore. Instead of aspiring to an identity that glitters with youth and talent, it is time to see oneself distinguished by experience, brains, the mature virtues of balance and judgment. Knowing what to try to be, as well as what not to be, is crucial to the fifties' crisis of identity. And there are good reasons why this transition is more difficult than those of other stages. Just consider the factors that are at play:

- *The person you've been.* For many people, their forties look great when they are in their fifties. It's not only that energy and drive were higher—indeed, may have been at a peak—but achievement may have been most impressive. For some, looking backward is a highly emotional experience. The rueful tinge that colors most nostalgia in this case can be punishing. You see yourself as you were, and don't want to be anything else. But the inexorabilities of biology interfere.

- *Intimations of a lesser you.* Even people whose capabilities at 50 are high get some intimation of a falling off that lies in the future. It's hard to tell just when it will begin, but this may be the first occasion when time has switched from being a friend to being the enemy.

Unlike identity crises experienced earlier, Stage V's are likely to be the first in which the new identity is less potent, less promising, and, most of all, most likely to be accepted with dismay.

- *Alleviants can only alleviate.* It makes sense to do the things that deter aging. But not everyone will admit to any decline—and they resort to cosmetic surgery to, as they see it, "stay as sweet as they are." Then there are the proponents of physical-fitness programs—the joggers, the swimmers, the tennis players, the sports enthusiasts whose love of their sport has always had a strong element of "it's making me better than I otherwise would be"—a perfectly rational observation.

The point is not that aging is an implacable if erratic

process, or that debilitation is just around the corner. What is involved here is the Stage V awareness that change may no longer be progress and can put one at a disadvantage, both in terms of self-image and in the objective world as well. And some people, unwilling to accept negatives, may attempt to put the lie to the calendar and to the date on their birth certificate.

Some people use every ounce of their brainpower and caginess to try to maintain the pretense that they are twenty years younger. They do this for all kinds of reasons, personal and professional. Their identity crises take the form of "Why am I no longer that vibrant person I used to be?" The fact that that person of the past was never quite that vibrant is not germane.

The frog who laments that he is no longer a prince is fantasizing. The frog who tries to continue to be a tadpole is ignoring the fact of growth.

The question "Who am I?" always has job-related ramifications. People tend to hold on to job-related self-definitions that they formed in their twenties or thirties.

The person without a sure grip on identity is unsure of role and of the appropriateness of behavior. When we are highly conscious of our actions, we become clumsy. Think about each discrete motion involved in putting on a coat—instead of just doing it automatically—and you become thoroughly tangled in the garment. Creating a false front to interpose between you and the world almost guarantees strain and phoniness.

The identity crisis that comes in the decade of the fifties is apt to be climactic in that, if not handled properly, it can affect the rest of one's life. A substantial part of proper handling involves getting the question "Who am I?" in perspective.

First of all, the question is apt to reflect nostalgia. We may really be asking, "Why is it so hard to remain what I used to be?"

There is an odd mixture of feelings about the *fact* of questioning identity. On one hand, it's fashionable. It's

Stage V (50-60): The Consummation Decade

"in." You're a clod if you don't go through an identity crisis. Quest for self denotes sensitivity.

But at the same time, it's an admission of weakness, an admission that V.P., Marketing, Paul Valentine, sought to avoid by aiming for the top job in his company.

"Marge Adams is sure to get the spot," a friend told Valentine. "A treasurer with a law degree, that's a damn impressive qualification. In my opinion, the big guys in New York have been grooming her for president. I'm sorry, Paul, I know you had some ideas of your own."

Valentine's agitation forced him to his feet and he glared across the desk. "It's been my brain and my push that has made this plant grow. I deserve the top spot. I'm going to do my own selling. If anyone, including Marge Adams, thinks Marge Adams is a better man than I am, I'm going to prove different."

Next day, which was Friday, Paul Valentine was on a plane to New York. He had phoned Dace Caldwell, chairman of the board and grandson of the founder of Caldwell Refrigeration. Dace had said, "Of course, Paul Valentine. What can I do for you?"

Paul had decided what he would say in answer to that question: "There's a crucial organization matter that's coming up. I wanted to alert you to a letter about it I'm putting in the mail."

After a moment Caldwell said, "Why not come up and spend the weekend with us? If it's important enough for you to make this call, it's important enough for us to get together. It will be just family, but we'll make you feel at home."

It's do or die, Paul thought, and accepted.

At about noontime, Paul Valentine was ensconced in the Caldwell town house on East Sixty-eighth Street. The place was well stocked with Caldwells. Dace's new and very young wife was there, and Penny Schwall, Dace's daughter, and husband Frank, and a cousin everyone called Biggie.

Shortly, Dace led the way into the study and gave Paul the chance to say his piece. Paul launched into a recital of the situation down in the Atlanta plant as he saw it. He made an effort to seem fair and objective, praising Marge Adams's potential and saying how great it was to have such a capable woman on the staff.

"But in all fairness, you couldn't expect a thirty-five-year-old woman, bright as she is, to absorb the nuances of the refrigeration business in just a few years. . . ." Then he proceeded to describe his contributions, advanced some of the thoughts he had for the future development of the plant.

Caldwell listened attentively, asked a few questions: What did Paul think of the effectiveness of the MIS setup? Did he think that computer services were adequate? What were his ideas for updating them? Where did he think the company's future growth lay? Would he continue with the retail line of appliances they had started two years ago or scrub it?

Their meeting was interrupted by Paulette Caldwell. "Stow the shoptalk, men," she said. "We've decided that we are going to the new disco that's opened on the West Side."

Caldwell thought a moment, smiled, and said, "Why not?"

Half an hour later, in two limousines, the Caldwell ménage was off for a night on the town. Paul, bewildered by the sudden abrupt leap into café society, showed his flexibility by asking Paulette to dance as soon as they were shown to their table. Naturally graceful, he had a good style, and wanted Caldwell to see his youthfulness in action.

After ten minutes on the floor with Paulette, he was ready for a rest, but Penny asked him to dance since Frank had started off with Paulette.

"I don't see how you do it," Biggie said, his 250 pounds firmly fastened to his chair. "Waiter, another vodka martini."

An hour later, Paul was badly winded and the drinks had made him queasy. Caldwell and Biggie were playing a coin-matching game. Frank Schwall, two years out of col-

Stage V (50-60): The Consummation Decade 247

lege and a very good dancer, took turns partnering Paulette and Penny. The outing had become a nightmare.

Suddenly Paul knew he was in trouble and made for the men's room. Under the bright light, he saw, despite slightly out-of-focus vision, that the dye he'd put on his sideburns to cover the gray didn't match the rest of his hair. Back at the table, he readily accepted Biggie's suggestion that they return home and let the "young ones" continue the evening.

"Got your note," Dace Caldwell said, coming into his room next morning. "Sorry you have to go back so soon."

"It's really been fun," Paul said, "but I've got things to do before Monday morning." He hoped Caldwell would assume they were business matters. His host assured him he'd think over what Paul had told him.

Paul said his good-byes and Caldwell accompanied him to the waiting limousine. On the way out to JFK, Valentine wondered: Had Caldwell asked him up to test him, or merely to demonstrate that he, Valentine, didn't have what it took—not the youth, not the stamina, nor the savoir faire to merit the presidency of Caldwell Refrigeration?

He ran the previous evening through his mind: the conversation in the study, the pointlessness of the disco visit. Was that planned? If so, he had been tested and flunked. The evening had showed him up as the hold-the-line 55-year-old man he was.

He told no one about the visit, but suspected that some of the key people knew. And he never heard directly from Caldwell. Another Stage V careerist had gotten stuck on a plateau. Some months later, everyone was agreeing that President Marge Adams was just what the organization needed. Valentine was given to understand—by the new president—that his position as head of Marketing was secure, and would he please start work on a drastically new approach for next year.

His striving has shown him who he wasn't. Now President Adams had given him a challenge that gave him a chance once again to test his identity.

37.

Looking Back and Accepting What You See

LIKE our height, weight, and hair color, our ambitions change with age. Who doesn't remember the universe-beating dreams of our late teens? Would-be writers dream of giving Shakespeare a run for the money; dancers expect to make Nijinsky or Pavlova seem second-raters. And Neil Armstrong—why, he stopped at the moon.

Our aspirations mature. Those having to do with work tend to peak in Stage IV, then continue in more realistic modes. By the time you reach Stage V, aspirations may still be for upward movement—getting to be a vice-president or even president. But some people lower their sights. Their goals can no longer be described as aspirations. Perhaps *hopes* is the best word: hopes of being promoted up one more notch, transferring to a more interesting job, or just staying put.

Whatever the record shows, in our fifties, despite all we may have accomplished, the gaps tend to stand out starkly. The goals *not* achieved are the ones we think about most.

Stage V (50-60): The Consummation Decade

George Palen's case illustrates a rueful review of things done and undone.

George Palen was a 58-year-old assistant to the head of a book club. An author manqué, an editor manqué, he found himself one day indulging in a remembrance of things—job-related things—past.

There was so much that George felt sorry about—things he had done wrong, screwed up, omitted, failed to do better. And so many people he had let down.

After some time spent wallowing in the more dismal moments of the past—a kind of "This Is Your Life" as hosted by the Marquis de Sade—the nebulous cloud of missed chances and mistakes crystallized into one memory, by no means the most significant.

Whatever, he wondered, had happened to Steve K.? He hadn't thought of Steve for years. But the one time he had been fired from a previous job, friend and colleague Steve had stabbed him in the back. It had been a shocking betrayal. From then on he tried to have nothing to do with Steve. Occasionally Steve would call: How about lunch? Sometimes he would have lunch. It was usually a guarded hour and a half; neither man broached the Big Topic of George's dismissal, which, Steve asserted, had taken him completely by surprise.

A couple of times Steve had needed his help. Steve had replaced him—so long ago—after the firing. That hadn't worked out; Steve had ultimately been let go himself. George—at one of the strained lunches—expressed sympathy he did not feel. (La Rochefoucauld said, "All of us have enough fortitude to bear the misfortunes of our friends.") Steve continued, from time to time, to call. The overtures all came from him. Sometimes he needed help in what was becoming a shambles of a career. Sometimes he just wanted to reminisce. Sometimes he seemed to be looking for something: sympathy? understanding? forgiveness? George always kept his distance. At last Steve stopped calling; even stopped sending Christmas cards.

George Palen was suddenly struck by a thought: Why not call Steve for lunch? A moment later he was amazed at himself: What an outlandish idea! Steve—who had stabbed him in the back? As an antidote to his sentimentality, he set himself to recalling the enormity of Steve's treachery.

And he couldn't remember. Not at all. Oh, he remembered his anger, and his disappointment, and his pain. But what had the guy *done*? What was the nature of the betrayal?

"If I can't remember the damn thing at all," he told himself, "then maybe it wasn't so bad." Later, he began to permit himself the heretical thought that maybe he had gotten it wrong, all those years ago, and that maybe Steve had been truthful about his innocence. Finally George thought, who gives a damn. He called for lunch.

Now they meet regularly. They talk with animation of the old days; the good times mostly. And they talk about their present difficulties. They are even getting around to talking—with nostalgia and laughter—about the dimly remembered event that separated them. Forgiving yourself and others for the misdeeds of the past—that's maturity.

When regret is focused in a ruptured friendship, the gulf can be bridged again. But the crisis of regret often encompasses much broader matters—like one's whole life.

Did you "sell out" long ago? Who didn't? "There was just one way for me to get started," says a currently famous neurosurgeon. "I was too broke to hang out my own shingle. So I joined a group. And, boy, did I see the seamy side of medicine! It was bad."

This doctor does not say today—at 52—that he has no regrets. "We all have regrets," he told us. "To say you don't is unrealistic."

But he did what he had to do, he feels. He established himself in the community—albeit that meant playing ball. He became familiar with a system in which "dons" of the medical Mafia allocate territories without much regard for the needs of the public or the profession.

"But I was good. When I broke away from the group, I

was too well known for them to deny me hospital privileges. I was powerful enough to be a 'don' myself."

A crisis of regret is often brought on by selective reminiscence—concentrating on the bad things in the past without regard to the good. One promise broken, or one principle betrayed, outweighs a virtual lifetime of productive work and good citizenship. It's like a grain of sand in the eye.

When the crisis of regret is concentrated in one finite entity—a person who can be talked with or a situation that can be corrected—do something about it. When it is broad and diffused, you can try to make it go away by reviewing, without skimping yourself, the accomplishments you have made against difficulties.

Peace is wonderful, when you make it with yourself. It makes many things possible in the future that otherwise would shrivel up in the acid bath of regret and bitterness.

A recent publicity story about designer Karl Lagerfeld boasted that he had "destroyed the past." In one sense, any innovation or change destroys the past. In the case of George Palen and other retrospective careerists who dwell on disappointment and failure, it can be urged, "Destroy the past, or it may destroy you."

38.

Retirement on the Job: A Crisis of Adjustment

THE stereotyped view of the retirement crisis is that the individual suddenly has nothing to do and falls to pieces at once. That view sometimes gains adherents even though it is not supported by experience or observation. How many people do you know who have actually fallen apart upon retirement just because they had nothing to do?

There is not much hard evidence that retirement—in the sense of cessation of the job—is a major problem for most people. The gerontologist Robert Atchley studied more than 3,700 retired teachers and telephone workers. Most of his subjects did not display a high degree of work orientation. Retired female teachers were the only ones who defined themselves in terms of their past jobs. These people, on the whole, did not miss work all that much.

However, this is not to say that the thought of retirement does not cause problems. For one thing, the basic reminder of mortality that it brings can be enough, combined with other factors, to set off a severe crisis. And it seems to be the case that worry about approaching retirement can be a lot more critical than the actuality. "What will I do?" is an agonizing question when you start to brood about it at age 55.

Luckily, there is something enjoyable and constructive that can be done. People cope successfully with the thought of retirement, early or otherwise, by starting to use "the other brain." The individual who looks around in the mid-fifties and does not have a clue about what can be done when the job ceases is in need of activity in the "other brain."

Peter Drucker suggests that you need a true outside interest—"not just water-skiing"—in which your capacities are extended, you work against high standards, and you are judged by specific and substantial criteria. This may be a field totally outside the work you do. Drucker remarks that it did not hurt the British World War II general Archibald Wavell to be known as a good minor poet.

The "other brain" can be used as both a source of pleasure and a means of assuring occupation and income when retirement comes. This is a case in which the discovery of the right outside interest not only resolves the crisis of concern over retirement but also makes you a happier and more effective person.

Retirement in its fullest sense is a matter to be considered in the next section. It first becomes a critical issue in the decade of the fifties. It becomes an issue because, as a person gets into the latter half of the decade, there are questions to be considered. One question is that of early retirement. A lot of people imagine that they would like to retire early, but they can't afford it. Most pension plans—along with social security—provide for smaller payments if you retire at 62 rather than the 65 on which the plan is based.

This book is not the place to take up the objective pros and cons of early retirement. (Auren Uris's book *Over 50* does a thorough job of that.) Here we are examining crises of working life, predominantly emotional crises.

And the subject of retirement reaches crisis dimensions when it precipitates thoughts about what used to be ignored and then became unthinkable. "When you are twenty-five, you're immortal," Mary Froman says. "When I was in my thirties, I was just hitting my stride. Yes, there were all kinds of problems, including that particularly messy divorce from Sid. No way would I ever want to go through that again. And I hardly knew when I hit forty, what with the excitement of starting my own shop and all the rest of it. Love and sex were, frankly, side issues. There was surely no shortage. Always available."

The deal that Mary made when she sold her operation to a big company would have enabled her to quit working at age 48. She preferred to continue; "I never even gave any other course a thought." Her two children were just about grown. She enjoyed a long-standing, comfortable relationship with a man whose career was quite independent of hers. At the time of the merger, her lawyer told her that, as part of the package, he was insisting that she be admitted to full participation in the company's executive retirement plan, even though she would not have been in the firm long enough to qualify totally under ordinary circumstances. "I just laughed. I told him to forget it. He never mentioned it again, but I had it."

While there was never a perfect mesh between Mary's unit and the company that had absorbed it, things went along all right. Then came the day when the chairman and chief executive officer asked her what she thought about taking early retirement. "He slipped it in casually," Mary recalls, "and to slip something like *that* into the conversation casually takes some doing." They had been talking about hiring and promotion in Mary's unit, and about future leadership, and the question that came then was "Well, if you had to say right now who would you pick to succeed you? None too early to think about it, you know."

None too early! To Mary, it was absolutely too early. Suddenly she saw everything in terms of the calendar. That night she mentioned it with a laugh to Ted, with whom she lived. "Yeah, it's something to think about, all right," he said. "It won't be too long before I have to give it some

Stage V (50-60): The Consummation Decade

thought myself. How do you feel. . . ?" But Mary wasn't listening. All at once she was thinking, *He's five years younger than I am!*

From that moment on, things got very, very tough for Mary Froman.

That Freud, of all people, should have written that there is no representation of death among unconscious ideas is strange. Astounding, unless we have read about Freud's own life and know the degree to which—as pointed out by Ernest Jones and others—he repressed the thought of death and suffered accordingly. One has only to recall the aborted journeys to Rome, which Freud himself finally admitted he did not want to reach because of reaction at some psychic level to the old saying "See Rome and die."

Freud fought his fear of death in his lifework. He declared that there was no time perception in the unconscious; in *Reflections on War and Death*, he added that in the unconscious we are all immortal.

We fight the clock and the calendar in various ways. The psychoanalysts Edmund Berglet and Geza Roheim report the case of a 50-year-old woman who invariably arrived half an hour late for her analytic appointment. Anytime the analyst left the room, she would turn the hands of the clock back a few minutes. When the hour ended, she always complained that the analyst was cheating her out of time.

Another patient—diagnosed as psychotic—says, "I was trying to make [the sundial] stand straight at twelve o'clock, and to stop the sun while hurrying in the sky." This person stopped, not the sun, but himself. He became immobile. He simply quit.

And that's one thing that can happen. Assailed by the "last time" syndrome, the individual simply quits. The 50–60 decade is a time when there is much discussion and thought about early retirement. That's *official* retirement, with the pension plan and all the appurtenances (which we shall discuss).

But not all the retirees get a gold watch. They quit on the job.

It happened to Martinescu—the whole thing: the melancholy, the "last time" syndrome, the unauthorized retirement. At 57, Jan Martinescu went, as he always did, to the annual meeting of his trade association. The action, as always, took place in the corridors and hospitality suites. Martinescu had a wonderful time. He saw a lot of old friends, exchanged a lot of good old stories. He shunned most of the official agenda, as all convention-wise veterans do. But he showed up for the final session. Sitting there with a weeklong weariness not unmixed with hangover, he heard the windup speaker say, "And in ten years, when we once again hold our convention here in New Orleans, I hope they finally manage to do something about all those unofficial chambermaids. . . ." The joke was not particularly funny, but everyone laughed. Just about everyone. Martinescu was impaled on the words *in ten years. In ten years he would not be going to any more conventions.* In ten years he would be through . . . out . . . washed up.

Back at work, he began to apply the "last time" touchstone to things as they came along. "Is this the last time I'll be involved in a full-scale new product introduction? No, of course not. We've still got Starburst in test market, and we'll be inserting it nationally in two years, three at the outside. But not necessarily. Look at AppleTime. We had AppleTime in test for ten years. Geez, this just *might* be my last shot at a real big product introduction. I better go all out on this one."

And then, in a moment, inevitably, "What the hell for? What difference does it make?"

From then on, he began to check out of his job. If there was an optional trip, he took it. Whereas before subordinates had found that getting delegated authority was like extracting a fang from a swamp adder, they were now bewildered to find all kinds of big problems dumped on their desks without warning. At meetings, Martinescu went through the motions very skillfully. He said the right things, kept the ball rolling. That there was no substance to what he said was not really a startling fact. Substance was not necessarily a big feature of the meetings anyway.

Stage V (50-60): The Consummation Decade

The person Jan Martinescu did the best job of fooling was Jan Martinescu. He was under the impression that he was still giving his all. He was quick to find rationalizations for everything he was doing—or *not* doing—now: "For God's sake, I have to give these young guys a chance to do things on their own. Otherwise, how do I ever find out if they have anything on the ball?"

When you retire on the job, work is no longer something you are involved in, or even something you have to do. The work scene becomes somewhat unreal. You don't see things sharply. The meaning of events is perceived principally in terms of how they measure the days of your life.

On-the-job retirees reminisce a lot. There are few conversations that cannot be brought around to provide an opportunity to regale the listener(s) with stories about the old days. And of course inevitably the individual becomes a bore. Colleagues will go to great lengths to avoid the occasion of another anecdote.

On-the-job retirees are somewhat unpredictable. No longer anchored solidly to the work, they skitter from one chore to another. The sense of proportion diminishes. A thoroughly unimportant task will supersede an assignment of supreme urgency.

People in this state are hard to get through to. They don't seem to hear things the first time. They overlook the tiny details. They daydream. They don't return your telephone calls.

And so finally somebody says, "Have you noticed Katherine [or Andy, or Dora, or Jesse] lately? How not-with-it she [he] is? Do you think she [he] is getting senile?" Senility is one of those ailments (like amnesia and nymphomania) that are quickly diagnosed by lay persons on the basis of extensive observation of medical shows on TV.

Then the person becomes a headache for the bosses. No matter how much good and faithful service has been put in, the firm can't put up indefinitely with somebody who is "out to lunch" much of the time.

How does on-the-job retirement affect the actual performance of the person? Actually, it may not affect objective performance all that much. Most jobs do not require a show of constant concentration and frantic activity. Woolgathering individuals may be able to do the job in their sleep. In fact, they are doing it in their sleep. You can almost hear them snoring.

But that's the trouble. In many lines of work, success is based to a great extent on qualities that are extraneous to actual performance on the job. This is peculiar to the American work culture. There is tremendous emphasis on cosmetic or semicosmetic qualities like aggressiveness and ability to "come across" at meetings and so forth. The major criteria by which people are judged in many corporations have more to do with the constellation of traits that add up to "promotability" than they have to do with actual performance. This leads to the ridiculous situation in which you may be superb in your present job, but if you are not altogether suited for the next job up, you will ultimately be fired because you have lost your "promotability." And in many firms it is suicide to admit that you're contented with your present job and would like to stay in it. This indicates that you have contracted the loathsome disease called "lack of ambition." People will shun you. They will not take chairs close to you at the meetings. And sooner or later you'll be replaced by someone who is not as good at the job but who is eminently promotable. That this misplaced emphasis is one of the reasons for our slipping further and further behind the Japanese is just beginning to come through dimly to American business leaders. However, they don't know what to do about it.

The criteria of "promotability" may be reasonably logical when applied to a young person. However, we often continue to apply them to men and women well into middle life. It is as if a track coach could be hired only if he ran the hundred in 9.3. And so there is a booming business in hair coloring, face-lifts, and general rejuvenation for desperate individuals who would like to act their ages a little more but know it would be professional hara-kiri. The individual who retires on the job may be doing nothing more than opting for a more sensible way of getting the job done. But this results in vulnerability.

Stage V (50-60): The Consummation Decade

On-the-job retirement does not usually involve pain; only a kind of dull, restless feeling. There is no feeling of crisis. One certainly thinks things are going along with reasonable smoothness. This may well be so; but the person doesn't give the *appearance* of concentration or energy that is desired.

This is a crisis that, if caught in time, may be susceptible to simple measures. One person we know threw off her lethargy by changing the order of the day: correspondence last thing before going home instead of first thing in the morning; a brown bag and brisk walk at lunch instead of the usual restaurant repast; even an overnight trip by train instead of the nearly inevitable air shuttle.

This sort of unofficial early retirement can be insidious in that it provides a culture in which other, more serious crises may breed. Essentially, the hazard is lack of involvement and lack of direction, inviting all the ancient strictures about the evils of idleness.

Yes, idle hands *can* do the devil's work. For example, smoking, a safely abandoned habit, suddenly becomes irresistible, and the weed warned against by the surgeon general on cigarette packs reclaims a past victim. Drinking is another pitfall that stands ready to lure the directionless to compensate for guilt and loss of identity.

Consequences also turn up in the form of failing job performance. Irritations with people flourish—one's boss or colleagues. Good relationships are replaced by disagreements and feuding.

Perhaps the most punishing consequence of all can be boredom. The need to drag oneself out of the house to a milieu that has lost interest and meaning becomes a daily torture.

In short, the person who becomes disconnected from work without becoming connected to anything else is fair game for anything from the fidgets to a nervous breakdown.

For some loss of direction, procedural refreshment mentioned earlier—changing the order of the day, etc.—can be effective medicine. But for severe cases, more incisive steps are needed to rebuild involvement and enjoyment of the job. If you have the right kind of boss, discussing the possibilities of more challenging assignments may work. In some cases, a transfer into another job or department with assignments of greater interest to you may help.

One 59-year-old who felt she had lost the ability to be involved in her work made a move that turned out to be productive. She went to her boss and described her state of malaise. The boss understood what she was saying. He smiled and said, "Mildred, if you could have any assignment in this company that you wanted, what would it be?"

Mildred blinked, thought for a few moments, and, helped by a sudden flash of insight, was able to say. "Yes, there is something. You know shopping has always meant something special to me. I'm one of the few people I know who finds a trip to the supermarket as interesting as seeing a good movie. What are the chances of my being an assistant to Mr. Kreger in Purchasing?"

The boss though it might be a good idea. It was.

Still A Lot of Life Left

Despite the Mildreds and the general middle-aged malaise that depresses the outlook of many, there are still a substantial number of Stage V people who are self-satisfied, pleased with job achievement, and don't turn green at the thought of going back to work after weekends. Their emotional high is in part a reflection of their general sense of well-being. A strong constitution, an absence of any debilitating ailments, and, most important, a feeling that they are "doing a job" lifts their spirits.

From this group come the feisty, assertive individuals whose strivings have not come to an end. To them, the rung above their present one beckons with all the challenge of Mt. Washington. They are the people who say to themselves, "There's still a lot of life left in this body." And many of them go on to prove it.

Stage VI (60–70): The Wrap-up Years

39.

Over the Top

STORYTIME. And whether it's high drama or low comedy, we make our final judgments about a tale by the way it ends. For most careerists, Stage VI is wrap-up time, an occasion for assessing a life on the job.

The stereotype of the employee who mounts this stage triumphant, fulfilled, can be accurate. After all, he or she has survived, probably has the esteem of colleagues, the appreciation of his or her employer.

For some, the rosy picture suits. But for others, Stage VI is a bullring: Once entered, no matter how capable, confident, strong, or wily the actor, the end will see him dragged out dead. It is this black-and-white, victor-or-vanquished dichotomy that splits the Stage VI ranks.

Following are some key feelings people just entering Stage VI voiced about their career outlook:

Executive vice-president of a large metropolitan newspaper: "For a while I was a token woman executive, but I shed that image long ago. I've got ten good years to give.

I'm going to make the people around here sit up and take notice."

Foreman of a finishing department for a furniture manufacturer: "I lost out on a promotion to division manager last year. I guess they thought I was too old. I haven't accomplished half of what I hoped. I'm just going to put in my time."

Head librarian: "My work has been my life. I've loved every minute, but when I finish this job and retire, what's left?"

A buyer for a grocery chain viewed eventual retirement more optimistically: "I look forward to closing up shop. 'Free at last,' as Martin Luther King said. It's going to be a ball."

Examine the conflicts faced by the Stage VI group and it becomes clear that the nature of the battle, the character of the enemy, has been transformed. The simple lions of peer competition and upward mobility have been replaced by a loathsome assortment of dragons, lizards, and venomous reptiles. Somewhere on the way from being 50 to becoming 60, careerists have broken contact with previous antagonists. Preoccupations with values, attitudes, goals, status, which caused great stress, have been replaced by new and more implacable foes:

Aging, both of visage and body, balefully limned in every mirror.

Infirmity, either in the minor form of stiff joints, and loss of grace and coordination, or in diminishing acuity of the senses and memory impairment.

Organization values that tend to give preference to the younger and more vigorous.

The fears of severance from the organization as retirement impends. "It's an operation, a cutting," says a hard-driving executive, "like a lobotomy." Severed from the organization with which he has identified for years, he sees retirement as a depersonalization that will leave him a vegetable.

These downbeat views don't tell the whole story. There

Stage VI (60-70): The Wrap-up Years

are both positive as well as negative viewpoints in the group.

The states of mind of typical Stage VI people are essentially oil-and-water opposites: hope and fear, pessimism and optimism. For some, there is an upsurge of aspiration and creativity; for others, a burnout compounded of failure and depression. And stoking the fire under the emotional stew is last-lap awareness; knowing that, for better or worse, the finish tape is just ahead.

The hopes are obvious; ending a career on a high of accomplishment and recognition. Whether you end up as president or only a vice-president, or a senior member of your group, you probably want the esteem of co-workers and a clear path to a well-financed and pleasant retirement. If the flames of your ambition rage unchecked, you may decide that after retirement at 70 you will remain a working stiff and seek other employment—become a consultant with your present employer or others, go into business for yourself, and so on.

For many, career prospects are buoyed up by an inner peace and self-appreciation. After all, by now your capabilities have been developed and tested. You know that you can deal with problems and people, and have made at least one of every kind of decision. Your judgments of situations, and of people, have been honed repeatedly. Years of perception and assessment make you feel you can cope with anything that comes along. You see no reason why your last decade on the job can't be the icing on the cake.

Some people are lucky enough to have some form of built-in security that will ease the worries that plague many in these years. Such made-to-order circumstances include:

You own the place. If the traditional *Prop.* follows your name on company indicia, you're probably impervious to any of the turns of tide or fortune that might dislodge others.

You're the works. Occasionally a person—through either special expertise, experience, or skill—is that rarity, the indispensable employee. It's more likely that a whole management echelon will be death-rayed rather than that a key employee whose talents are an essential resource will be let go. Charles Steinmetz, the genius of General Electric, is the prototype of many whose contribution is essential to the present and future of the organization.

Like the 800-pound gorilla, these people can have things pretty much the way they like. Their hold on the organization is such that nothing can budge them against their wishes. For example, George Meany stayed on as head of the AFL-CIO until he was 86. No one ever mounted a successful effort to loosen his grip.

At the top levels of industry, similar precedent-shattering tenures have occurred: William S. Paley ruled the roost at Columbia Broadcasting well into his seventies, and you could fill a book with the names of key people in industry whose only nay-sayer will be the angel Gabriel.

There can be other reasons for individuals having a lock on their jobs. People may either pack considerable political clout or be protected by those who do. "X knows where the bodies are buried" is another way that people have of explaining that an individual won't be shoved down or out until he/she is ready to go.

"Tess, you'll always have a job here as long as you want one," an executive secretary is told. Tess finds the promise easy to believe. Being privy to some past high jinks of her boss, she accepts the offer with a complicated smile made up of one part sneer, one part resentment, and one part mockery.

The company is sentimental and rich. Organizations can be as considerate of their older employees as loving children are of esteemed parents. If the coffers are well filled, the powers that be indulge their self-image, give it a lord-of-the-manor tinge, by taking care of loyal retainers to the end.

Whatever the cause, many on the sixth plateau feel secure in their jobs and work along contented, with the weekly interruption of an account-building trip to the bank.

Despite such instances of security and adjustment, however, insecurity and dread also exist among sixth-decade individuals. The threat is usually awareness of their dependence on their jobs. Anything that may sever the connection is viewed as the devil's fiery sword. Some possibilities:

The Willy Loman finale. Those of us who saw the original Broadway production of Arthur Miller's *Death of a Salesman* know that there was scarcely a performance at which the sound of sobbing from the audience at the end failed to drown out the voices onstage. In salesman Willy Loman, suffering the fatigue of a man pushed beyond endurance by a demanding job for which his energies and skills were no longer adequate, audiences saw their own burnout, their own way to the grave.

Failing health. Ailments more specific than Willy Loman's soulsickness can take people out of action. The number of debilitating and destructive health handicaps is large among the sixties group. Whether it's a bad heart or a sight impairment, dulled mental faculties or arthritis, aging is no friend. A nurse who loses mobility because of a broken hip, a sound engineer going deaf, may have to replan their lives without the benefits of a regular job.

Organizational earthquake. There is a threat of change that can cause tremors at the very highest echelons. An organization that is acquired by another may find 80 to 90 percent of its personnel fired by the parent company. High-salaried people are particularly vulnerable, and no amount of experience, no exhibition of piety or wit, is going to change a word of "Sorry, you're fired."

The threat of youth. Companies plan; they *must* plan to bring new blood into the organization. To some, bright young faces in the corridors and company cafeteria are a heartening sight. To older people, it means the enemy has been invited inside the fortress. It's like a law of physics: The greater the push upward from the younger folks, the faster the rate of separations among older ones.

The uneasiness, even the dread, that Stage VI people may feel about their job longevity is usually concealed. Perhaps the anxiety is best measured by the increasing number of face-, eye-, and neck-lifts for both men and women in their sixties. If you prefer a liquid measure, check on the increasing sales of hair dye, especially the products that promise an end to gray hair and a return to one's natural color.

An instance that took place in a wholesale shoe house some years ago best catches the age-youth battle-to-the-death.

Larry was one of the stockboys—a "boy" well over 60—who had been a salesman, drunk himself out of a job, then had been rehired by a kindhearted employer for the one spot in which help was needed. Ten years later, he was still there, but now terrorized by the specter of getting canned.

In the business turndown, several people, notably older ones, had been let go. Larry came up with a way to demonstrate his youthful vigor—and thereby his continuing employability. He took a packing case—one about knee-high—and ripped the top flaps off. He practiced a while, more or less out of sight in the back of the stock room. One day, the boss, an old acquaintance, appeared on the stock floor to check a special order.

"Hey, Mr. Hertz," Larry called, "watch this." He produced his carton and, standing alongside, jumped into it without touching the sides.

"And watch this," he said, and leaped out of the box, coming up grinning and nodding.

In the boss's favor, let it be said that he patted the stockboy on the back: "Younger than springtime, Larry," he said, and walked down the steps wet-eyed.

40.

The Group, Broadbrush

STAGE VI people: They are 60 years old at the start of the stage. Wherever they are in terms of achievement is pretty much a freeze frame. Their place in the career sun is established.

And except for the unimaginative, there is awareness of the decade's end marked by a large LAST EXIT sign. Those who stay the full term will be 70, the Bible's three score and ten measuring the human life-span.

But today's seventies are a mixed bag. While some are infirm, hard-of-hearing, dim of sight, suffering from one or another motor disability, a large proportion are miracles of persistent youth—sports-loving, sexually active, matching the professional drive of the best in any previous stage.

Gwen Clay is an industrial sales rep and tennis addict. At 66, she is looking into job possibilities in California, where she can enjoy her game year-round.

Executive Harry Belden at 62 is in competition with a 40-year-old and feels he has the edge: "I'm the best man to take over the new division. I know more about marketing than anyone else around, and my experience in production gives me the clout that's exactly what the job needs. Ed Peck doesn't have a chance."

People at various levels of accomplishment—presidents, chairpersons of boards, clerks, janitors, people put out to pasture in low-level jobs such as guard, messenger, and so on, were interviewed. Some of the attitudes were as expected; others surprising. For example, you'd expect disappointment and a sense of failure at the lower echelons, self-satisfaction at the higher ones. These turned up, but also the reverse.

Peter Medocq, head of a corporate division in a large conglomerate, told us: "They keep piling on the perks. I'm glad to have them. But they don't compensate for my not getting the presidency. It was goddamn politics that kept me from the job in the last turnover. Now I'm five years older, and out of the running."

Studs Terkel quotes an elevator starter he interviewed, a man pleased with his profession: "When I see a celebrity [coming into his building], I go home and tell my wife about it. She'll tell all her friends and relatives. I don't want to retire. I'd be lost if I had to stay home and don't see the public all day long."

Aspiration and expectation are major factors in feelings about career accomplishment. Those who consider work a means of economic survival have no shattered aspirations to haunt them. A middle manager whom you might think would be fulfilled by years of intelligent and productive service may harbor a giant-size emotional wound because a vice-presidency remained elusive.

Other attitudes our interviews uncovered include:

Self-satisfaction: Jeno Paulucci, at 48 the owner and president of Chun King Corporation, manufacturers of canned and frozen exotic foods, is a self-made man in the old American tradition, working his way up from fruit-stand tender to building a worldwide exporting business. "Doing things the hard way is best," he says. "You have to put out more, but the victory is sweeter."

Tunnel-vision contentment. This view was registered

Stage VI (60-70): The Wrap-up Years

by a lathe-department foreman in a metals fabricating plant:

"Look at me, sixty-one in three months and I'm in the same job today that I was ten years ago, and doing it better than any squirt around. Sure I feel good. I like the feeling that I'm a tough long-laster. . . ."

His view shows how attitudes about self and the world of work can yield favorable feelings on the basis of what, to others, would be seen as failure or, at best, dying in a dead-end job.

Bitterness. "They're burying me alive," a bank executive told us. "When computers came in, I took courses, spent all kinds of hours studying new systems and procedures recommended by the consultants. Two years ago, they brought in a whiz kid who is technically my assistant, but she's running the show. My long years of experience amount to nothing. I'm hoping to stick until seventy, but it's a race between giving up—this situation is bad for my health—and the bank dropping me."

Resignation. "They're never going to fire me," a VP, Purchasing, says. "They remember that twenty years ago I was brought in by my cousin, who is on the board of directors. But every minute of every workday is a pain. I occasionally read something with the phrase *work satisfaction* in it and I'm halfway between laughing and throwing up. But there is nothing I can do. I can't afford to quit, so I'll just stick around as long as the paycheck is there."

Elder statesman. For many Stage VI people, there is a secure and satisfying niche. With the conscious or unconscious connivance of their superiors and colleagues, they are decked out with the mantle of wisdom and esteem of their years and their experience. "They still need me," a vice-president of an electronic-parts company says. His responsibility is designated by the title VP Dealer Services. His actual assignment includes anything from thinking up contests to arranging for female companionship for his boss's field trips.

But other individuals who might qualify for "elder statesman" status operate less ambiguously. They are indeed the repository of considerable experience that continues to be a resource for their organizations. One is in the newspaper field, a large city daily, and a member of the president's executive staff. "Some of my competitors," he says, "are M.B.A.s fresh out of school, and smart, smart, smart. At first I was scared, thought I was going to be trampled down by the future. But I soon realized that these youngsters couldn't get in school what I had learned over the years as reporter, foreign correspondent, city editor. We may be hurt by TV, or, worse, acquired by some broadcasting outfit. But as long as we operate as a newspaper, I'm the cheapest inside consultant they've got."

The disparity of fates and attitudes is further diversified by the "eternal youth" factor, the health/attitude development in which today's 60-year-olds have the vigor of a traditional 40-year-old, and an eagerness to enjoy it that is unprecedented.

And despite the omnipresence of retirement, Stage VI is as loaded with situations—rewards as well as ordeals—as any other. The problem is how to make these years of fulfillment instead of misery. It is in this attempt that Stage VI people run into crises that threaten the closing years on the job.

A basic question is "How do I play my cards so that I leave at the top of my career, feeling good about myself and what I've accomplished, instead of being put out like the garbage?"

Offhand you might think one retires loaded down with honors and the respect and admiration of peers. It does happen. But also—it doesn't. For some individuals, the period from 60 to 70 is one long skid downward. One by one, responsibilities are stripped, sometimes titles downgraded, ditto pay.

And there is *concern about the future*—that life after life-on-the-job ends: "What will I do after I retire? How will I spend my time?" Even when answers are promising, uneasiness persists. After all, the familiar is going to be replaced by the untested. Even a limited observation will

Stage VI (60-70): The Wrap-up Years

produce evidence that some people retire into the misery of joyless idleness.

And *financial problems* threaten. There is almost always a cut in income after retirement. The average person must make do with social-security payments and a pension, if one is forthcoming. Average figures show that these sums represent about 40–60 percent of working income. The cut of itself is bad enough. In periods of inflation, it can badly damage standards of living and life-style.

Another crisis: "What will happen to my on-the-job friendships?" It's a question that few voice but often worry about. Daily associations that have enriched work over the years seem about to end. Many do, but some people learn how to transform on-the-job friends into the off-the-job variety.

The final crises of these years is the very simple fact that the job must, one day, be given up. There are laws on the books that prevent discrimination against people because of age. These regulations apply mainly to hiring and firing, and to salary and advancement on the job. But no laws can regulate the biology of aging, or affect the hidden battle waged between young and old in every workplace in which the two age groups are represented.

Observers of this conflict know that advantages tend to cancel themselves out. Youth, vitality, inexperience with failure are often assets; age and experience of both success and failure also have their advantages. Both the young and the old have had the opportunity to say, "You win some and you lose some."

But a practical consideration comes into play eventually. No matter how brave the knight and how skilled in weaponry, eventually a courier taps him or her on the shoulder and says, "Get ready to hand over your job."

The fighters, those with a lifetime of happy conflict, have been known to shoot bringers of the unwanted message and fight retirement all the way up to the board of directors.

But organizations, even when they might like to do

otherwise, know that special privilege given to individuals, however mighty, undercuts the whole retirement procedure. Notably wishy-washy boards have turned adamant on this one.

And so, willingly or otherwise, the Stage VI individual must adjust and in some cases officiate at the final dismantling of his or her own career: perhaps choose and train a successor and act as though it's a pleasant duty.

But let's go back a bit in time, to the beginning of the Stage VI experience, to a phenomenon that starts just about the time the 60–70 lap does.

41.
The Age Gap

"Just got back from my publisher's office," a writer friend says. "It was devastating. Almost every face I saw belonged to someone in their twenties. I made a turn in the corridor and almost bumped into a thirty-fiveish man. Suddenly he looked like the old man of the sea. Here I am sixty-two. How the hell am I supposed to feel other than obsolete?"

While it's true that publishers' offices seem to be entirely staffed by the long-haired, blue-jean set, the writer is influenced by a sensitivity common to 60-year-olds—it may happen earlier or later—who suddenly become aware of the fact that they are surrounded by colleagues as old— or as young—as their grandchildren. Those who are particularly age-conscious start viewing these young people with the same sense of threat as a tourist in the jungle who distinctly sees nonexistent natives with poison arrows skulking in the underbrush. This is not to say they don't exist at all, but not then and not there.

We talked to a woman with a particular insight into this age-difference situation. "I'm an age alien," she says.

"I have worked in this utility company for thirty years. My first day on the job, we moved into a brand-new building. Top management is now talking of leaving 'this old wreck' and moving into more modern quarters. I'm an antique.

"In my job, instead of feeling at home, I wonder what I'm doing here. It's terrible to feel like an intruder in a place you've lived for thirty years. And what can I do about it? How should I act?"

She continued: "If you are an alien from another country, you can help get yourself absorbed into the new culture. You solve your language problem, dress to conform, start palling around with the natives, maybe even marry one. But age aliens are stuck with an irreversible quality. As far as having friends among your young colleagues, sure, it's possible. But the friendship is never one between equals. Sometimes you're looked up to, but that's because you represent a parental image. And in other cases you're tolerated or patronized."

There are two logical reasons why Stage VI people tend to be socially isolated. One is the differences in attitude and values between themselves and their young colleagues. The other reason, although usually veiled, is stronger and more personal.

In her book *Decades,* Edith M. Lynch describes a common conflict: "Usually, aggressive employees do feel their progress is blocked by an older person's retention of a key spot. A poll of graduate students . . . indicates that the primary concern of a majority of students is that there will be no spot to move upward to as long as the 'old man' or 'old woman' keeps working."

The young workers' resentment of individuals who remain on the job after 60 may have a variety of causes. In addition to the resentment of a senior who may block a promotion pathway, there is the impatience with what are seen as old ideas and obsolete experience.

Perhaps there is no one as pathetic on the work scene as the Stage VI individual proud of his or her professionalism and experience who is treated with not-too-well-con-

Stage VI (60-70): The Wrap-up Years

cealed condescension. His or her most inspired statements at meetings may be listened to patiently but are then brushed aside by the aggressive young whizbangs, and when the meeting is over, "One more 'As I see it' or 'Here's how we used to handle it' and I'm going to burst out laughing, or crying," a member of the youth clique mutters.

Out of this welter of feelings—of alienation, loss, bewilderment, resentment—comes a crucial question for Stage VI individuals: "How should I act?" It's a critical hinge-point for what the individual will do, feel, and accomplish in the last years on the job.

To those who feel their age and are put down by condescending attitudes on the part of younger colleagues, there may seem to be only one answer: acceptance. Hold your nose, make the best of a bad situation, and hope that the other-life of retirement will be better.

But there are other possibilities open to those who will not permit their egos to be crushed or their careers to end in a thin stream of bubbles pushing up through the organizational sediment.

The other side of the coin to the one that bears the image of the Age Alien carries a different face: a visage reflecting power, even arrogance, self-satisfaction, and self-confidence.

Among the Stage VI people are a goodly share of men and women who feel that they are at the top of their form, at the peak of their abilities. Their experience, their past victories, give them a feeling of superiority that generally shows up in aggressive action.

One man, a vice-president of management services for a large manufacturing company, says, "If you can't lick 'em, lead 'em." An example of what he means is his current and successful effort to reinforce his grip on his job. He has just reorganized his department, firing one person, transferring two others, and hiring three replacements who are now "his people."

In football there are players, either offensive or defensive, who are so quick, strong, and aggressive that they are a major force in what happens on the field. Sportswriters refer to them as "Monster men." There are some individuals in business who are similarly strong and aggressive and intend to dominate. They run full tilt into Stage VI, unfazed by the number 60 or the sight of the finish tape that will end their racing days. They talk like Tim Gordon. Listen:

"You've heard of the born-young-again sixties? That's me. I feel as good as or better than I ever have. I can outthink, outrun, outwork the young people around. Some of them really haven't caught on to this business even after two or three years."

Occasionally, Stage VI people are centers of attention they don't particularly relish. . . .

Dealing with the Shouldering Herd

"Al Shultz called," Gretchen Morley's secretary tells her. "He'd like to have lunch with you one day this week."

Morley nods and goes into her office. Suddenly her secretary hears a strange noise and rushes to the doorway. There's her boss hunched over the desk, shaking with laughter.

"Are you all right, Miss Morley?"

The red-faced, wet-eyed executive nods and after a few moments explains. "Al's the fourth person in the last few days who's eager to have lunch with me. Can you explain my sudden popularity?" The secretary shakes her head and Gretchen Morley smiles. "It's a sure way to become a celebrity. I'm popular because they all want my job and think I can help. I wish I could, but I just got the news from Mr. Horton—they are looking outside for my successor. I could play a dirty trick on the whole bunch by taking them up on their lunch invitations, but I'd just get fat and feel guilty afterward."

Some people are in a bind over the very situation that Gretchen Morley is able to take so lightly. Their recommendation *can* be a major factor in who succeeds them.

Stage VI (60-70): The Wrap-up Years

And for the conscientious individual, it can be a real sticker. Here are some posers that make a crisis of the matter of succession:

"Appoint the subordinate I like best?" But he or she may not be the best suited for the job.

"Recommend the best qualified?" But that means passing over Alice, my best friend, who is counting on me.

"Recommend the hardest worker, the most loyal and dedicated?" But what about Carl, who is studying hard to make the grade?

"Recommend Fred, who is my boss's choice? The boss has made it clear that's what he expects. If I don't, that will mean trouble with my boss, who has a say about some of my retirement benefits, which are negotiable." But if the boss's choice is an exercise in favoritism, being unfair to a more deserving employee may become traumatic to a conscientious retiree.

One of the executives who had to go to the mat with the problem of picking a successor says, "There is an opportunity to indulge in enlightened favoritism, tapping your best friend for the promotion. But the cleanest solution, and the one that ended my losing sleep, is to play it straight. Let people know you're going to try to be objective and select the person most deserving and best qualified for the job. Of course, that still leaves the decision flexible—much of the judgment is subjective—but at least you have set the parameters that promise reasonable evenhandedness."

The Ozymandias Nightmare

Listen to the words of a middle-echelon manager with twenty-two years of service in the personnel department of a large department store. After her retirement, she was brave enough to bite on the well-intentioned invitation "Come back and visit," and called her ex-boss, who couldn't make lunch but urged her to "drop in, it will be great to see you."

She did, and the conversation was warm, nostalgic. The boss hit the right buttons of reminiscence: "Remember the time you . . ." etc.

Then it was time to leave, and the visitor walked down the corridors, musing on the number of unfamiliar faces and the change of occupancy of the offices.

"Suddenly it struck me," she said, "what I was doing. I was looking for something, for somebody. Then I realized, *it was for myself.* And I wasn't there. And not only was the 'me' I sought not there, but it was as though she never had been."

There is an aspect of retirement that largely explains the chill it brings to the spirits of those who face the final parting. Put yourself in the mind of the soon-to-be ex-employee. After the farewell lunches, the ritual handshaking tour to bid colleagues farewell with the pro forma agreement to "keep in touch," the final and official retirement ceremony comes to a tomblike quiet. And looking back, you see no mark or sign of your presence or handiwork on the organization.

It is doubtful that Percy Bysshe Shelley had workers in mind, still less likely that he thought of Stage VI people when he wrote "Ozymandias." Many a high-school student has been made momentarily old by reading the poet's haunting comment on human vanity and the wish for immortality, or at least to be remembered.

Shelley's poem is set in the words of a traveler from an "antique land" who describes a monument he has seen, remnants of a huge figure lying in fragments in the desert. Here are the last lines:

And on the pedestal these words appear:
"My name is Ozymandias, king of kings;
Look on my works, ye Mighty, and despair!"
Nothing beside remains. Round the decay
Of that colossal wreck, boundless and bare
The lone and level sands stretch far away.

Stage VI (60-70): The Wrap-up Years

For the middle-echelon personnel manager, as with Ozymandias, the need to be remembered is a sticking point that darkens the parting from the organization. It's a crisis for which there may be little amelioration. How? How to be remembered?

Many captains of industry, generals and privates as well, yearn to leave their mark. Countless men and women have hoped that work done, goals achieved, will forever stand to win the plaudits of the yet unborn. For these, awareness of the brevity of human life and works strikes at the heart.

The monument builders are a recognizable subgroup among Stage VI individuals. They want the feeling that something notable will mark their existence and their contribution. There is some satisfaction for a few: a bronze plaque that names them for outstanding service; a portrait on the corridor wall. But perhaps the best the average person can hope for is to be remembered with warmth by ex-colleagues. That's at least as well as Ozymandias fared.

Others want to get out as quickly and quietly as possible. Their desire to live on in the minds of their successors is nonexistent. These are the individuals who, despite pressures and pleading, refuse to participate in a retirement ceremony. Reluctantly they may go along with a friendly lunch with several of their friends and cronies among their co-workers—and that's it.

Some people see retirement as the end of their career.

Others see it as the beginning of a new life.

42.

Retirement: The Final Identity Crisis

It comes to the surface in different ways and at various times during the 60–70 decade. Gradually for some, in a blinding instant for others comes the realization that the end of the road is in sight, clearly in view or just around the bend.

"I've got ten more years to live." That's the way one 60-year-old purchasing head of a southern paint company sees his last decade on the job.

Entering Stage VI finds most individuals with a last-lap feeling. For better or worse, retirement will part them from their company. Some see it as for better—a life of self-indulgent activity in retirement. Others see it as the worst—a transition from being somebody to being nobody.

Emotionally, it's a long way from 60 to 70. Some people, fighting to benefit from the last shreds of youthful vigor, will take early retirement and leave at 62 or 65: It was a pronounced trend until the late 1970s, when inflation undercut the financial plans of those retiring with fixed incomes. But others go full term—and then, if the company

Stage VI (60-70): The Wrap-up Years

permits, stay on either in their old jobs or take on special assignments under the umbrella title "consultant."

There is a wide range of feelings expressed by those for whom retirement looms. And although the prospect of leaving their employer does not necessarily dominate their every move and thought—for some, incredibly, it doesn't actually "happen" until the last week on the job—people do look down the tunnel, see the light at the other end. For some, it is bright and beckoning; for others, murky and ominous.

"Who and what will I be after my job ends?" That's a key question that pre-retirees ask themselves, and it continues to haunt some of them after they have ended their working days. Consider:

The scene is a preholiday cocktail party with thirty or so neighborhood people standing around getting genteelly plastered. Some of the people have known each other as close and good neighbors; others meet as total strangers.

In one corner, a group has gathered, and after some remarks about the weather and the washout of the road at the intersection, the conversation takes a "who-are-you" turn:

"My name's Josh Whitten," a young man says to an older one. "I live in the corner house." Then *the* identification question: "What do you do?"

"My name is Hank Rowe. That's my wife over there, the one with the silver hair. I'm retired."

In Rowe's last words lies the acknowledgment of a crucial fact: He feels depersonalized. Ask a person who he is or what he does and the mere statement of a job title or activity—"I'm an engineer," "a salesman," "a boat designer"—provides a key to one's identity.

For many people, retirement ends all that. An economic and social castration has terminated the individual's status. Whether he or she was an engineer, teacher, or dress designer, without some job designation the individual feels afloat, cut off, bereft of the one thing that for some forty years has been the single most reliable source of self-definition. For the last time, identity has been lost. Whether or not it will be regained—by work, or reassessment of self, or love of a good man or woman—depends on the ego strength of the individual.

Interestingly enough, it seems to make little difference at what rung of the ladder people were when they severed their organizational connections. Asked the question "What do you do?" both an ex-president and an ex–company guard will give the same answer: "I'm retired." And this may be the answer even though their postretirement life is full and active. They may run a consumer-affairs office in the local government; lead a life of enlightened leisure; travel; or wallow knee-deep in a scholarly area such as archaeology. And yet, severed from an organization that gave them status, and a microcosmic world in which to have an identity, they are left with a sense of loss and desolation.

For some, the organization meant more than just a position and a regular paycheck. The company affiliation was a source of power and privilege. Here's how Mortimer Feinberg of BFS Psychological Associates, a New York consulting firm, put it in an article in the *Wall Street Journal*:

> It isn't easy for a CEO to face retirement. Hereafter he will have no aide to do his leg work, no secretary to receive his phone calls, no company limousine waiting at the airport and no chauffeur to carry his bag, no well-appointed office with carpeted floors, decorator-chosen paintings on the walls, the refrigerator and bar in the corner. More important than the paraphernalia is the substance they symbolize—power and station and constant reassurance. No longer will there be meetings over which to preside, with the singular attention that is riveted on the acknowledged leader when he chooses to speak. No longer will a sea of faces turn toward him as he enters the toom. The pension may match the salary, but no perks of retirement can make up for the loss of influence and control.

What can possibly fill the gap? Answer: your inner resources, your ego, sense of self, the things you can still do to make life satisfying and meaningful.

43.

The Final Crisis of Self-Assessment

How do people feel about their accomplishment, totting up the score? Some of the group can look back to two score and ten on the job, others perhaps less, but the process is the same. The brain, that infinite computer, adds, subtracts, multiplies, and divides, and comes up with a bottom line that sums up how an individual feels about a lifetime of labor.

The night sweeper can make the calculation as readily as the CEO, and come up with as meaningful a statement. But for the careerist, for whom a significant element of the self (self-identity, sense of self-worth) has been tied up in the working life, the bottom-line calculation can have enormous meaning. And depending on the degree of contentment and satisfaction felt, it can have major impact on the success or failure of the years to come. Here are some of the views we heard.

- *The happy warrior.* "Business is my game, exciting, fulfilling, a great source of enjoyment." (This executive had made this statement before, in conversations with business-press reporters and writers.) "I'm one of the few people I know who, if I got a second shot, would like to come back as myself and do it all over again exactly the same way."

This game player will be sitting pretty in his retirement if he is able to rest on his laurels. A key factor is his ability to lead what he considers an active and rewarding life. But if his sense of game playing isn't satisfied, he will turn itchy, and either he will find himself some occupation to siphon off his energies or he'll suffer the relentless boredom of those retirees for whom there can be no substitute for the stimulating pressures of work.

- *The overachiever.* A businessman who made it big in the garment trade: "Look at me, I'm the original poor boy who made good—no education, no prospects. But I'm a fighter. I didn't let anything stand in my way, certainly not hard work. And just last month I gave the museum my art collection and the money to build a separate wing to put it in. Only in America? Maybe. But certainly from those like me who made it happen, you understand that you are your own fate."

His degree of self-satisfaction augurs well for this business achiever. Like a latter-day Alexander, but unlike his predecessor in appetite, he doesn't feel the need to seek new worlds to conquer. Leaving the scene of his victory behind, he may bore the pants off anyone who will listen to his stories of conquest, but *he* isn't bored by these tales. He reminds himself of just how great he was, and in reliving those times, he feels he still is.

- *Won the world, lost his soul.* "I worked very hard and got very far," says the president of a suburban utility company. "Between my wife and me, we run this town. But it took three psychiatrists to finally help me understand that, while I was busy keeping my nose to the grindstone, I lost the ability to enjoy life. My current psychiatric helper is trying to undo the damage, but I'm still the guy you see on the beach in Hawaii sitting in the shade and reading computer printouts."

Most of the people who say "I'll never retire" are half-

Stage VI (60-70): The Wrap-up Years

people, like this president. Perhaps they are more akin to worker ants than to *Homo sapiens,* suited only for labor, and without the desire to do anything else. They want to go out with their boots on. Their resolve is wise.

- *The Martin Eden outcome.* Jack London's autobiographical novel tells the story of Martin Eden, an uneducated sailor who is suddenly introduced into upper-class surroundings, invited to dinner by a grateful young man he has saved from muggers in San Francisco. The affluence, the gentility, the beauty he sees become personified in Ruth Morse, sister of the young man he saved. Here is Martin Eden's reaction:

> Here was the intellectual life, he thought, and here was beauty, warm and wonderful as he had never dreamed it could be. He forgot himself and stared at her with hungry eyes. Here was something to live for, to try to win, to fight for—ay, and die for. The books were true. There were such women in the world. She was one of them. She lent wings to his imagination, and great, luminous canvases spread themselves before him, whereon loomed vague, gigantic figures of love and romance, and of heroic deeds for woman's sake—for a pale woman, a flower of gold.

Then, in keeping with the romanticism of the story, the sailor sets about winning the girl and all she stands for. He chooses a rocky road, that of professional writer. He slaves, goes sleepless, hungry, lives in a hovel, studying, writing, educating himself and honing his skills. After horrendous suffering, which includes being finally rejected and ostracized by Ruth and her family, success bursts upon him like an avalanche. His books and stories eventually begin to be accepted, and suddenly he becomes the literary sensation of the day.

With coincidental suddenness, the people who snubbed him rush to court his favor—including Ruth and her family. And Martin Eden, in a revulsion of feeling reminiscent of Goethe's young Werther, becomes bitter, disillusioned, and, finally—when Ruth throws herself into his arms, with the assistance of a brother who waits in the street outside

Martin's hotel during the attempted seduction—depressed unto death. Reaching the nadir during a trip to Tahiti, he drowns himself.

Perhaps, in a more romantic age, careerists who achieved impossible goals only to find them unworthy or meaningless might also slip into the sea in a final act of sore-winnership. Being tougher-minded, we are likely to react to this final disappointment with a drink and the resolve to have one hell of a retirement.

Excellent resolve. Retirement, particularly if it's not cramped by meager funds, is apt to be just the right milieu for those who basically yearn to be nonmaterialists. These are the people who set out to explore the world, take up astronomy, painting, buy acreage in the wilderness and build their own homes, or go in for animal breeding and subsistence farming. On the rebound, they want to indulge their lust for activities that are basically nonmaterial.

The people who answer "Having a ball" when you ask how their retirement is going include a fair percentage of those who resented the hard-edge quality of business. They may have reached elevated goals, reaped rewards for contributions made, but basically they didn't play the game with the exuberance of the Happy Warrior. Stopping work meant putting down a yoke. In the unstructured world of retirement, they can seek personal answers and perhaps come into their own. Perhaps belatedly. But better late than never.

- *The work scene as wasteland.* Barbara Grey's company threw a big party for her retirement, a jolly affair with all the stops pulled out. Clearly, Barbara was liked by all.

She said, "I started as an assistant doing all the dog jobs and ended as an officer of the company, senior executive in charge of customer relations. But I had a brain I never used. Maybe I made the wrong move way back. I would have made a good doctor. But in the company, I should have aimed higher. With study and a bit of hustle, I could have achieved more, probably in marketing. But I did it the easy way and never extended myself. Funny, this is the time when it comes to me.

"The people are great. They were the good part of the job. But the pettiness, the infighting, the fawning from below and the currying favor with the power people—*yech!* I didn't want to lower myself by making my job that important in my life. I'm curious to see how I do as a retiree."

Unfortunately, hoping to right the balance in retirement is mostly futile. A good retirement doesn't compensate for the feeling that life on the job was without a sense of achievement or fulfillment.

It's a stark fact to understand early: You don't solve career problems in retirement. Those must be faced up to stage by stage. Each phase has its own crises that must be dealt with in order to attain goals and satisfactions.

In retirement, you solve the problems of—retirement.

44.

A Few Words About Retirement Planning

For the foresighted, retirement planning starts years before the move takes place. Retirement considerations may begin to form as much as five or ten years in advance of actual departure. Certainly, a key factor, finances, have to be given considerable thought long before the parting, to optimize investments, for example.

Retirement these days is very different from what it was. Previously, the symbols of the retiree were a gold watch, a rowboat, and a fishing pole. Now they're more likely to be (by request of the employee to his boss when asked, and he or she usually is, nowadays) not a gold watch but a typewriter, or a pair of skis, or collection of cookbooks. And instead of the rowboat—a world cruise.

There's an interesting reason—rather, two reasons—for the change. First, we've learned a lot about the retirement process, and we learned the hard way. Mortality tables told us what was what. Quite simply, the death rate among retired people shot up alarmingly. Clearly, some-

Stage VI (60-70): The Wrap-up Years

thing happened in the change of daily patterns and preoccupations.

It was not only that on-the-job daily routines kept people physically and mentally occupied. Their work seemed to provide a *reason* for living, a retirement for many meant idleness rather than leisure. The drive and energy that had gone into work, certainly the satisfactions and rewards of the job, were not being adequately replaced. And out of this realization came a new technology—perhaps a vainglorious phrase, but it represents an important activity—retirement planning.

The second reason is equally arresting. As a result of increased youthful vigor and modern health practices, retired individuals today have a longer life expectancy, and more years of good health ahead of them. Retirement no longer means a few years of survival but, in typical cases, lives lived to the mid-eighties or -nineties and often marked by rewarding activity.

The new 50-year-olds are vital at a stage in life that used to be thought of as middle age. Actuaries assert that a man of 65 today has a life expectancy that a 53-year-old had in the 1920s. Putting it another way, a man of 65 has a life expectancy of 78.7; and a woman 83.1. And that expectancy is constantly rising. By the year 2000, it will reach 80 for men and 84.5 for women. And for the wise-living individual, the average is often surpassed.

These figures suggest that retired individuals have a potential for a whole new life experience. And apparently the aged are to inherit the earth: As the demographics of our society change, there is a shift from a youth orientation toward one favoring the interests and values of mature adults.

Retired people tell you, "You don't know how it really is until you do it yourself." Largely true. No matter how good the travel folders, distant places always pack a lot of surprises.

But vicariously it is possible to empathize with those who have taken the retirement step, and to learn from people whose experience can be revealing and useful. The retirement ranks are never-ending, and postretirement fates highly varied. But one case history will show how one person translated working skills and accomplishments into post-working life, and how this reflected on the past. The case of Geraldine Wigren:

Gerry Wigren got her promotion to director of internal information services of a large insurance company about ten years before she retired. At the age of 65, her pension was substantial enough to permit her to leave the company. In addition, her husband, who had died some years before, had left her financially secure.

Retirement to her meant first a rest, then a life of easy enjoyments—travel, with sojourns in foreign places that interested her. Certainly London and Paris, but also the Mediterranean and Scandinavian countries.

Things went according to plan. But unexpectedly, after she returned from a two-month visit to Spain (her sister Beth, newly widowed, went with her), she discovered that her next trip, to France, did not beckon irresistibly. She postponed it once, then realized that her travel urge had weakened. Distant shores seemed less exciting than some of the possibilities at home.

After a couple of weeks, her thinking finally turned up a plan of action. Her husband's last days had been spent in a large hospital in town. In her visits, she had had the chance to see up close just what hospital life was like, both for the hospital employees and for the patients. Her methodical mind had churned up a number of "Why-don't-they's"—mostly things that the hospital could do to improve the services to the patients.

She put a call through to the hospital director, Gordon Bassett. Getting him on the phone was a bit difficult—Gerry Wigren correctly assuming that hospital directors are prime targets for patients and their relatives who want to register complaints ranging from cold bedpans to exorbitant charges. But for someone with her business experience, evading the telephone screen was simple: "Mr. Bassett will want to speak to me," she told a secretary. "Tell him I'm a friend of Grace Howell's." (Grace Howell was on the hospital's board of directors), and, well, she wasn't a friend exactly, but she had met the woman at a charity cocktail party.

A few days later, she was in Bassett's office, sketching out her ideas for unifying and improving patient services. "I think you have enough volunteers right now," she told the director, "but I don't think they are efficient. My idea is to reorganize—unify, really—these really splendid people so that they can do more in less time. The end result, of course, is to make your patients more comfortable, increase their well-being as much as possible, and take some of the strain off your professionals and service people."

Gerry Wigren expected Bassett to drool, and he did. "It all sounds very impressive," he said, trying to repress his enthusiasm. "How do we go about it? Will you . . ."

"Yes, I'll be glad to help implement the plan. Of course, there are dozens of details. . . ."

"Can you give me some idea . . ."

"Generally, I'm interested in the direction suggested by the American Hospital Association's 'Patient's Rights' statement. Patients, at the very least, should have protection against some questionable hospital practices."

The director said, "The AHA's concept is a bit unrealistic and costly. But as a principle . . ."

"You can depend on me to be practical as well as visionary."

"I can see it on the office door," Bassett rhapsodized, "Geraldine Wigren, Chief of Volunteer Services. . . ."

Gerry laughed. "Maybe, after a while."

"I had hoped you could start soon."

"I'm ready to start tomorrow—but not as chief of anything. I don't want to get my head handed to me the first day on the job. Starting at the bottom is the best move. I don't know a thing about hospital operations from the inside. You find a spot for me—anything, answering phones, helping the dietician. After some months, I'll be in a position to be more realistic in my thinking, and we can start to plan."

The director agreed. "You're tackling a tough problem. I don't want to minimize it," he said.

Gerry nodded. "Just keep that office available," she said.

Her ideas eventually bore fruit. About a year later, she was made head of patient services, but it was a more complicated setup than she had envisioned, involving not only the volunteers but also representatives of most of the professionals and worker groups, and also union representatives.

Months after she had taken on the responsibility, the reorganization was still incomplete. One afternoon she had a long discussion—*argument* is really the word—with a union representative about an area of service that seemed to fall between the volunteers and the employees. Realizing the exchange was getting nowhere, Gerry suggested that they continue the meeting the next day. There had to be some benefit, she thought, in letting the union officer cool off.

After he left, she sat back in her chair and relaxed, musing about her "job," which her friends rightly told her was one long headache. "But I love it!" she suddenly told herself. Even this wrangle with a somewhat unreasonable man was vital, meaningful. She was dealing with real problems. This was living! The organizational skills she had honed on her old job, her insights into people, knowing how to plan, how to motivate and direct, they all came to hand. And the one element she realized now she had missed in her job, the sense of making a social contribution, was a major reward for her travail. She liked what she was doing, she liked herself. Now *there's* a postretirement benefit I never thought of, she thought.

What she meant was, the executive skills she had developed were personal skills. In her retirement, she had become a new person by applying her abilities in the service of others. And the fact that they were strangers didn't diminish but added to her satisfaction. She was helping mankind. And thinking of herself she smiled and thought, "And womankind as well."

45.
Another Kind of Retirement

A development that is a growing phenomenon promises special advantages. Early *working* retirement. Here people, especially those with accrued pension benefits, leave in advance of the mandatory age with the intention of taking on income-earning activity: another job, either in the same or different field; consulting in an area of their expertise; starting a business of their own or buying into one.

Early working retirement is one way of avoiding what in some instances would mean winding up a life on the job with years of abrasiveness and frustration. Should you take the option? The answer often comes down to whether it is practical for *you*. Whether it is worth looking into depends on many considerations—everything from your family situation to your feelings about your job. However, in most cases there are two keys to practicality:

Financial advantages may tip the balance for those who have become vested in their organization's pension plan. A combination of pension plus income from a second career could compare favorably with staying on the job.

The *psychic rewards* are as important a consideration. A lumber-company manager says, "I used to like my job, but the management and policies of my company changed. I no longer felt at home after twenty-eight years. If I took retirement at age sixty-two, I would get not only a good-sized pension but also a separation bonus that my company was offering to old-timers. I got a job in commercial construction, and after six months I knew I had made my smartest career move."

Since early working retirement offers a useful view of a transition into a second career at a crucial stage, we were fortunate in meeting two people whose experiences, although different, are both exemplary.

Jack Beane was an electronics engineer and a good one. His ideas and designs for new equipment and electronic parts for computer elements justified a large salary, which his employer gladly paid.

But the larger Beane's bank account and investment portfolio grew, the more dissatisfied he became with his profession and his participation therein.

One night he and his wife Rachel had a serious and crucial talk. Jack enumerated for the three or four hundredth time his dissatisfactions with his job, then dropped his bombshell:

"We've talked about buying a farm and living close to the land. Now that Pete's off to law school and Helen has been accepted at Massachusetts Institute, let's make the move. I've been reading the acreage ads and right here in our own county there is still good farmland available. What do you say?"

Rachel Beane had her say. The role of farm wife had its romantic appeal, and her assent was followed by hours of excited planning.

Jack Beane told his employer he was going to take early retirement, and added, "Don't worry, I'm not going to work for a competitor." Since the company had a good pension plan, twenty years of tenure gave him a good-size annuity. Between that and his investment income, the

Stage VI (60-70): The Wrap-up Years

Beanes were in a good situation. And savings were sufficiently large so that they could look around for a land purchase right away.

Three months later, the Beanes were the owners of sixty acres of land, a main house, barn, and several sheds.

Corn and chickens were to be their main crop, in addition to Rachel's large vegetable garden, which was to be mostly for their own needs. A five-acre apple orchard had been neglected by the Adamses. Jack called in the county agent and they walked the acres together, examining the trees. The agent's suggestion was simple: "Take down all the trees and put in new ones. The varieties you can get today are much better bearers. New trees will bring you in more per bushel than any you have now, and the fruit will sell better."

So the Beanes became farmers. Fortunately, they were able to buy a considerable amount of farm equipment. Jack and Rachel did almost all the work themselves except during the planting and reaping season.

The first year, the corn crop didn't do too well because they hadn't enriched the soil enough. The second year, things were really looking up. They weren't quite breaking even, but Rachel's daily trip into town with the station wagon to sell the eggs, and the deals they made with local stores to sell their corn, improved their cash flow.

Jack was pleased. "At the price we're getting for early corn, it's almost like bringing in oil."

But the third year was disappointing. The work seemed endless. A drought cut into the corn yield. Bringing water down to the new orchards with tank trucks to help the trees survive was costly. Woodchucks feasted on their cabbages and other assorted vegetables. They worked hard and results were disappointing, but they assured each other that next year would be better.

But it was a hard winter. And just as spring came around—as determined not by the calendar but by the readiness of the earth—Jack came down with a bad case of pneumonia. "Total bed rest," the doctor said.

Jack and Rachel discussed the situation with uneasiness. "I've got to start preparing next week," he said. Rachel volunteered to have the tractor gone over. On a fateful Monday morning, Jack got out of his sickbed, dressed, and went out into the spring rain, mounted his tractor, and began the patterned ride over the fields. Two hours gone, his harrow struck a hidden rock and snapped one of the blades.

Jack stopped the machine and looked about him at the muddy field, the unfriendly sky, and then considered his own physical condition. His chest felt bound in steel, tears streamed from his eyes.

Fifteen minutes later, he was back in the living room getting out of his rain gear and wet clothes. Rachel hovered.

"This is it, Rach," he said. "Out there in the field, I got a picture of myself. If I can't afford the luxury of being sick, I'm in the wrong job."

The Beane story has a happy ending. They were able to sell the farm profitably. They had bought it for $150,000. They were able to sell off forty-five acres to a developer for $1.2 million. In the four years since they had bought the property, the area had suburbanized and land values had exploded.

Jack is now vice-president of a company that manufactures electronic parts; and Rachel, whose spirit of enterprise also survived, deals in antiques from the old farmhouse they still own and enjoy.

Other full-time retirees turn in less happy reports: "I've never gotten used to retirement. The day I stopped work, *I* stopped." But for some, there is a halfway house that seems to offer special advantages. We recently interviewed a person who took this road.

Another instance of early working retirement illustrates another approach and another outcome.

Franz Edelman, of Trenton, New Jersey, was associated with RCA for thirty years, his last position and title, VP, Business Systems and Analysis. He loved his job, liked his company.

When he hit the 56-year mark, he decided that, as

Stage VI (60-70): The Wrap-up Years

satisfying as he found his RCA connection, there were other things he aspired to professionally. He wanted to test out his ideas, his skills, his capabilities in a larger and less protected arena. Would he be as successful in meeting a broader range of challenges on his own, without Papa RCA to fall back on? He decided to try.

With that decision made, he gave himself three years to prepare for the move. In that time, he did several things:

- He did some hard thinking about what he wanted to do after he left. Consulting was his choice, along the lines he had been working on for RCA.
- Since he felt that professional contacts would be important to him, he began to jot down the names and affiliations of people he met when he gave a talk or attended one, or during any of the other functions at which he met fellow professionals. When he was ready to retire, his list ran to some 500 names.
- He took advantage of the services RCA provided to ease retirement shock. These ranged from discussions about his financial situation to booklets covering everything from travel to volunteer services, from health to hobbies. Out of his financial talks came the decision to take his pension in a lump sum, an option sometimes available to retirees, and one that Edelman saw as a good move for him.

Of top management's attitude, Edelman says, "People were supportive and encouraging. I was told to spend my last three months pretty much as I liked, while continuing to have use of all facilities—office, secretarial and so on." This was a helpful and much appreciated convenience.

A key part of Franz Edelman's retirement plan was to develop consulting clients. His chief device was a mailing to his list of contacts announcing his departure from RCA and his entry into the consulting field. He didn't solicit business; he simply assumed that those who were interested would get in touch with him. His strategy was successful, so much so that within four months he was booked ahead for a full year of his time.

"I did make one tactical error along the way," he confesses. "At one point, my time was so limited, I made no secret of being fully booked. That frightened off potential clients and inquiries fell off. I realized that advertising one's unavailability was not a sound business tactic."

He originally had intended to work half-time, but requests for his services made that unrealistic. "I felt I was doing something that the field needed badly, and I wanted to spread the word. Besides, I enjoyed being successful and sought-after."

Edelman's special interest is what he calls "IRM," Information Resource Management, which he defines as the education of general management in the new ways of computers and information systems. To many, particularly those at the top, these developments were seen as mysteries and threats. "I present the new technology in practical and functional terms, show how they can be integrated into traditional operations. Just demystifying and clarifying the benefits of MIS/dp can be a major gain in many instances."

Edelman saw a new education industry coming into existence, aimed at improving understanding, acceptance, and integration of computer and information technology with other business functions.

"In the old days," Edelman says, "people who took early retirement did so because of dissatisfaction with their working situation. They disliked something about it—lack of freedom, an incompatible boss, disagreement with company policies, or the nature of their daily tasks."

In his case, the opposite was true. He respected his employer, liked his work, but sought a broader field in which to exercise his professional skills and interests. Here are the guidelines he developed for himself that helped steer a winning course:

- *Anticipate some negative consequences.* "My experience has been favorable, but others haven't been as fortunate. For example, I talked with an MIS director who retired and got a job, somewhat similar to his previous one, with a smaller company. He was dissatisfied; his work didn't have the same challenge as his previous job. However, there were some advantages—easier commuting, a good boss—and eventually he came around to accepting a trade-off between the pluses and minuses."

- *Money unpredictability.* "Unless you have a new job or a situation assured, there may be a risk in the economics of change. You have to watch this factor and prepare to make adjustments if the money part isn't to your taste. For example, one executive who had tried to get into consulting on his own finally teamed up with a going concern, with considerably improved results."
- *Your marketability.* "People lose track of the passage of time. And if they do any amount of job-hopping, they may find that the salary they command may decline, because in part the business is changing, or their particular kind of expertness is less in demand." He suggests that one try to anticipate this factor instead of having it appear as an unexpected obstacle.

Curtain Call

In these contrasting case histories, one sees both the chanciness and opportunities of starting a second career with the benefits of a pension, maturity, and a sense of what you would like to do as a professional encore. And if the encore goes over even better than the original—sweet victory indeed.

Stage VI is a wrap-up mainly in a chronological sense. It is the decade in which you conclude your life on the job, and make a transition to activities that generally represent a balance between the practicalities and your final aspirations for yourself. This period, as you can tell by your observations of friends and relatives, offers activities, challenges, rewards. And perhaps there are handicaps of age that must be taken into account, and coped with.

There is a crucial shift that is central. For some, the capabilities that one used at work continue to be useful, as was the case for Gerry Wigren. But for others, it is the mental and spiritual resources—such as understanding, a paternal feeling for others, a willingness to pass along the benefits of your experience and wisdom—that become major preoccupations. Perhaps these acts of grace are the real consequences of life on the job. When all else falls away—the procedures, the routines, the mechanics and forms of work—it is the effects of these on the human spirit that is the ultimate meaningful consequence.

Out of the Wilderness into the Sunshine

Negotiating the rocks and rapids of a career requires a different set of skills than those needed to do the job itself. You can be very good at doing everything demanded by the occupational requirements of a particular profession; yet at the same time, you can fail, not because you haven't done your job well but because you have not been equally professional in handling the crises of your career. Managing a career is a job in itself.

Crises are the flash points, the testing you meet at each stage. The fact that crises are predictable—and that one can often anticipate the stage during which certain kinds of crises will be met—facilitates career planning.

But it is never easy. And it is very seldom handled perfectly. Most people make their share of mistakes, mishandling certain crises, dodging others when they should be faced, failing to resolve issues and moving into the next stage of working life still trailing useless umbilicals.

But you get through. And you don't yearn—except in weary and angry moments of isolated frustration—for a life that would be altogether insulated from crisis.

You know that's impossible. To try to completely avoid problems would be like trying to completely avoid fate. There is the often-told story of the rich merchant of ancient Baghdad who was told that Fate was coming to announce to him his death.

"I will escape," the rich man vowed. "Fate will not find me. I will flee to Samarra."

A little while later, a man met Fate moving along a road. "Excuse me," said Fate, "but I cannot tarry. I have an appointment to keep. Even now a man is hurrying to meet me—in Samarra."

And even if, by some miracle, one could live a life without crisis, would it not be less challenging, less yielding of victories? Claire Fine is a successful executive who goes on Outward Bound trips. She says, "When I'm crouched there, clinging to the side of a mountain, I sometimes think, Why the hell am I here? I paid good money for this! Who needs it?"

She adds, "I need it. It's uncomfortable, rugged, often undignified, hard work, sometimes dangerous. But when I come through, *I feel strong and good about myself.*"

Another business person says, "The commodities market is a mountain. I climb it every day."

It's tough just to survive the stages of working life. When you do more than survive, when you meet the challenges with strength and honor, you are fulfilling yourself as a human being and becoming a better human being. What you have to show is what you have become.